REFLECTIVE TEACHING

The Study of Your Constructivist Practices

Second Edition

James G. Henderson
Kent State University

Merrill, an imprint of
Prentice Hall

Englewood Cliffs, New Jersey   Columbus, Ohio

Library of Congress Cataloging-in-Publication Data
Reflective teaching: the study of your constructivist practices/
    [edited by] James G. Henderson. — 2nd ed.
            p.   cm.
        Includes bibliographical references and index.
        ISBN 0-02-353521-0
        1. Teaching. 2. Teaching—Case studies. I. Henderson, James George.
    LB1025.3.R437 1996   95-36399
    371.3'32—dc20   CIP

Cover photo: Telegraph Colour Library for FPG International
Editor: Debra A. Stollenwerk
Developmental Editor: Linda Ashe Montgomery
Production Editor: Julie Anderson Peters
Photo Editor: Anne Vega
Design Coordinator: Julia Zonneveld Van Hook
Text Design: STELLARViSIONs
Cover Designer: Retter/Patton & Assoc., Inc.
Production Manager: Laura Messerly
Electronic Text Management: Marilyn Wilson Phelps, Matthew Williams, Karen L. Bretz, Tracey Ward
Illustrations: Tracey Ward

This book was set in New Baskerville by Prentice Hall and was printed and bound by Quebecor Printing/Book Press. The cover was printed by Phoenix Color Corp.

© 1996 by Prentice-Hall, Inc.
A Simon & Schuster Company
Englewood Cliffs, New Jersey 07632

Earlier edition, entitled *Reflective Teaching: Becoming an Inquiring Educator,* © 1992 by Macmillan Publishing Company.

Photo credits: Scott Cunningham/Merrill/Prentice Hall, p. 156, Barbara Schwartz/Merrill/Prentice Hall, p. 204; Anne Vega/Merrill/Prentice Hall, pp. 2, 48, 74, 104, 132, 182; Tom Watson/Merrill/Prentice Hall, p. 24.

Printed in the United States of America

10 9 8 7 6 5 4 3 2 1

ISBN: 0-02-353521-0

Prentice-Hall International (UK) Limited, *London*
Prentice-Hall of Australia Pty. Limited, *Sydney*
Prentice-Hall of Canada, Inc., *Toronto*
Prentice-Hall Hispanoamericana, S. A., *Mexico*
Prentice-Hall of India Private Limited, *New Delhi*
Prentice-Hall of Japan, Inc., *Tokyo*
Simon & Schuster Asia Pte. Ltd., *Singapore*
Editora Prentice-Hall do Brasil, Ltda., *Rio de Janeiro*

Foreword

Learning to Teach Through Telling Our Stories

What does it mean for each of us to learn to teach? It is this question this book asks each of us to consider. The book, designed for preservice teachers, asks questions that many of us who name ourselves teachers continue to ask as we learn to live and tell our stories as teachers. What stories do we live and tell of ourselves as teachers? On what personal and professional knowledge landscapes (Clandinin & Connelly, 1995) were these stories constructed? On what professional knowledge landscapes will these stories of ourselves be lived out? What is the link between the personal, the practical, the professional? How do we, as teachers, link theory and practice in our personal practice and professional knowledge? What do we ask of the teacher education programs in which we learn to teach?

These are questions that are too often set aside in teacher education programs as we find ourselves pushed to view teaching as a set of technical, expert skills separate from who we are as people, from the children with whom we work, and from the contexts within which we work. The authors in this book, through their rich teacher narratives of experience, make spaces for us to consider these questions.

While it is a book of ways to think, of processes through which to work, of scaffolding frameworks, it is the images, metaphors, and stories that stayed with me; images of children, of teachers, of schools, of theory. Let me share some of them here so that, as you read the book, you can find the stories that resonated for me and find others that resonate for you.

The text, for me, comes most alive in the stories. These are stories to live by. Many of them made me, as Hannah Arendt might say, "stop and think" about what it means to live my teacher's life. For example, in a narrative written by Jon Secaur, he states that "meaning is found in the whole, not in the parts, and the meaning one draws from the parts is intimately tied to one's perspective." Had he left it at that I may not have remembered my own stories of teaching. But he did not, for he then introduced me to Diane, a student in a class he was teaching. She was a student who was not getting 'it' and he tells his story of that situation. As she struggled with his explanations, he realized that

> I didn't understand her question, anymore than she understood my answer. . . . I wanted them to hold that same image, watching the work turn from that neutral and removed point of view. Instead, I felt that image crumble; she was seeing from a radically different perspective. But I had no idea what it was. I needed to see the problem from her point of view, and so I went looking for some parts from which we could reconstruct a new whole.

How many times has that happened to me in my teaching? How often has there not been a space to tell the story and to think through what happened? Jon, in his telling, makes that space for me.

As I read Janice Hutchison's narrative, I met Summer, a student in difficulty. In this story, Janice and Summer learn to create an environment in which Summer can learn. Summer's words are included to describe her experience. She writes in a journal entry to Janice

> The reason I'm succeeding so well in your English class is because you don't act like you don't have time to know me as a person and not just a student. When a teacher who doesn't know me gives me some bad vibes, I give them right back; and that was the problem with Miss R. When I got into your class, you didn't do that for me. You gave me a chance, and I thank you for that.

Through Jennifer Waldbauer and Sharon Klimm, we meet three teachers working together, who introduce us to Melissa, "an ordinarily quiet student." Melissa, a student who "left her private thought-world to enter a discussion", asks a question that "could have led to a whole line of inquiry and learning". They describe the activity and watch Melissa

> through much of the feelings/reflections activity. She seemed to have so many feelings, good and bad, jumbled inside. She fumbled with her feeling cards as she tried to sort through her emotions. Perhaps she could put her grieving process into hibernation so that others around her could heal. . . . In this small and safe setting, Melissa smiled and opened up a little.

I remembered, as I read, the children like Melissa I had known. Had I told their stories? Had anyone been there to listen and to give my story back so that I could learn to make more educative spaces for other children like Melissa? Waldbauer and Klimm made that space for all of us in their telling.

There are many other stories filling the pages of this book. The authors both tell us and show us how to pay close attention to the stories they live and tell. In this way, they tell and show us, as readers, how to live and tell our own stories and to consider how they will be lived out with students in our schools. They give us a framework that orients us to the study of ourselves as teachers which is, of course, what this book is about. There are references to theoretical resources such as John Dewey and Maxine Greene and connections that the authors make with such readings. These are important ways to make sense of our lived and told stories. But in telling their own stories, the authors begin to make a space that is safe enough for us to tell our own stories and to tell them in ways that will enable others to respond. For it is in the telling and in the response and then in the retelling that we awaken to and transform our lived teaching stories.

This book does not, as do so many books on learning to teach, encourage us to set our own stories aside and to become blank slates for what theory and research tell us teaching should be. Rather, this book challenges us to begin with ourselves, our own stories of what we know and to ask questions of those stories. Situated within the constructivist paradigm, all of the authors ask us to think about the relationships among what we think, how we think, who we are.

In the final two chapters, we learn about the importance of living in the community with other teachers on the landscape. In our terms (Clandinin & Connelly, 1995) we learn about how important it is to construct safe places in out-of-the classroom places in order to build community to engage with others. The challenge will be, for readers of this text, to find those safe places for the telling, retelling, living, and reliving of their own stories. It is a challenge that is important to all of us as we continue to learn to teach.

D. Jean Clandinin
University of Alberta

REFERENCES

Clandinin, D. Jean and Connelly, F. Michael (1995). *Teacher's professional knowledge landscapes.* New York: Teacher's College Press.

Preface

Two Educational Reform Trends

This second edition of *Reflective Teaching* has been substantially rewritten in response to two emerging and related reform trends in education.

There is increasingly widespread support in the United States and Canada, as well as many other countries throughout the world, for today's students to receive **constructivist educational services**. This type of education stresses teaching for meaning-making rather than for memorization or practice of rote skills. It calls for students to construct their knowledge as active inquirers into the subjects they are studying. Teachers who provide a constructivist service may incorporate some memorization and rote-skill learning into their lessons, but they will do so only to assist the overall goal of furthering their students' active understanding.

The second reform trend is easy to state, but it is actually quite complicated. There is a call for schools to become **centers of inquiry**. In other words, teachers should daily function as students of their own professional work. They should think for themselves and not simply follow the directions of others—supervisors, administrators, policy leaders, and textbook publishers.

In response to these two emerging reform trends, this text is designed to help you become a career-long student of your constructivist educational practices. The book is based on a central premise that can be phrased as a rhetorical question: If you, as a teacher, are not thoughtful about your professional work, how can you expect your students to be thoughtful about their learning?

The text promotes a particular study method that is called **liberal professional inquiry**. You will be learning a certain way of being reflective about your teaching, and this approach is explained in chapter 1. Chapter 1 also provides an overview of the rest of the book.

Six Assumptions

Six assumptions have guided the creation of this text.

1. *Background in teaching strategies.* We assume that you have already acquired a sufficient background in teaching strategies to be able to use this book. There are many instructional skills texts in the market, covering techniques from a behaviorist, constructivist, or other philosophical orientation. Without having acquired some of this technical background, you may have difficulty following the study guidance in this book.

2. *Motivated to teach.* The study approach in this book takes for granted that you are motivated to become a career-long student of your teaching. Clearly, this text would be of little interest to those who perceive teaching as an eight-to-three job with summers off. Such people may be willing to develop the necessary technical background to function as competent, efficient teachers, but that's the extent of their motivation. This book's study method is quite challenging and requires a deep commitment to the education profession.

3. *Personal/professional knowledge.* We believe that personal and professional development cannot be separated. Hence, the hyphenated term **personal-professional knowledge** will be used consistently throughout this text. Research has clearly established the central importance of personal beliefs and circumstances to teacher thinking. The study method in this text is designed to impact your core beliefs. You should not be surprised to find that you may be reflecting on some of your basic values and private circumstances as you work with this book. Furthermore, you will find that the teacher narratives included in this text are quite personal.

4. *Contextual teacher inquiry.* We recognize that teacher inquiry is contextual. What is relevant for professional study in one setting may not be relevant in another. You will note that the teacher narratives in this text not only possess personal features, they are also highly situational. The teacher reflections in these narratives emerge out of specific, unique circumstances.

5. *Peer support.* Teacher inquiry requires social support. Don't expect to get too far with your personal-professional studies if you act on your own. You will need the help of others in many ways. Unfortunately, many teachers today go about their educational work in isolation from their peers; and this will need to change if schools are to become true centers of inquiry. This basic assumption guides all the study material in this book; but it is highlighted in chapter 8, where you will learn ways that teachers can support one another's study.

6. *Proactive professional growth.* The study method in this text is linked to a proactive transformative teacher leadership. If schools are truly to become centers of inquiry, that is, places where teachers function as students of their constructivist practices, many structural changes will need

to occur. Teachers will need to be actively involved in fostering these transformations; otherwise, the necessary reforms may not happen. If teachers do not fight for the quality of their professional lives, who will fight for them?

7. *Active meaning-making.* We assume that the phrase *constructivist teaching* can usefully serve as a general cover term for *teaching for active meaning-making*. Another cover term might have been employed. For example, Zemelman, Daniels, and Hyde (1993) use the phrase *best practice* to refer to teaching for active student understanding. The use of constructivist teaching as a general referent does not mean that we subscribe to an exclusive cognitive psychology view of human meaning-making. As you will note in the book, educational constructivism is treated as a complex ideological topic that can be interpreted in multiple ways. We believe that constructivist teaching can be understood through many lenses, and we are working with a broad view of human meaning-making that is well expressed by Eisner (1994):

> Humans both understand and reason about the world in a variety of ways. These ways manifest themselves in the forms of representation they are able to use. Hence I believe that one major aim of education is the expansion and deepening of the meanings individuals can secure in their life, and since I believe that humans have different aptitudes with respect to the forms in which meanings can be made, I believe that school programs should provide ample opportunity for youngsters to become "literate" in a wide variety of forms. This will increase the meanings all students can secure and [it will] expand educational opportunities for those students whose aptitudes are most congruent with those forms now neglected. (p. 87)

Glossary

Four terms in this preface are printed in boldface: constructivist educational services, centers of inquiry, liberal professional inquiry, and personal-professional knowledge. All terms that are printed in **boldface** are included in the glossary at the end of this text. You are invited to study this glossary; it will help you understand the book's conceptual structure. Since reflective teaching is such a complex and slippery topic, key explanatory concepts must be carefully defined and consistently used. The glossary will provide you with concrete definitions for the text's organizing ideas.

Acknowledgments

This book is the result of extensive professional collaborations guided by one writer. As the author-of-record for this text, I wish to acknowledge the hard work of the following individuals: Patricia Hertel, Janice Hutchison, Sharon Klimm, Mary Jo Marksz, Susannah Miller, Charlene Newman, Jon Secaur, Linda Topp, Jennifer Waldbauer, and Lee Williams. Their specific contributions are noted in the book's Collaborating Authors page. The second edition builds on the collaborative work of the first edition. The following individuals contributed to that book: Thomas Barone, Patricia Hertel, Mari Koerner, and Carol Melnick.

I would also like to acknowledge the many helpful and constructive comments from the peer reviewers: Terrance R. Carson, University of Alberta; Jeanine M. Dell'Olio, Hope College; Carol A. Mullen, OISE, Canada; Iris Nierenberg, Ball State University; John E. Steinbrink, Oklahoma State University; Donna Strand, Baruch College; John Taylor, East Tennessee State University.

Finally, I wish to thank the following people at Merrill/Prentice Hall for their important contributions to this text: Debbie Stollenwerk, Linda Montgomery, and Julie Peters. A special word of gratitude to Linda Belew for her careful and sensitive editing and to Linda Topp and Cindy Bowman for their proofreading.

Though this book could not have been created without the dedicated work of many people, its overall conception, organization, and phrasing are the responsibility of a single author. Any errors in the text are mine alone.

James G. Henderson

REFERENCES

Eisner, W. W. (1994). *Cognition and curriculum reconsidered* (2nd ed.). New York: Teachers College Press.

Zemelman, S., Daniels, H., & Hyde, A. (1993). *Best practice: New standards for teaching and learning in America's schools*. Portsmouth, NH: Heinemann.

Collaborating Authors

Critical Incident and Autobiographical Reflection Writers

Contents

CHAPTER 5 Enacting Constructivist Transactions   105

CHAPTER 6 Creating a Classroom Learning Community   133

SECTION

3

Fundamental Topics   155

CHAPTER 8 Professional Collaboration   183

CHAPTER 9 Transformative Teacher Leadership   205

APPENDIX **A** **The Teacher-Character
Ideological Map**   **223**

APPENDIX **B** **Simulated Cases**   **229**

1

Foundational Topics

These two introductory chapters provide you with a foundation for the reflective teaching orientation of this book. Chapter 1 presents the book's rationale and an overview of the remaining chapters. Four characteristics of progressive decision-making are described and illustrated. These characteristics are based on a careful synthesis of current philosophical literature on human rationality. At the heart of this synthesis is the integration of three interrelated forms of teacher reflection: pragmatic reconsideration, critical reasoning, and critical engagement. Chapter 2 discusses the ideological foundations of the teaching profession. Four fictional teacher-characters provide an ideological map of the diverse perspectives in the field of education. Their comments offer insight on educational constructivism, critical reasoning, and critical engagement.

1

Studying Your Constructivist Practices

This book invites you to become a career-long student of your constructivist practices. The purpose of this chapter is to provide an overview of that invitation. In
the spirit of inquiry that guides this text, this chapter is organized as a set of specific responses to the following open-ended questions. As you read these questions, consider your own response to each.

1. Why should you become a career-long student of your teaching?
2. What are constructivist teaching practices, and why and how should they
   be studied?
3. What is a good way to provide advice for the career-long study of teaching?

What are your thoughts about these inquiries? You may want to keep them in
mind as you read this chapter.

Career-Long Study

Studying your teaching can help facilitate your personal and professional development. Sirotnik (1989) writes that schools should become **centers of inquiry**,
not targets of other people's inquiry. He makes this point for a very important

reason. If you are always the target of someone else's thinking, you may become good at following orders but not at developing abilities that will guide your personal-professional growth. Sergiovanni (1992) notes that when teachers engage in continuous professional study, they no longer need to be told how to teach. They become responsibly empowered professionals. Sergiovanni (1992) writes:

> A commitment to exemplary practice means staying abreast of the latest research in practice, researching one's own practice, experimenting with new approaches, and sharing one's insights. Once established, this . . . results in teachers accepting responsibility for their own professional growth, thus reducing the need for someone else to plan and implement staff development programs for them. (p. 43)

Teacher inquiry—studying your own teaching—is also an important consideration in discussions of educational reform. The improvement of teachers is central to the improvement of education. Barth (1990) stresses this connection as follows:

> Those who value . . . education, those who hope to improve our schools, should be worried about the stunted growth of teachers. Teacher growth is closely related to pupil growth. Probably nothing within a school has more impact on students in terms of skills development, self-confidence, or classroom behavior than the personal and professional growth of their teachers.
>   . . . Inquiry for teachers can take place both in and out of the view of students, but to teacher and student alike there must be continuous evidence that it is occurring. For when teachers observe, examine, question, and reflect on their ideas and develop new practices that lead toward their ideals, students are alive. When teachers stop growing, so do their students. (pp. 49–50)

An example of two teachers' differing approaches to the same topic will help clarify the value of teacher inquiry. Jack Dusett is a sixth-grade teacher preparing to teach a social studies unit on Christopher Columbus's "discovery" of America. Mr. Dusett wants to take a questioning approach with his students. In effect, he wants his students to relate their own experiences and interests to the content of the unit. He turns to the teacher manual for a social studies text that he will be using in this unit, and he discovers some useful guiding questions. For example, he decides to use the following questions from the manual:

> If Christopher Columbus hadn't discovered America in 1492, how might the history of the United States have been different? Have you ever discovered something in your neighborhood, such as a new playground, a new movie theater, or a new restaurant? How did this discovery make you feel? How do you think Christopher Columbus felt when he discovered America?

The students learn about Christopher Columbus's voyage to the new world, but they are not overly excited about this social studies unit; in fact, they generally perceive Mr. Dusett as a mechanical, unimaginative teacher. Furthermore, because he isn't particularly inquiring about his work, Mr. Dusett's teaching has remained fairly constant from year to year. Past students have also felt that he was mechanical. In fact, Mr. Dusett has developed the reputation of being a very routine instructor—a reputation that will probably not change unless he begins a more systematic study of his teaching practices.

Karen Smiley is also a sixth-grade teacher, but her practices are guided by a deep commitment to personal-professional study. As she plans her unit on Columbus, she looks for materials that help her critically examine the topic. She reads Kirkpatrick Sale's *The Conquest of Paradise: Christopher Columbus and the Columbian Legacy* (1990), which questions Columbus's motives and ecological values. Based on this examination, she decides to include activities that will broaden her students' multicultural perspectives. She shows students a segment of an old cowboy movie in which Native Americans are portrayed as savages. Then she asks students to list adjectives that express how they feel about Native Americans. While teaching the unit, Ms. Smiley presents information from the Native American as well as the European point of view. When the students have completed the unit, she asks them to make another list of adjectives expressing how they feel about Native Americans. She analyzes and discusses any differences between the two lists with her students. She also wants to know how her students feel about her teaching. To get feedback on her work, she conducts an open-ended classroom conversation on the following types of questions:

> We challenged the motives behind Christopher Columbus's "discovery" of America. What do you think about this type of challenge? Do you ever challenge your friends' motives? Do you think it's good to be so questioning? Did you enjoy our approach to this social studies unit? Is there anything I could do to make social studies more interesting for you?

Ms. Smiley's inquiries aren't limited to the context of her classroom. She has developed an inquiring relationship with several colleagues who enjoy exchanging ideas and evaluating one another's teaching practices. Once or twice a week they gather after school to discuss their experiences. Together they examine the quality of their teaching with the idea of constantly improving their instruction. At one of these meetings Ms. Smiley discusses her unit on Columbus. They collaborate over the virtues of her curriculum decisions. One colleague arranges to observe several of Ms. Smiley's lessons and shares constructive feedback with the group. All of the teachers look forward to learning new ideas and approaches from these group inquiry experiences. They have talked about changes in their school that would encourage more professional collaboration, and they are beginning to consider ways to provide leadership for such institutional reform.

As you can see, there is a qualitative difference between Jack Dusett and Karen Smiley's reflective practices. Mr. Dusett's commitment to thinking about his teaching is quite limited, while Ms. Smiley is dedicated to the professional study of her practices. Her deeper commitment results in the continuous improvement of her work. She constantly seeks opportunities for mutual questioning and discovery among both her students and her peers. In fact, she hopes that in time her entire school will become an inquiring community in the spirit of Dewey's (1939/1989) vision of democratic learning organizations: "Self-governing institutions are the means by which human nature can secure its fullest realization in the greatest number of persons." (p. 101)

Constructivist Teaching Practices

A constructivist teaching practice can be defined as any deliberate, thoughtful educational activity that is designed to facilitate students' active understanding. Cohen, McLaughlin, and Talbert (1993) describe this type of professional service as central to the educational reform policies of all major subject areas. They write:

> Education reform goals challenge America's schools and teachers to move away from transmitting knowledge and facts to promoting students' deeper understanding of academic subjects—understanding based in active engagement with subject area concepts. This vision of teaching and learning, called *teaching for understanding* to distinguish it from traditional modes of instruction, would promote students' critical thinking skills and authentic learning. (p. xi)

In a recent publication of the Association for Supervision and Curriculum Development, Brooks and Brooks (1993) provide an overview of constructivist teaching:

> Constructivism stands in contrast to the more deeply rooted ways of teaching that have long typified American classrooms. Traditionally, learning has been thought to be a "mimetic" activity, a process that involves students repeating, or miming, newly presented information. . . . Constructivist teaching practices, on the other hand, help learners to internalize and reshape, or transform, new information. (p. 15)

There are many sources of insight into learning-for-understanding. One of the most significant sources is research in cognitive psychology. Resnick (1983) summarizes three principles that emerge from this research:

> First, learners construct understanding. They do not simply mirror what they are told or what they read. Learners look for meaning and will try to find regularity and order in the events of the world, even in the absence of complete information. This means that naive theories will always be constructed as part of the learning process.
>
> Second, to understand something is to know relationships. Human knowledge is stored in clusters and organized into schemata that people use both to interpret familiar situations and to reason about new ones. Bits of information isolated from these structures are forgotten or become inaccessible to memory.
>
> Third, all learning depends on prior knowledge. Learners try to link new information to what they already know in order to interpret the new material in terms of established schemata. (pp. 472–473)

As Brooks and Brooks (1993) note, the guiding questions of constructivist teaching practices are:

- Can students demonstrate comprehension of concepts, not memorize information?
- Can they imaginatively solve problems, not rotely follow procedures?
- Can they inquire into complex issues, not parrot rehashed beliefs?

Brooks and Brooks (1993) also identify five principles for constructivist teaching:

1. Students should engage in active inquiry activities that are based on meaningful problems.
2. Inquiry material should be organized holistically, through the use of broad concepts, so as to encourage diverse problem-solving styles and strategies.
3. Teachers must encourage students to cultivate their own points of view on the instructional topics.
4. Curriculum materials must be responsive to students' problem-solving suppositions.
5. Evaluation should be authentically linked to students' inquiry experiences.

Constructivist teachers see their students as active participants rather than passive recipients during the learning process. In metaphoric terms, students are not just vessels into which the teacher pours knowledge. Rather, students are viewed as **conscious agents** possessing a present- and future-oriented intentionality and a background of prior knowledge and dispositions (Searle, 1992). The constructivist teacher invites these conscious agents to become fellow inquirers on a journey of discovery—perhaps eventually to become contributing members of a particular community of inquiry. If certain students don't respond to a specific inquiry invitation, the constructivist teacher reflects on three general questions: (1) What are these students' actual learning intentions? (2) What prior knowledge and/or dispositions prevents them from accepting my learning invitation? and (3) Was my inquiry invitation sufficiently compelling?

To summarize, the teacher understands **constructivist learning** as a complex interaction between students' personal purposes, their prior knowledge and dispositions, and the requirements for specific subject-matter inquiry. Figure 1.1 shows a diagram of this interaction. Do you have experience with constructivist teachers? Such teachers didn't ask you to memorize facts and practice rote skills. Instead they found ways to inspire and facilitate meaningful inquiry learning.

Figure 1.1
A Constructivist View of Learning

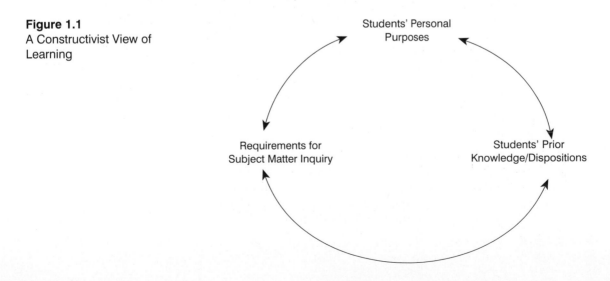

Students' Personal Purposes

Requirements for Subject Matter Inquiry

Students' Prior Knowledge/Dispositions

Why Study Constructivist Practices?

As a reflective teacher, you want to be careful to not embrace a new teaching strategy—constructivist or behavioristic, for example—until you have thought about your purposes for using it. You want to avoid technicizing your work, that is, thinking only about the means and not the end result of what you do. Elaborating on the dangers of **technicism**, Posner (1992) writes:

> Technicism focuses on the techniques of the perspective, examining only their relative effectiveness and efficiency without serious regard for their goals. . . . A preoccupation with technique diverts attention from the theoretical assumptions from which the technique derives and by which it derives meaning.
>
> It is possible to technicize any perspective, although some are more prone to technicism than others. The extreme case is the behavioral perspective. It focuses on developing effective behavior modification techniques. While claiming to be only a technology, it contends that its techniques are appropriate for any educational ends and are therefore value-neutral, and it regards behavioral psychologists as the experts in, and therefore the proper authorities on, educational decision-making. These characteristics reveal its inherent technicism. (pp. 262–263)

To avoid technicizing your constructivist practices, you must thoughtfully examine your purposes for engaging in this type of teaching. Three general goals will be presented in this section. You will need to adapt each goal to the setting in which you work. Furthermore, other valid purposes may occur to you as you gain experience with constructivist teaching. The three goals are:

- To help students actively understand subject matter with reference to their past experiences and personal purposes.
- To help students actively understand themselves.
- To help students actively understand participatory democracy.

The first goal is simply a restatement of a point made in the previous section and illustrated in Figure 1.1: that the constructivist teacher sees learning as a complex interaction between students' personal purposes, their prior knowledge and dispositions, and requirements for specific subject-matter inquiry. Imagine you are a high school English teacher covering a lesson on Shakespeare's play *Romeo and Juliet*. What can you do to help your students understand this literature classic in light of their experiences and motivations? The drama in this play is set in motion by the conflict between the Montagues and the Capulets, two households in Verona, Italy:

> Two households, both alike in dignity,
> In fair Verona, where we lay our scene
> From ancient grudge break to new mutiny,
> Where civil blood makes civil hands unclean.
> From forth the fatal loins of these two foes

A pair of star-cross'd lovers take their life. . . .
(Shakespeare, c. 1595–1596/1952, p. 285)

How can you use your knowledge of your students to make this "ancient grudge" worth studying? What experiences have they had with civil strife? Could they discover any value in studying a longstanding conflict between two households in Italy? Constructivist teaching requires you to find answers to such questions. If you are successful in creating meaningful lessons with the *Romeo and Juliet* subject matter, you will have accomplished the first goal.

The second constructivist goal builds directly on the first. As you deliberate over your students' experiences and motivations, you may want to contemplate the quality of their self-knowledge. How well do your students know themselves? In arguing for this goal, educational philosopher Maxine Greene writes: "I would like to think of teachers moving the young into their own interpretations of their lives and their lived worlds, opening wider and wider perspectives as they do so" (Greene, 1986, p. 441). In another publication, Greene (1978) describes this goal as facilitating students' "wide awakeness."

To return to the *Romeo and Juliet* example, suppose you decide that one purpose for teaching this play is to help your students better understand themselves. In Maxine Greene's terms, you want them to be more wide-awake by the time they have finished studying this subject matter. What do you do? By understanding the play, will they also come to better understand themselves? Or, must you do more? What else can you do to facilitate self-insight? How can you encourage your students to look into their own hearts, minds, and souls? When contemplating these questions, you are reflecting on the second constructivist goal.

The third goal of helping students actively understand **participatory democracy** builds on the first two goals. A social philosopher and political scientist describes participatory democracy as a "process of ongoing, proximate self-legislation . . . [resulting in] the creation of a political community capable of transforming private individuals into free citizens and partial and private interests into public goods" (Barber, 1984, p. 151). This political process could serve as the referent for the creation of a democratic classroom community. Teaching for active understanding of subject matter and self-understanding necessarily involves teacher-student reciprocity. The teacher must help facilitate students' emerging understanding—not promote his or her own. The teacher must work with a sense of constructivist equity: "Within the constraints of the lesson's subject matter, I understand in my way; now, I want you to understand this material in your way."

This teacher-student reciprocity can serve as a springboard for teaching participatory democracy. Consider again the *Romeo and Juliet* example. Suppose you decide that one purpose for teaching this play is to encourage the resolution of conflicts through dialogue. How might you cover the content in the play? How could you encourage your students to work with you and with one another as self-aware individuals? Imagine such highly developed and "wide-awake" people. How would they relate to one another? Wouldn't they be respectful of human diversity; as necessary, wouldn't they also be willing to establish common ground with others? In Barber's (1984) language, wouldn't they function as "free citizens" who would willingly help co-construct a sense of the "public good"? While covering the *Romeo and Juliet* material with your students, how would you teach these values? How would you establish a classroom environment that encourages this democratic interaction? What behavior would you model for them?

You may not know how to respond to the reflective questions in this section. Don't worry about this. This book has been designed to help you explore these types of instructional inquiries. As you read the chapters in this book, you will be receiving a great deal of advice on how to teach for active subject matter understanding, self-understanding, and democratic understanding. The handbook that accompanies this text will provide you with additional opportunities to learn about this comprehensive approach to constructivist education.

You will be learning a study approach that can be characterized as **liberal professional inquiry**. Beyer, Feinberg, Pagano, and Whitson (1989) provide an elegant summary of this type of teaching study:

> . . . we argue that a liberal education is, or should be, practical, preparing the student for active participation in the making of the world—for doing and being at the same time. Fundamental to this project is the development of a moral imagination, in teachers as well as students. Persons who act out of a moral imagination . . . act in accord with practical reason. In this, we are urging a reconceptualized view of liberal education as well as of professional practice. In our view, the practice of teaching should be taken as a central object of liberal study, and liberal study should be taken as the object of teaching. "Profession" describes at once a knowing and a doing; it describes a practice rather than a technical application. The sense of "profession" as we encounter it in the literature of professionalization is a debased one. There the professions seem to be narrowly concerned with the inculcation of habits and the development of skills from which competent practice within a vocation will result. While those concerned with the study and the teaching of the liberal arts tend to see themselves as engaged actively in the life of the mind, in developing in students certain desirable habits of mind and heart, those concerned with professional training are often inclined to see themselves as simply certifying some sort of technical competence among graduates who have been taught to accomplish specific vocational tasks through the deployment of acquired skills. Such a notion of "vocation," too, is debased. For one should not ignore the etymological . . . relationship of both words to the sense of calling. (p. 14)

This lengthy quote captures much of what this book is about, and you are encouraged to return to this quotation from time to time as you study this text.

You may believe there is a difference between liberal arts and education courses. These feelings are certainly legitimate given the current distinction between the liberal arts and professional education in many colleges and universities. Keep in mind, however, that this book collapses that distinction. In this text, you will be encouraged to think of the "practice of teaching . . . as a central object of liberal study and liberal study . . . as the object of teaching" (Beyer et al., 1989, p. 14). Think about what this means: Through careful liberal professional study, you learn to practice a certain type of teaching. By practicing this teaching, you liberalize yourself and your students. You help yourself and your students to be more eclectic—to understand a topic from many different points of view (Schwab, 1978).

This view of liberal professional inquiry is based on a certain understanding of liberalization—of how people should be free. Barber (1992) captures the essence of this sense of freedom and its relationship to education:

> Democracy is the rule of citizens, and citizens alone are free. For citizens are self-conscious, critical participants in communities of common speech, common value, and common work that bridge both space and time. As freedom yields community, so the forms of community and commonality alone yield freedom. Education makes citizens; only citizens can forge freedom. Democracy allows people to govern themselves; indeed, it insists that they do so. Education teaches them the liberty that makes self-government possible. (p. 265)

In this book, you are practicing a study method designed to facilitate your growth as a teacher who can help students—and others, as you will learn—cultivate the discipline of democratic self-government. Think back to the three constructivist goals: teaching for active subject matter understanding, self-understanding, and democratic understanding. This text will encourage you to incorporate all three goals into your teaching deliberations. This may be a challenging developmental ideal, but what are the alternatives? Should teachers only facilitate subject matter understanding? This type of learning should help their society's economy. But what about its civics? Should teachers facilitate self-understanding without encouraging a strong, participatory democratic ethic? What would be the quality of life in a society composed of personally insightful but highly private individuals?

How to Study Constructivist Practices

You will be invited to study your constructivist practices as a **progressive decision-maker**. Teachers who are progressive decision-makers exhibit four key characteristics:

1. Their decisions are sensitive to the context of the situations in which those decisions are embedded.
2. Their decisions are guided by a continuous cycle of fluid planning, empowered enactment, participant observation, and a pragmatic reconsideration of their knowledge.
3. Their decisions are informed by personal-professional knowledge that is under continuous critical examination.
4. Their decisions are enhanced by informal and formal study projects.

We now turn to a careful examination of these four characteristics because they form a frame of reference for this book. Teaching-as-progressive-decision-making is this text's guiding ideal. The better you can comprehend and appreciate this view of enlightened teacher reasoning, the more you will understand the book's study advice.

Context Sensitivity

Teachers must make decisions in the context of their interactions with their students. If they are not sensitive to the many subtleties and nuances associated with their students' meaningful learning, they will not be successful as constructivist educators. They must base their actions on their best perceptive and judicious abilities. Van Manen (1991) calls this *pedagogical thoughtfulness*:

> Children are not empty vessels who come to school merely to be filled with curricular content by means of special instructional methods. Moreover, children who come to school come from somewhere. Teachers need to have some sense of what it is that children bring with them, what defines their present understandings, mood, emotional state, and readiness to deal with the subject matter and the world of the school. . . . It is possible to learn all the techniques of instruction but to remain pedagogically unfit as a teacher. The preparation of educators obviously includes much more than the teaching of knowledge and skills, more even than a professional ethical code or moral craft. To become a teacher includes something that cannot be taught formally: the most personal embodiment of a pedagogical thoughtfulness. (pp. 7, 9)

Teachers must also be sensitive to other contexts. They must understand the perspectives of those who supervise their work, the expectations of their students' parents, the norms and values in their school's surrounding neighborhood, and the social trends of the society in which they work. Teachers have a lot to consider as they engage in decision-making. Their work is embedded in many subtly unique and overlapping contexts.

This book contains many teaching stories, and you will notice that each narrative is embedded in its own unique context. The study advice in this book is general in nature. It will be up to you to adapt the advice to the specific setting in which you work. The idiosyncrasies in the narratives should serve as a reminder that progressive decision-making requires **context sensitivity**.

Decision-Making Cycle

When teachers function as empowered agents rather than as subjects of other people's decisions, they are free to engage in a proactive **decision-making cycle**. This cycle has four phases: (1) a fluid, open-ended, experimental type of planning; (2) teaching-learning enactments that flow from this planning; (3) sensitive participant observations of the consequences of these enactments; and (4) a **pragmatic reconsideration** of knowledge in light of these consequences. The final phase may involve some personal discomfort. When reconsidering their personal-professional knowledge, teachers may experience some cognitive dissonance (Festinger, 1957) before altering their ideas and beliefs. **Cognitive dissonance** is a feeling of discomfort engendered by experiences that are perceived to be in conflict with fundamental constructs. For example, suppose a teacher believes that he treats students fairly. Then, through careful observation, he discovers that he consistently pays more attention to certain children—maybe white males, high-achieving middle-class females, or athletes. A strong feeling of dissonance is likely to occur. The teacher can resolve this dissonance through a reconsideration of basic constructs or future plans and actions. Figure 1.2 provides a schematic illustration of the four-phase decision-making cycle. McCutcheon (1995) provides an example of a teacher engaging in this decision-making cycle. This brief narrative illustration begins with the participant observation phase:

> . . . Mark Schaefer, third-grade teacher . . . recently observed that his students did not understand the definition of even numbers in his school system's mathematics curriculum and that he was to implement the concept that "even numbers are numbers that can be divided by two." Compared to previous classes he taught in Mapleton, he viewed these students as somewhat less capable, but he was momentarily perplexed because not even his brightest students in class understood this definition until they had learned about division (which was not to occur until fourth grade, according to the graded course of study). He saw it as a sequencing problem in the graded course of study. He used this reflection in his [planning] decision to remind students of the chant, "Two, four, six, eight, who [sic] do we appreciate" and to return to the definition later in the year after he introduced division (he was permitted to exceed the grade objectives). Following the [enacted] teaching of the chant, students were able to sort numbers into odd and even on worksheets [that] he made. . . . (p. 40)

Three related foundational concepts provide important insight into the decision-making cycle: pragmatic intelligence, action research, and experiential learning. The concept of **pragmatic intelligence** is drawn from the philosophical tradition of pragmatism. This tradition includes the works of Ralph Waldo Emerson, C. S. Peirce, William James, W. E. B. Du Bois, John Dewey, and Richard Rorty.[1] John Dewey is arguably the most influential member of the pragmatist group. In *How We Think* (1910/1933), Dewey analyzes pragmatic intelligence. Grimmett (1988) provides a precise summary of Dewey's analysis. First, we experience "a state of doubt, hesitation, perplexity, or mental difficulty. . . . " (p. 6).

Figure 1.2
The Decision-Making Cycle

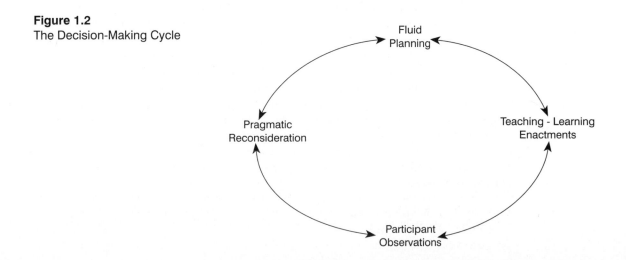

We then seek to resolve this problematic experience in a suitable way. We arrive at a tentative conclusion that is based in part on our past experiences with solving problems. This conclusion also infers to some degree that what we did in the past to solve our problems will work again. We act tentatively because we do not know if our inference will lead to a productive solution. Sometimes our problem-solving inferences are correct, and sometimes they are not. Because we act tentatively, we are willing to engage in further inquiry and, as necessary, reconstruct our knowledge until we arrive at a conclusion that we believe is "trustworthy" (Dewey, 1910/1933, p. 47). This means that we must be "willing to endure suspense and to undergo the trouble of searching" (Dewey, 1910/1933, p. 16). This suspense is based on a paradox of pragmatic intelligence (Grimmett, 1988, p. 8). We cannot know if our tentative efforts will be successful until we act, but it is difficult to act without knowing exactly what to do. To be intelligent problem solvers, we must persist despite this paradox. **Action research** also has a long history, and Kurt Lewin is a central figure in this intellectual tradition. In *Resolving Social Conflicts* (1948), Lewin discusses the key dimensions of good action research: analyze a problematic situation, gather additional useful information, define the problem, hypothesize a solution, act to solve the problem, observe the results of your actions, and make a judgment as to how best to proceed. In the past half century, there have been many adaptations of Lewin's work in teaching and teacher education.[2] Kolb (1984) provides a sophisticated analysis of the process of **experiential learning**. He notes that during experiential learning "one moves in varying degrees from actor to observer, and from specific involvement to general analytical detachment" (p. 31). You can best realize this type of learning when you maintain a balance between acting and observing and between participation and thoughtful detachment. Examine the decision-making cycle as illustrated in Figure 1.2. You will note how it is guided by this principle of dual balancing.

Though this book cannot provide specific guidance for idiosyncratic and unique teaching settings, you will receive general advice on how to move through the decision-making cycle as a constructivist educator. The study guidance in chapters 3–6 focuses on four constructivist practices: solving complex learning problems in a constructivist way (chapter 3); creating a constructivist curriculum design (chapter 4); enacting constructivist transactions (chapter 5); and creating a classroom learning community (chapter 6). Chapters 3–6 follow the same pattern. In each chapter you will read a vignette that introduces the constructivist practice. Next you will study a protocol of that practice. The protocol is a general application of the decision-making cycle and is designed to facilitate your experi-

---

[1] For a sophisticated review of pragmatism, see Cornel West's *The American Evasion of Philosophy: A Genealogy of Pragmatism* (1989).

[2] For a concise overview of this history, see J. McKernan's "Action Research and Curriculum Development" in the *Peabody Journal of Education* (1987); for a current discussion of action research in teaching, see M. Cochran-Smith and S. L. Lytle's *Inside/Outside: Teacher Research and Knowledge* (1993).

ential learning on that particular constructivist practice. You will then read a narrative written by an experienced teacher that illustrates the protocol. The narrative provides a personalized and contextualized description of the pragmatics of the chapter's constructivist practice.

Hopefully this material will help you practice the decision-making cycle as a constructivist educator. As you study chapters 3–6, keep in mind that the constructivist practices are presented separately to facilitate your professional learning. In the real world of teaching, the four constructivist practices are usually closely integrated. It will be up to you to find a meaningful way to apply this study material to your own teaching circumstances.

Critical Examination of Personal-Professional Knowledge

Our examination of the second characteristic of progressive decision-making revealed that the decision-making cycle includes a pragmatic type of reflection. The third characteristic—the continuous critical examination of **personal-professional knowledge**—incorporates two other types of reflection. These are called **critical reasoning** and **critical engagement**. Both types of reflection are necessary because teachers' pragmatic decisions are grounded in rational and intuitive considerations. In other words, progressive teachers base their decisions on justified reasons and on more personalized tacit knowledge, conscious and unconscious feelings, and guiding metaphors.[3] Critical reasoning is the process of examining one's reasons for particular decisions. Ennis (1987) writes that "Critical thinking . . . is a practical reflective activity that has reasonable belief or action as its goal" (p. 10). You can practice this type of thinking in diverse ways. Consider your own style of critical reflection. When you confront competing interpretations on a topic, how do you justify your position, and what do you include and exclude in your justifications? For example, are you deductive, acting on the basis of general principles? If so, what are these principles? Or, when you are rational, do you tend to be inductive, carefully studying a situation before deciding how to act? What is included in your inductive observations? Are you more tacit in your approach? Do you act; and when necessary, think of your reasons for acting afterwards? Is your critical reasoning eclectic? When formulating or defending a position, do you combine reasoning strategies and cover a wide range of topics? Is your critical reasoning situational? Do you reason differently in different circumstances?

Critical engagement is a correlate of critical reasoning. It is the complementary process of considering or becoming attuned to the tacit awareness, feelings, and metaphors that inspire your teaching. It is being led more by your heart than by

---

[3] There is a great deal of research on the type of knowledge and understanding that guides teachers' decision-making. For a good overview of this research, see McCutcheon (1995), especially pages 44–45.

your head. This type of critical work is aesthetically immediate rather than ana-
lytically detached. Through critical engagement you open yourself to your highest intentions, your best virtues, and your deepest sense of inspiration. The great
poet John Milton writes:

> Virtue could see to do what virtue would
> By her own radiant light, though sun and moon
> Were in the flat sea sunk. And Wisdom's self
> Oft seeks to sweet retired solitude,
> Where with her best nurse Contemplation
> She plumes her feathers, and lets grow her wings
> That in the various bustle of resort
> Were all too-ruffled, and sometimes impair'd.
> He that has light within his own clear breast
> May sit i' th' centre and enjoy bright day;
> But he that hides a dark soul and foul thoughts
> Benighted walks under the midday sun;
> Himself is his own dungeon.
> *(Milton, 1632/1952, pp. 41–42)*

Teachers often face situations that require them to make wise educational decisions, and critical engagement can enlighten their decision-making with aesthetic
sensibility.

Critical engagement is as open-ended as critical reasoning. There are many
ways to become aesthetically attuned, and what is nourishing and invigorating to
one person may be ordinary and uninspiring to another. Aoki (1992) encourages
this type of reflection as follows:

> I ask you now to think of a really good teacher that you have experienced in your
> time. Allow him or her to be present before you. I believe that the truth of this good
> teacher of yours is in the measure of the immeasurable. And, now, say to him or her:
> he *is* the teaching; she *is* the teaching. And after you have said these words, allow the
> unsaid to shine through the said. Savor now the elusively true, the mystery of what
> teaching essentially is. (p. 27)

Does Aoki's meditative invitation inspire you? If not, what would? In what ways
can you identify deep feelings that will energize your teaching life? How will you
practice critical engagement?

You may not have a good feel for your critical reasoning and critical engagement preferences. You may not have yet cultivated a definitive way to critically
examine your personal-professional knowledge, and you may be interested in
several models as to how to proceed. In chapter 2, four imaginary teachers will
introduce themselves, each representing a dominant ideological position in the
teaching profession. They function as distinctive, headstrong, and contrary characters in a novel, and so they are called **teacher-characters**. They have each cultivated a distinctive **critical style**, a unique way to critically examine their teaching.

They will discuss their approaches in chapter 2. These ideological discussions have been created as study material to help you ascertain your critical style. The four teacher-characters also provide commentary on the four constructivist practices in chapters 3–6; the purpose of this ideological commentary is to help you critically examine your personal-professional knowledge.

Chapter 7 will present a broad, career-long overview of this book's study method. You will read the developmental stories of two experienced teachers who have reflected on their growth as progressive decision-makers. Their autobiographical reflections are guided by a consideration of four teaching virtues associated with constructivist practices. The four virtues are teaching as a **calling** and as **caring**, **creative**, and **centered** work. They will be called the **4C virtues** because they all begin with the letter *C*. The autobiographies have been written to help you appreciate the value of sustained professional study.

Because the referent for the autobiographical accounts are the 4C virtues, they are crafted to highlight critical examination. There is a reason for this narrative emphasis. In today's fast-paced world, professional work often stresses the pragmatic over the critical. Unfortunately, this understanding of professionalism can be dangerously unbalanced. It can result in businesslike, matter-of-fact decision-makers who lack a deep sense of the virtues of their work. They function without a refined appreciation for the aesthetics and ethics of the services they provide.

This type of skewed professionalism is particularly problematic when teachers attempt to facilitate the three constructivist goals of subject-matter understanding, self-understanding, and democratic understanding. This type of educational service requires a teachers' best pragmatic and critical development, and this book has been designed to encourage this type of comprehensive personal-professional growth.

Chapter 7 also includes teacher-character commentary on the 4C virtues. Their analysis should help you further craft your own critical style. It should also serve as a reminder that considerations of best practice in education are inherently diversified. Tolerance for diversity is an important consideration in chapters 8 and 9, the final two chapters of this text. An overview of these two chapters will be presented shortly.

Continuing Study Projects

The fourth key characteristic of progressive decision-making is engagement in informal and formal study projects. Personal-professional growth is also fed by the stimulation of new knowledge. Chapters 3–6 and 8–9 each conclude with a list of further readings to help facilitate your continuing education. However, since meaningful project work tends to be specific to each situation, this general study book cannot possibly provide the personally tailored guidance you will need. You will ultimately need to rely on your own best context sensitivities.

AN IMAGINARY CRITICAL INCIDENT

The following fictionalized episode provides a brief illustration of the four characteristics of progressive decision-making:

Carolyn Dickson has been teaching French at Lewis and Clark High School for twelve years. During her first year of teaching, she made a personal vow to reflect on her teaching practices at least four hours a week. She decided that if she could discipline herself to exercise four hours a week, she could certainly devote the same amount of time to her chosen profession. Over the years she has kept her vow by engaging in a variety of formal and informal study projects, such as study groups, workshops, and university courses.

As part of her commitment to professional development, Carolyn subscribes to three journals. One journal recently carried several articles on cultural pluralism. After reading them, Carolyn began reflecting on her teaching. Though her school's population included African-American, Hispanic, Native American, and White students, her classes were predominantly White. She wondered what she could do about this.

Suddenly, Carolyn had an idea. She began to think of the culturally diverse populations in many French-speaking cultures in the Caribbean, such as Haiti. She thought of the varied population in French Canada. Perhaps she could prepare one or more inquiry units on these societies. Maybe over time, the inclusion of these units would encourage minority students to take French.

Carolyn wondered if this experiment would work. Would it be worth the time and effort? She believed that she would only know the answer to this question after careful planning, observation, and further reflection. She decided to start with a unit on Haiti. This was a logical choice since this country had received so much news coverage in recent years.

As Carolyn began her planning, she further considered her reasons for teaching this unit. It would enable her to break away from her current emphasis on Parisian French. After all, French is spoken in many different ways throughout the world. It would also enable her to work with literature from countries besides France. She could also tap into local resources she hadn't used before. For example, there was a small Haitian subculture in her city. She soon discovered that some members of this ethnic group were willing to help; but if she hadn't been working on this unit and trying to expand her teaching horizons, she wouldn't have made the contacts.

As Carolyn contemplated the potential power of this inquiry unit on Haiti, she felt fortunate to live in a culture that had democratic traditions. Haiti, with its history of military dictatorships, was such a contrast to her society. Carolyn was inspired by the image of diverse social groups working out their differences in a peaceful way. Haiti was trying to build this kind of society. This would be an important point for her students to understand. Maybe then, they could better appreciate the value of the democratic struggles in their own society. All in all, the more Carolyn thought about this unit, the more excited she became. She thought to herself, "I can hardly wait to begin this experiment. I wonder what I will learn about myself and my students?"

You have now been introduced to the study method that will be used in this book—and in the workbook that accompanies this text. You will be guided to approach your constructivist practices as a progressive decision-maker. You will be given the latitude to develop your own reflective approach, but with the encouragement that you undertake a balanced pragmatic and critical study.

An image may help you visualize the study method advocated in this book. To repeat a point made at the beginning of this chapter, you are studying your teaching so as to facilitate your personal-professional growth. In effect, you are working on constructing your best teaching self as a constructivist educator. This developmental work could be likened to weaving a fabric using three types of fiber. The three types of fiber represent the three forms of reflection introduced in this chapter: pragmatic reconsideration, critical reasoning, and critical engagement. The three fibers are pictured in Figure 1.3. Teachers can use slightly modified versions of each fiber, and they may weave in many different ways. The result is that each teacher weaves his or her own distinctive fabric. Each teacher's development unfolds in its own unique way.

Figure 1.4 portrays a medley of weavings, representing the developmental diversity that results from the study method in this book. It may take you time to learn how to function as a progressive decision-maker. This book presents a study method that requires hard work and perseverance. This chapter began with an

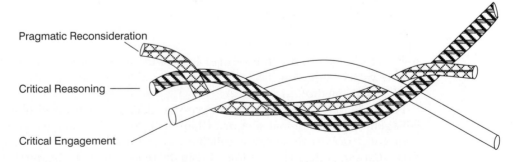

Figure 1.3
The Text's Three Forms of Reflection

Figure 1.4
Teachers' Development: A Medley of Weavings

invitation for you to become a career-long student of your constructivist practices. Rome wasn't built in a day, nor will you be able to take full advantage of this book's study method in a day.

Few individuals can practice progressive decision-making without systematic collegial and institutional support. Chapter 8 presents strategies on how to study your constructivist practices in collaboration with other teachers. Chapter 9, the final chapter, addresses the topic of **transformative teacher leadership**. This is a type of leadership in which teachers function as agents of fundamental change. They work to help initiate and sustain progressive decision-making and to facili tate the necessary organizational changes that must accompany this sophisticated reflective practice.

To conclude this section, keep in mind the underlying referent for this text's study method. Through continuous pragmatic reconsideration, critical reasoning, and critical engagement, you are liberally educating yourself in a particular way. You are developing your abilities to govern your own teaching—you are democratically empowering yourself and positioning yourself to help others with democratic self-government.

Metacognitive Guidance

The study advice in this book has been organized as **metacognitive guidance**. Metacognition is the conscious monitoring of one's thought processes (Haller, Child, & Walberg, 1988; Wittrock, 1986). Think of metacognition as a mental prompt analogous to a shopping list that you use when you go to the store. You don't mechanically follow this list, but you use it to remind yourself of things you may need. A metacognitive strategy is a mental reminder. The more you begin to regulate your thinking by following conscious thinking strategies, particularly in a supportive collegial environment, the better you will be able to integrate these strategies into your everyday teaching (Vygotsky, 1978).

Metacognitive guidance in education can be pictured as scaffolded instruction. A scaffold is an "adjustable and temporary" support system (Palincsar, 1986, p. 75). In effect, this book provides you with scaffolding for becoming a career-long student of your constructivist practices. Use it in this spirit. As you begin to internalize this structured assistance—to integrate the metacognitive guidance into your continuing professional inquiries—discard the scaffolding. In the future, you may want to use metacognitive guidance in your teaching. You can easily engage in this practice by providing your students with a relevant but temporary thinking scaffold they can use to monitor their inquiries during specific constructivist lessons.

CONCLUSION

You have now read responses to the three questions that opened this chapter. Do you agree with the way these questions have been answered? If so, why? If not, why not? Keep in mind that as you read this book, you will be encouraged to think for yourself. Functioning as an independent thinker is at the heart of empowered professional inquiry. However, such independence requires a strong sense of responsibility. In this book, you will be urged to consider your responsibilities as an educator in a diversified, ideologically complex democratic society.

REFERENCES

Aoki. T. T. (1992). Layered voices of teaching: The uncannily correct and the elusively true. In W. F. Pinar & W. M. Reynolds (Eds.), *Understanding curriculum as phenomenological and deconstructed text* (pp. 17–27). New York: Teachers College Press.

Barber, B. R. (1984). *Strong democracy: Participatory politics for a new age*. Berkeley: University of California Press.

Barber, B. R. (1992). *An aristocracy of everyone: The politics of education and the future of America*. New York: Oxford University Press.

Barth, R. S. (1990). *Improving schools from within: Teachers, parents, and principals can make the difference*. San Francisco: Jossey-Bass.

Beyer, L. E., Feinberg, W., Pagano, J. A., & Whitson, J. A. (1989). *Preparing teachers as professionals: The role of educational studies and other liberal disciplines*. New York: Teachers College Press.

Brooks, J. G., & Brooks, M. G. (1993). *In search of understanding: The case for constructivist classrooms*. Alexandria, VA: Association for Supervision and Curriculum Development.

Cohen, D. K., McLaughlin, M. W., & Talbert, J. E. (1993). Preface. In D. K. Cohen, M. W. McLaughlin, & J. E. Talbert (Eds.), *Teaching for understanding: Challenges for policy and practice* (pp. xi–xvii). San Francisco: Jossey-Bass.

Dewey, J. (1933). *How we think: A restatement of the relation of reflective thinking to the educative process* (2nd ed.). Boston: D. C. Heath. (Original work published 1910)

Dewey, J. (1989). *Freedom and culture*. Buffalo: Prometheus Books. (Original work published 1939)

Ennis, R. H. (1987). A taxonomy of critical thinking dispositions and abilities. In J. Boykoff Baron & R. J. Sternberg (Eds.), *Teaching thinking skills: Theory and practice* (pp. 9–26). New York: W. H. Freeman.

Festinger, L. (1957). *Theory of cognitive dissonance*. Stanford, CA: Stanford University Press.

Greene, M. (1978). *Landscapes of learning*. New York: Teachers College Press.

Greene, M. (1986). In search of a critical pedagogy. *Harvard Educational Review, 56*, 427–441.

Grimmett, P. P. (1988). The nature of reflection and Schon's conception in perspective. In P. P. Grimmett & G. L. Erickson (Eds.), *Reflection in teacher education* (pp. 5–15). New York: Teachers College Press.

Haller, E. P., Child, D. A., & Walberg, H. J. (1988). Can comprehension be taught? A quantitative synthesis of "metacognitive" studies. *Educational Researcher, 17*(9), 5–8.

Kolb, D. A. (1984). *Experiential learning: Experience as the source of learning and development*. Englewood Cliffs, NJ: P T R Prentice-Hall.

Lewin, K. (1948). *Resolving social conflicts*. New York: Harper and Brothers.

McCutcheon, G. (1995). *Developing the curriculum: Solo and group deliberation*. White Plains, NY: Longman.

Milton, J. (1952). Comus. English minor poems, Paradise Lost, Samson Agonistes, Areopagitica. In R. M. Hutchins (Ed.), *Great Books of the Western World* (pp. 33–56). Chicago: Encyclopaedia Britannica. (Original work published 1632)

Palincsar, A. S. (1986). The role of dialogue in providing scaffolded instruction. *Educational Psychologist, 21*, 73–98.

Posner, G. J. (1992). *Analyzing the curriculum*. New York: McGraw-Hill.

Resnick, L. B. (1983). Mathematics and science learning: A new conception. *Science, 29*, 472–473.

Sale, K. (1990). *The conquest of paradise: Christopher Columbus and the Columbian legacy*. New York: Knopf.

Schwab, J. J. (1978). *Science, curriculum, and liberal education: Selected essays*. (I. Westbury & N. J. Wilkof, eds.). Chicago: University of Chicago Press.

Searle, J. R. (1992). *The rediscovery of mind*. Cambridge, MA: MIT Press.

Sergiovanni, T. J. (1992). Why we should seek substitutes for leadership. *Educational Leadership, 49*, 41–45.

Shakespeare, W. (1952). Romeo and Juliet. In W. G. Clarke & W. A. Wright (Eds.), *Great Books of the Western World: Vol. 26. The plays and sonnets of William Shakespeare* (pp. 285–319). Chicago: Encyclopaedia Britannica. (Original work published circa 1595–1596)

Sirotnik, K. A. (1989). The school as the center of change. In T. J. Sergiovanni & J. H. Moore (Eds.), *Schooling for tomorrow: Directing reforms to issues that count* (pp. 89–113). Boston: Allyn & Bacon.

van Manen, M. (1991). *The tact of teaching: The meaning of pedagogical thoughtfulness*. Albany, NY: State University of New York Press.

Vygotsky, L. S. (1978). *Mind in society: The development of higher psychological process* (M. Cole, V. John-Steiner, S. Scribner, & E. Souberman, Eds. and Trans.). Cambridge, MA: Harvard University Press.

Wittrock, M. C. (1986). Students' thought processes. In M. C. Wittrock (Ed.), *Handbook of research on teaching* (3rd ed., pp. 297–314). New York: Macmillan.

C H A P T E R

2

Critically Examining Your Constructivist Beliefs

For all of us, there is an important connection between what we believe and how we arrive at these beliefs. The purpose of this chapter is to help you critically examine the content of your constructivist beliefs and help you identify the process you use to clarify these beliefs. Try the following experiment with one or two close friends or family members. Ask each person for an opinion on some topic. Then ask, "How did you arrive at that opinion?" You should be able to see a close connection between the substance of their beliefs and their method of believing. The fact that this relationship exists should not be surprising. What we think and how we think are integral parts of who we are.

Think back to chapter 1. You were told that the study advice in this book is metacognitive: it is a sequence of mental prompts or scaffolding designed to help you think. In this chapter, four contrasting teaching ideologies, each represented by a fictional teacher-character, will serve this scaffolding function. The four teacher-characters will first introduce themselves. Following these brief biographical sketches, they will discuss the content of their constructivist beliefs and the critical process they use to clarify their beliefs. In terms of the language we used in chapter 1, these teacher-characters will present a synopsis of their personal-professional knowledge on educational constructivism, and they will describe their distinctive **critical style**, their way of critically examining their teaching.

25

Hopefully, these contrasting perspectives will help you examine your own constructivist beliefs as well as your preferred critical approach.

An Ideological Overview

The four teacher-characters appear in chapters 2 through 7. Their collective views provide an overview of dominant ideologies in the teaching profession. The examination of **ideology** can be traced to the work of Antoine Destutt de Tracy in the early nineteenth century. McLellan (1986) describes de Tracy's pioneering work as follows:

> de Tracy proposed a new science of ideas, an idea-logy, which would be the ground of all other sciences. Rejecting the concept of innate ideas, de Tracy explained how . . . [a] rational investigation of the origin of ideas, free from religious or metaphysical prejudice, would be the foundation of a just and happy society. (p. 6)

Since de Tracy's original work, many systems of ideological analysis have been created. It is beyond the scope of this book to explore all these systems, which include the work of Karl Marx, Karl Mannheim, and many others. If you are interested in this history, McLellan's *Ideology* (1986) would be a good place to start.

The teacher-character scaffolding, which begins in this chapter and ends in chapter 7, is based on the following understanding of ideology:

> Individuals behave according to the manner in which they perceive reality. . . . [Their] belief systems provide a foundation for the selection and sorting processes involved in perceiving, categorizing, excluding, judging, inferring, defining, and intending. . . . Once these socially learned complex systems are internalized, they become referents for behavior. Such an affirmation does not deny spontaneity or creativity but rather asserts that spontaneity and creativity occur within a person's ideological frame of reference. (Bernier, 1981, p. 293)

It is assumed that you have already formed some opinions about "good" teaching—that, to some degree, you have already developed a perspective on teaching before reading this text. Hopefully, the contrasting points of view of the four teacher-characters will help you examine your teaching beliefs. There is no expectation that you should internalize this text's ideological overview. In fact, if you tried to do so, you might succumb to the problem of naive eclecticism. **Naive eclecticism** is the superficial adoption of selected elements of an ideology without a critical examination of your practices and underlying beliefs. Naive eclecticism is cosmetic; it can be likened to the adoption of a fad. It would be a surface response to, and a misuse of, the teacher-character scaffolding in this text. Naive eclecticism is linked to self-deception rather than authentic inquiry. In succinct terms, it lacks depth and does not lead to developmental change. It results from a lack of pragmatic and critical reflection.

You may, of course, want to try out some of the contrasting advice in this text before internalizing it. This pragmatic experimentalism, guided by the decision-making cycle described in chapter 1 and exemplified in chapters 3–6, is not the same as naive eclecticism. It is a sincere effort to consider the merits of particular teaching perspectives. You may ultimately discard a particular point of view because it doesn't work for you in your teaching circumstances, but that type of trial effort should not be compared to the faddish, superficial adoption of a belief.

The four teacher-characters in this book represent only one ideological overview on beliefs about "good" teaching. Other comprehensive systems of ideological analysis could be used to support the study of teaching. After you read this book, you may want to entertain such possibilities.[1] For a discussion of the ideological scholarship that guided the creation of the four teacher-characters in this book, see Appendix A at the end of this book.

Teacher-Characters: Autobiographical Introductions

The four teacher-characters will now introduce themselves. As these imaginary individuals speak, you will notice symbols next to their names conveying the essence of each character's ideology. Johnny Jackson's symbol is the image of an *open book*, which conveys his rationalist orientation. For Amy Nelson, the *personal computer* symbol denotes controlled, efficient information processing and economic achievement. Dennis Sage's symbol is a *teacher clasping the hand of a student*. This image stands for his faith in the power of personal relationships in education. For Silvia Rivera, the *scales of justice* symbol represents passion for social justice.

Johnny Jackson, High School English Teacher

I grew up on the south side of Chicago in the early 1950s. My dad was a school custodian, so our family didn't have a lot of money. Still we took advantage of all of the city's cultural resources. It seems as though every weekend we went to a museum, a play, a special art exhibit, or whatever. I guess my mom was the main motivator for these family outings. She grew up in Alabama, and she had a thirst and passion for education. She made sure I worked hard as a student. I can still see her face the day I told her I had been accepted at the University of Chicago.

---

[1] For an overview of the ideological systems that have been developed in the field of curriculum and teaching, see the introductory essay in the *Handbook of Research on Curriculum* (New York: Macmillan, 1992). This essay, entitled "Conceptions of Curriculum and Curriculum Specialists," is written by Philip Jackson, who is also the editor of the text.

I majored in English at the University of Chicago, and I'll never forget one professor who taught a course on James Joyce. Our study of Joyce's (1914/1934) novel *Ulysses* was a revelation to me. I couldn't believe so many ideas could be packed into one book. The juxtaposition of the simple everyday lives of the characters with the **great ideas** of Western civilization was stunning to behold and contemplate—and it still is!

I'm chair of the English Department at a highly respected college preparatory magnet school in the Chicago Public School System. I have a master's degree in English Literature from UC, and I have often thought about going on for a Ph.D. so that I could teach college students. But deep down I realize that my calling is with adolescents. I enjoy turning them on to a vast cultural world they know little about—not because they're not bright enough, but simply because they haven't received the proper exposure. I seem to have my mother's missionary zeal for education—particularly when it comes to the boys. I'm one of the few positive African-American role models in their lives. With the help of such creative writers as William Shakespeare and Alice Walker, I can help them discover their potential for a broad and enlightened identity.

Speaking of Shakespeare, I recently read a speech by Dr. Lee Shulman at Stanford University that, for me, captures the essence of the constructivist approach to learning. (By the way, Dr. Shulman is also a graduate of UC.) He describes an English teacher who introduces Shakespeare's *Julius Caesar* through an imaginative activity.[2] The teacher asks students to pretend that they are crew members on the starship *Enterprise* led by the highly respected Captain Kirk. Unfortunately, the captain begins to act strangely, and the crew starts to worry that he will ask them to use the power of the *Enterprise* against the very empire they are sworn to serve. What should the student crew members do? Should they become "revolutionaries" and work to remove Captain Kirk from power, or should they remain "loyalists"? The class discussion raises many feelings. (I know it would for my students because a couple of them have brothers and sisters who are associated with gangs.)

The day after the *Enterprise* discussion the English teacher tells students that they are going to study a play by Shakespeare that raises many of the same issues they covered yesterday. What an imaginative way to introduce *Julius Caesar*! Shakespeare describes the human comedies and tragedies that are part of our everyday lives, and this teacher found a way to build a meaningful bridge between this great dramatist and the students' past experiences. That's the kind of teaching to which I aspire.

---

[2] Shulman, L. S. (1989, January). *Aristotle Had It Right: On Knowledge and Pedagogy*. Keynote address at the annual national meeting of The Holmes Group. (Available from The Holmes Group, 501 Erickson Hall, East Lansing, MI 48824–1034)

Amy Nelson, Elementary School Teacher

My dad is a successful businessman, and I grew up in an affluent suburb outside of Cleveland. I'm 35 years old. I'm quite proud of my dad's accomplishments, and he has always been a big supporter of mine, too. Like when I won the all-school spelling bee as a fifth-grader. My strongest opponent was Bobby Watkins, and he never had a chance! I was the "power speller supreme," and I got a special kick out of beating a boy.

Both of my parents are well-organized, hard-working people, and thanks to them I know how to use my time well. Sometimes I think I get too task-oriented, but then I realize that life is short and there's much to accomplish. I'm glad I became an elementary school teacher because I can help the next generation acquire the proper work habits.

I like focused people who have goals in life. Sometimes I think I missed my calling and should have gone into business like my dad. But then I realize that many children today aren't lucky enough to be raised by two hard-working parents. They need someone like me to show them the way. I know this is true because former students have stopped by to thank me for that extra push they got in my class.

I'm one of the few women I know who reads the sports pages. My dad used to take me to the Cleveland Browns football games, and I still follow them on television. I like competition. If it's managed properly, it can build character and self-esteem—for girls as well as boys.

I'm currently teaching sixth grade and have a master's degree in Educational Administration and Supervision. My elementary school isn't very big, so our only administrator is the principal. I function as the school's informal assistant principal, for which I get paid extra money. I don't mind the additional responsibilities because I plan to apply for a principalship when there is an opening in my school district. Our school is located in one of the new "professional" suburbs outside Columbus, Ohio. Most of our children's fathers—and some of the mothers—work for the new high-tech firms that are prospering in Columbus. (These vital, dynamic businesses are one of the bright spots in our changing American economy.) Our students are expected to succeed, and they score very high on all the standardized achievement tests. We are quite proud of this record and have even included an insert in the Sunday paper highlighting the achievement levels of the students in our school district.

I'm also quite proud of my professional accomplishments. I have gone to innumerable workshops on teacher effectiveness, and I know how to maximize my students' academic achievements. I can talk for hours about performance objectives, advanced organizers, student engagement rates, lesson transitions, and so on.

One of my heroines is Dr. Madeline Hunter. I should say that I tend to respect all high-achieving women no matter how different their points of view. I applaud both Margaret Thatcher and Geraldine Ferraro. Dr. Hunter has synthesized educational research into very readable instructional principles and procedures. I highly recommend her book *Mastery Teaching* (1982), which will help you inquire into the topic of efficient student learning. Teachers can guide their students' constructivist learning. There are specific ways they can teach for understanding, thereby bridging the gap between their students' unfocused childhood interests and the high-profile, high-performance, problem-solving world of professional life. It is this world that is the hope for a strong America in the future.

Dennis Sage, Kindergarten Teacher

I sometimes wonder why I'm a teacher. I was raised by an artist mother in the San Francisco Bay area and learned to love the creative process. My mother was a photographer for a local newspaper, but that was just for money. She had to work because my dad left us when I was very young. I'm 28 years old, and I don't have any brothers or sisters. Mom built a darkroom in an old, dilapidated garage behind our house and did all her creative work there. She has won many prizes and had her work published in a variety of magazines and books.

I grew up as a member of a loosely affiliated community of artists. I learned how to paint, sculpt, dance, and play the trumpet. I guess that's why I like kindergarten teaching. You can be creative with the children without worrying too much about a bunch of standardized, bureaucratic expectations.

I've studied the works of the great naturalist John Muir, and I'm an avid backpacker. I believe contemplative inquiry is an important part of quality life, so I have a quiet story time with my students every day. I wonder sometimes what would have happened to our society if our forebears had decided to learn from Native Americans instead of trying to eradicate them. I enjoy studying people and learning about their idiosyncrasies. I might have become a novelist, but I didn't want to be a starving artist. I've seen too many in California.

Instead, I help my students prepare for the wonderful world of literature. They act out all sorts of dramas that we create together. I am fascinated by the Whole Language movement, and I deeply believe that teachers should help their students actively construct their own meanings from what they read. I sometimes think I should get a master's degree in reading and become a reading specialist or teach second grade.

I think I have gone to every creativity workshop there is. I just love learning about new ways to turn kids on to their own creativity. Have you read *Artistic Intelligences: Implications for Education* (1990), edited by William Moody? The most important bridge in life is between your everyday self and your innermost self, between your profane and sacred sense of life. I want to help my young students learn to balance these two sides of our human nature. I want them to feel special about themselves and their unique talents and experience the constant wonder of discovery.

I work for a rural school district in the western foothills of the Sierra Nevada mountains. My children come from all types of families. We've got everything from low-income, rural families to affluent, computer-age professionals in our school district. I guess I enjoy the pluralism in this part of California. It doesn't have the hard edge associated with urban diversity. Californians believe in "live and let live." I like that kind of individualism. It can mature into a deep wisdom about life.

One of my favorite educational writers is Max van Manen, who is a professor at the University of Alberta. In 1986 he published a short book entitled *The Tone of Teaching*. In this book van Manen (1986) describes authentic teaching as follows:

A real math teacher is a person who embodies math, who lives math, who in a strong sense is math. . . . A real English teacher tends not only to love reading, writing, and carrying poetry under one arm during coffee break; a real English teacher cannot help but poetize the world—that is, think deeply about human experience through the incantative power of words. (pp. 45–46)

I aspire to be this kind of "real teacher." I applaud teachers who have developed a strong educational presence with their students. They understand the aesthetic side of good teaching.

Silvia Rivera, Middle School Social Studies Teacher

I was born in Puerto Rico in 1961, and my family moved to New York when I was two years old. I have three older brothers and two older sisters. As I was growing up I observed all their problems adjusting to the United States. My brothers had a hard time finding work. It seems like there was just one barrier after another, and it basically boiled down to one big obstacle: prejudice against people of color. One of my brothers took the easy way out by joining a gang and getting involved in drugs. He's now serving time in Attica, and I visit him once a month. This is very painful to do, and I cry every time I have to say goodbye. He was always so kind and gentle to me when I was young.

I have very loving parents, and they have been quite supportive. They both had low-paying jobs, but they sent all of us to the same Catholic elementary school so that we would get a better education while growing up in the Bronx. This was a big financial burden, but they never complained. We spoke Spanish at home, but the nuns made sure that we spoke only English at school and would never mention our Hispanic background. We were treated as Catholic souls who were accidently born Puerto Ricans.

One nun was special for me. She taught me in sixth grade, and she helped me in many ways. She made me feel important, and she taught me to think freely and question things. As I got older, her ideas got me thinking about all the inequities inflicted upon women. We have fewer opportunities, are paid less, and are generally less respected than men. We are constantly vulnerable to sexual harassment. I also have questions about the male domination of the

Catholic church and the sexist machismo in the Hispanic community. If I raise these topics with my mother, she just shakes her head and wonders where I get such crazy ideas.

Thanks to an aunt, I managed to get my college degree and teaching certificate from Brooklyn College. She was unable to complete her college education, but she did everything she could to make sure I finished mine. She helped me with money and clothes, and she even let me stay with her one difficult year when I couldn't find a decent job. It took me seven years to get through college, and I couldn't have done it without my aunt. I've read that some educational reformers want college students to wait until they have their undergraduate degrees to learn to teach. Such ideas might be good for the rich, but not for the people I know.

I was certified as an elementary school teacher, but I've always had a keen interest in social studies. I've taken extra graduate courses in history, anthropology, political science, and multicultural education. I'm now a social studies specialist at one of the new middle schools in the New York Public School System.

I love turning kids on to social issues—just like that special nun I had in sixth grade. I emphasize multicultural education in my teaching because I want my students to see the important linkages between their distinctive ethnic heritages and the pluralistic society we are trying to become. Instead of celebrating cultural differences, most Americans hide behind sterile, stereotypical middle-class images of good behavior. I know that this is a complex problem compounded by our mass media and our politicians. Have you read *The Ideology of Images in Educational Media* (Ellsworth & Whatley, 1990)? Those in power like our cultural stereotypes; it helps them maintain their own status and privileges. Where is their Christian sense of justice? Don't they know that Jesus' mission was with the poor?

I want my students to be critical inquirers, not because it is good to be radical, but because it is good to be fair and compassionate. A democratic society should not have so many barriers. Whenever I talk this way to my parents, they get nervous. They say they know their place in society, but do they? Why can't Hispanics share equally in the fruits of our wonderful land?

I'm not sure whether I want to remain in teaching. One part of me believes that through education we can change the power structure in our society. I get inspired when I go to conferences on multicultural education and when I read such texts as *Empowerment through Multicultural Education* (Sleeter, 1990). But the other part of me wonders whether I should get more directly involved in politics and social action. I want to serve as a bridge to a world with more justice. Can I best do this as a teacher? I have a gift for gab, and I like people. Maybe I should become a lawyer and then be a public defender or even a politician. But I know I would miss my students. Maybe I'll just go on to get a master's degree in multicultural education.

Four Distinct Constructivist Perspectives

The four teacher-characters now discuss both the content of their beliefs and the critical process they use to clarify and refine these beliefs.

Johnny Jackson

Content

I believe in the value of constructivist teaching practices, a topic you will study in chapters 3–6. I view educational constructivism as helping students with their **academic meaning-making.** For example, I want students to practice their problem-solving skills in the context of learning such traditional disciplines as English, history, and mathematics. I think teachers should be wary of curriculum materials that guide them to teach thinking skills that are not integrated with the content of such disciplines. I don't separate process from content in education, and I disagree with those teachers who teach only general thinking skills. I don't like critical thinking programs such as *CoRT Thinking Lessons*, *Odyssey*, and *Techniques of Learning*. These programs may get students thinking, but what are they supposed to be thinking about?

I also disagree with teachers who overly "psychologize" education. I find them too preoccupied with their students' self-esteem and thinking competencies. I want my students to understand the great ideas of Western civilization. This is the type of substantive comprehension that will make them feel better about themselves. I want them to feel deeply connected to people like William Shakespeare and Leo Tolstoy. I want them to be inspired by the breadth and elegance of the brilliant minds that provide the scaffolding for their cultural heritage.

If students don't know their intellectual birthright, what do they know about themselves? I agree with Robert Hutchins's critique of the shallowness of modern societies. Hutchins (1952), the editor of the *Great Books of the Western World*, writes:

We are as concerned as anybody else at the headlong plunge into the abyss that Western civilization seems to be taking. We believe that the voices that may recall the West to sanity are those which have taken part in the Great Conversation. We want them to be heard again—not because we want to go back to antiquity, or the Middle Ages, or the Renaissance, or the Eighteenth Century. We are quite aware that we do not live in any time but the present. . . . We want the voices of the Great Conversation to be heard again because we think they may help us to learn to live better now. (p. xii)

When I teach, I constantly ask questions that invite the students to participate in the "Great Conversation." For example, when covering a piece of literature in class, I seek meaningful ways to inquire into culturally important ideas. The following types of questions guide the classroom discussions I have with my students:

- How does this literary work help you think about the meaning of justice in your life?
- Does this book help you appreciate the issues of life and death that we all must face?
- Did any of the characters in the story change? What does *change* mean to you?

These types of questions can sometimes generate wonderful classroom dialogue. When this happens, I feel as if I am in "constructivist heaven." I have been successful in helping my students understand the power of literature to guide their lives in a meaningful, rational, and civilized way.

Process

I'm an advocate of systematic rational procedures, and I believe that humans achieve their freedom through rationality. This is the main reason I admire Western European cultures. Generally speaking, Western Europeans have a high regard for intellectual pursuits, and they have a deep respect for teachers who encourage intellectual development in students.

I believe in the value of deductive and inductive logic. How many people can identify valid and invalid syllogisms in an argument? Did you know that Aristotle was the first philosopher to discuss the nature of syllogistic reasoning? I encourage students to join our high school's debate team because they will receive an invaluable education in the art of reasoning. Too many of today's students have untidy, undisciplined minds; they operate on the basis of emotional impulses. How can they succeed in life? Most of our social problems result from a lack of rational self-restraint. Educators must work to rectify this situation.

My preferred critical style is to analyze concepts. Conceptual analysis is part of the tradition of analytical philosophy. The educational philosopher Jonas Soltis presents ways to practice this type of analytical work in *An Introduction to the Analysis of Educational Concepts* (1978).[3] In his text, Soltis discusses three methods of conceptual analysis, and I have synthesized these methods into a critical protocol:

1. Examine the different meanings of a particular concept. For example, when people say they practice *critical reasoning*, what do they mean by this term?
2. Decide which meanings are based on informed judgment. An informed judgment is reasonable: it is based on reasons that other people can log-

---

[3] For a historical overview of the tradition of analytical philosophy, see Michael Dummett's *Origins of Analytical Philosophy*, which was published in 1994.

ically follow. It is not logical for someone to say that "It is sunny today; therefore, it will rain."

3. Look for informed judgments based on great ideas that have stood the test of time. These types of judgments are especially powerful.
4. Based on your analytical work, select the best meaning for a particular concept, and then use this meaning as the basis for your decisions.

I strongly believe in meditating on the classics of Western civilization. My inspirational referents are the great ideas that scaffold our culture. My critical engagement of who I am emerges from the study of the Western canon and from attendance at cultural events. Most television programming is low-brow nonsense and is therefore useless for my type of personal-professional attunement. Can you remember the most popular television show from ten years ago? Has it had an impact on your life? I am careful not to contaminate my thinking with too much "mental junk food," and I am always on the lookout for solid and enduring cultural nourishment.

Amy Nelson

Content

I am trying to develop myself as a constructivist teacher in accordance with my interpretation of educational constructivism. For me, *teaching for understanding* means teaching **thinking skills.** I agree with Brophy's (1995) summary of constructivist instruction. He argues that lessons must "include higher-order applications of content" (p. 73). These higher-order applications require an in-depth study of a small number of topics. This type of study will "stimulate students to process and reflect on the content, recognize relationships among and implications of its key ideas, think critically about it, and use it in problem-solving or decision-making applications" (p. 73). By taking this instructional approach, teachers help students develop a variety of thinking skills including the ability to explain, deliberate, and predict.

I like cognitive psychology research. I think it helps teachers cultivate the constructivist dimensions of their practices, but I want to see this research translated into specific behavioral guidance. Rosenshine and Stevens (1986) provide the type of constructivist teaching advice that I like:

It is best that checking for understanding take place frequently so that teachers can provide corrections and reteach when necessary. Some methods for conducting checking for understanding include:
• Prepare a large number of oral questions beforehand
• Ask many brief questions on main points, supplementary points, and on the process being taught
• Call on students whose hands aren't raised in addition to those who volunteer
• Ask students to summarize the rule or process in their own words
• Have all students write answers (on paper or chalkboard) while the teacher circulates

- Have all students write the answers and check them with a neighbor (frequently used with older students)
- At the end of a lecture/discussion (especially with older students) write the main points on the board and have the class meet in groups and summarize the main points to each other. (p. 384)

Rosenshine and Stevens's language is behaviorally precise. This is the type of orderly teacher talk that I can follow. I can work with teaching competency checklists. These protocols help me develop myself as a constructivist teacher concerned with my students' active understanding.

I think that *teaching for understanding* means helping students prepare themselves to work in a very competitive world. I agree with Reich (1991) that a global economic, information-based system is beginning to emerge and that, if the United States is to sustain a vital economy, it must educate millions of Americans for work as **symbolic-analytic work.** Reich describes this type of work as follows:

Symbolic analysts solve, identify, and broker problems by manipulating symbols. They simplify reality into abstract images that can be rearranged, juggled, experimented with, communicated to other specialists, and then, eventually, transformed back to reality. . . . Symbolic analysts often have partners or associates rather than bosses or supervisors. Their incomes may vary from time to time, but are not directly related to how much time they put in or the quantity of work they put out. Income depends, rather, on the quality, originality, cleverness, and, occasionally, speed with which they solve, identify, or broker new problems. . . . Symbolic analysts often work alone or in small teams, which may be connected to larger organizations, including the World Wide Web. Teamwork is often critical. Since neither problems nor solutions can be defined in advance, frequent and informal conversations help ensure that insights and discoveries are put to their best uses and subjected to quick, critical evaluation. (pp. 178–179)

I cultivate the constructivist quality of my teaching because I want to prepare students to function as symbolic analysts. I want them to be astute manipulators of symbols and collaborative problem solvers. In this way, they will have successful careers and will also contribute to our nation's economic vitality.

Process

I think that the critical examination of one's teaching decisions is very important. I am constantly working on my critical thinking skills, and I want to make sure that my students are similarly employed. I have developed teaching units on thinking skills from many sources. For a sampling of these sources, see Chance's *Thinking in the Classroom: A Survey of Programs* (1986), which lists the following critical thinking curricula: *CoRT Thinking Lessons*, *Productive Thinking Program*, *Philosophy for Children*, *Odyssey*, *Instrumental Enrichment*, *Problem Solving and Comprehension*, *Techniques of Learning*, and *Thoughtful Teaching*.

I agree with Lipman (1995) that critical reasoning is "skillful, responsible thinking that facilitates good judgment because it (1) relies upon criteria, (2) is self-correcting, and (3) is sensitive to context" (p. 146). As Lipman notes, criteria help us establish the objectivity of our critical judgments. For example, the architects use "such criteria as *utility*, *safety*, and *beauty* . . . [while] critical thinkers rely upon such time-tested criteria as *validity*, *evidential warrant*, and *consistency*" (p. 147). Good thinkers can articulate the criteria that support their critical reflections; they are willing to revise their critical judgments as warranted; and they are sensitive to situational considerations.

In the next chapter, I will be offering advice on how to solve complex learning problems in a constructivist way. If you follow my advice, you will be required to refine your thinking skills in accordance with Lipman's definition of critical reasoning. I hope that you will be motivated to become a competent, efficient thinker. Too many people's judgments are muddled. Lipman (1995) writes: "Much of our thinking unrolls impressionistically, from association to association, with little concern for either truth or validity. . . " (p. 149). I don't want to be an impressionistic thinker; therefore, I continuously work on my reasoning skills.

My critical engagement is strongly linked to my religious background. I am a Christian and have carefully studied the word of God. I don't broadcast my religion, but I am constantly heartened by the examples of good behavior in the Bible. My sense of morals is based on these examples. Every day I read selections of the Bible with the hope that this study will continuously upgrade my character. I try to be a good model to my students. I want them to be inspired by my daily conduct and understand that the behavioral rules in my classroom have a deep resonance in the life of Christ.

I am happy that more of our country's politicians are discussing such topics as "family values." If people had higher moral standards, many of our social problems would be solved. I am very concerned that too many children are not receiving the proper guidance at home. If they don't have the opportunity to work on their moral character, how will they succeed in life? I do what I can to teach the proper values at school, but I need help. I am a teacher, not a parent.

Dennis Sage

Content

I am a committed constructivist educator, and I believe that I should teach for understanding. My goal is to facilitate students' understanding of themselves. I want to lead my students into an awareness of the meaning of their lives. I want them to comprehend more than subject matter. I want them to appreciate their unique possibilities as purposeful beings who can exercise their **existential will** — that is, people who can decide what is "right" for them without feeling they must be guided by the expectations of others. I want to cite a passage written by the educational philosopher Maxine Greene. It is somewhat lengthy, but it beautifully captures my constructivist teaching purposes—my reasons for being a constructivist educator. Greene (1988) writes:

For Jean-Paul Sartre, the project of acting on our freedom involves a rejection of the insufficient or the unendurable, a clarification, an imagining of a better state of things. . . . Few people, quite obviously, can become virtuoso musicians or advanced physicists or world-renowned statesmen, but far more is possible for individuals than is ordinarily recognized. . . . The point is not that there are never any excuses; it is that, in classrooms as well as in the open world, accommodations come too easily. It is the case, as Sartre said, that there is an "anguish" linked to action on one's freedom, an anguish due to the recognition of one's own responsibility for what is happening. The person who chooses himself/herself in his/her freedom cannot place the onus on outside forces, on the cause and effect nexus. It is his/her interpretation or reading of the situation that discloses possibility; and yet there is no guarantee that the interpretation is correct. If there is proof to be found, it is only in the action undertaken; and the action itself closes off alternatives. There is always, as in the Robert Frost poem, a "road not taken." (p. 5)

This is how I understand my constructivist teaching challenges. I do not want my students to accommodate too easily. I want them to cultivate a growing awareness that there is much they can choose in life. This doesn't mean they shouldn't comprehend the subjects they are studying, and it doesn't mean they should be selfish or egocentric. It simply means that they should develop a sense of their life's journey.

I tell my students that my journey of meaning-making is to be with them as an educator. This is what feels right to me. I want them to feel right about their lives, to begin to discover their meaningful journey: their way. I enjoy the writings of William Pinar, a curriculum scholar. He writes about the role of the self in educational experiences. The word *curriculum* is a Latin term that was coined in the Middle Ages to describe educational programs. It is a noun denoting the course students should follow, as in a race course. In several writings, William Pinar changes this noun into a verb, which he calls *currere*. If curriculum refers to the course or courses all students should take, currere refers to students' ability to create their own meaningful direction in life.

Pinar (1994) has developed a method of autobiographical study based on the concept of currere. This study method has four phases:

Regressive. One returns to the past, to capture it as it was, and as it hovers over the present. (p. 21)

Progressive. Progressive derives from *pro* meaning "before" and *gradi* meaning "to step, go." In this phase we look the other way. We look, in Sartre's language, at what is not yet the case, what is not yet present. (p. 24)

Analytical. One takes photographs, and sets them aside. What is left? Describe the biographic present, exclusive of the past and future, but inclusive of responses to them. . . . Juxtapose the three photographs: past, present, future. What are their complex, multidimensional interrelations? How is the future present in the past, the past in the future, and the present in both? (pp. 25–26)

Synthetical. *Syn* means "together" and *tithenai* means "to place". . . . Look at oneself concretely, as if in a mirror. Attention on the breath, to underline the biological concreteness of being. Who is that? In your own voice, what is the meaning of the present? . . . Mind in its place, I conceptualize the present situation. I am placed together. Synthesis. (pp. 26–27)

I integrate these four phases into my constructivist teaching. As they proceed with their active study, I challenge students to relate their present learning to their past experiences and their future possibilities. Because I am a kindergarten teacher, I do this in very concrete, basic ways without much analysis or synthesis. Even with young children, though, I find that I can teach for existential self-awareness, or critical engagement with one's authentic self. In this way, I hope I am helping my students understand that they have a voice in the direction of their lives, that they have an existential will.

Process

My critical approach is grounded in aesthetic awareness. I continuously meditate on the artistry of my transactions with students, but I do this out of a sense of contemplative or meditative silence. I'm not a strongly analytical or behavioral type of person. Perhaps I can best convey my critical style with an example. Let's say you are a practicing Christian, and a Buddhist friend wants to better understand your religious inspiration. Are you going to show your friend the beliefs, rules, and regulations of your religion? Would this reveal the soul of your faith? What would you do? My approach would be to share some inspirational stories from Christ's life, but I wouldn't talk about the moral of these stories. I would instead attempt to evoke the quality of Christ's compassionate and sensitive interactions with others. I would want my Buddhist friend to feel the consciousness that Christ embodied.

My critical engagement emerges out of my relationships with my students. I practice different types of "heart-to-heart rituals" in my classroom. For example, every day after lunch my students and I gather in a circle to tell stories. I also attempt to cultivate powerful moments of aesthetic learning, which Lee (1993) describes in this insightful way:

It is a moment of great magnitude because of the transformative insight it affords the individual. It is a memorable learning experience for that person after which he or she is forever changed, It is the moment when Archimedes leaped from his bathtub, crying, "Eureka!" The world is suddenly arranged in a new pattern, with new possibilities. That which was dispersed and separate is gathered together and unified with its own emergent meaning. (p. 77)

I love the *Eureka* in education. Why can't such moments be an integral part of mathematics learning, or social studies learning? Why can't students have aesthetically powerful experiences in all areas of the curriculum? This is what I contemplate as a teacher. My meditations are on the spirit and the joy of learning.

To me, the purpose of critically studying your teaching is to better understand the aesthetics of teaching-learning transactions. Eisner (1991) expresses my view of good critical thinking in education: "*Criticism* refers to the process of enabling others to see the qualities that a work of art possesses" (p. 6). I critically reflect on my teaching so that I can discern the subtleties of my educational interactions with my students. Van Manen (1991) writes beautifully about what it means to be a critically thoughtful teacher, what it means to practice *pedagogical tact*, which he defines as "a mindful orientation in our being and acting with children" (p. 149). He opens his book on pedagogical tact with this poetic evocation:

> What is a child? To see a child is
> to see possibility, someone in
> the process of becoming.
> (van Manen, 1991, p. 1)

I am a critical student of my work so that I can better understand and facilitate the idiosyncratic beauty of each student's growth.

Silvia Rivera

Content

As a constructivist teacher, I want to help my students understand themselves as **historical agents**, not historical objects. This is a key distinction in my interpretation of educational constructivism that I need to carefully explain. I want students to understand that they need not feel powerless. I want my students to get out of the habit of using the pronoun *they*, as in the following examples: "I'm tired of doing what they want me to do." "They are asking me to do something idiotic; they have no comprehension of my situation." "They have all these rules and regulations that make no sense." I don't want my students to continually carp about how "they"—other people—are controlling their lives. I want them to feel that they can confront their disempowering circumstances, which they believe others are controlling. I want them to discover the emancipatory possibilities in their lives.

I practice this type of constructivism by adapting Freire's (1970/1971) problem-posing education, which he summarizes as follows:

Education as the practice of freedom—as opposed to education as the practice of domination—denies that man [sic] is abstract, isolated, independent, and unattached to the world; it also denies that the world exists as a reality apart from men. Authentic reflection considers neither abstract man nor the world without men, but men in their [problematic] relations with the world. (p. 69)

. . . Problem-posing education, as a humanist and liberating praxis, posits as fundamental that men subjected to domination must fight for their emancipation. To that end, it enables teachers and students to become Subjects of the educational process by overcoming authoritarianism and an alienating intellectualism; it also enables men to overcome their false perception of reality. The world . . . becomes the object of that transforming action by men which results in their humanization. (p. 74)

I work with Freire's educational orientation by asking my students to study oppressive social problems that have relevance in their lives. For example, I have asked my students to examine segregated housing patterns in their neighborhoods. Why do these patterns exist, and what can be done about them? We have inquired into problems of sexism in our middle school. Why are there more after-school sports for boys than for girls, and what can be done about this? I have taped segments of talk shows that address pressing social problems, and we have created our own talk show scripts based on our study of these videotapes.

I feel that I have not succeeded as a constructivist teacher if my students don't begin to understand that they have power over their social lives. And I pursue my educational purposes in very concrete ways. One of my problem-posing units was on the power students have to affect school policy. I worked closely with the principal on this unit. As a result of our classroom studies, the principal established a school-community committee to review school policies once a year and make revisions if necessary. This committee includes not only teachers, administrators, parents, and community leaders, but also students. My students and I feel quite proud about our influence on the creation of this committee. I tell my students that I live by the motto: "Leave the world a better place than when you entered." If my students can better understand this motto when they leave my class, then I have been a successful constructivist teacher.

Process

My critical style is informed by my commitment to **social liberation**. I despise injustice in all its guises, and I would leave teaching if I couldn't fight sociocultural oppression in my work. You may think I'm coming on too strong, but let me explain myself. I am wary of qualitative talk, and there are good historical reasons for my wariness. Do you know any aesthetically developed individuals who are ethically limited? Did you know that many Nazis were liberally educated with refined aesthetic tastes in music, sculpture, and the fine arts? Yet, look at what they did. They practiced genocide with technical sophistication. What does this say about the beliefs of my other three teacher-character colleagues? What does this say about their critical styles? What social policies result from thinking great ideas, practicing thinking skills, and engaging in aesthetic awareness? This is my critical question. I am concerned about my ethical development as a citizen of my society. I want to avoid letting my range of interests become too narrowly bourgeois and personalized.

A social vision lies at the heart of my critical examination. Imagine a society where citizens embrace the idea of unity-within-diversity and celebrate democratic, multicultural principles, activities, and institutions. They understand that they must struggle together to actualize an inclusive cultural pluralism; otherwise, their society can never become a great civilization. The educational philosopher Maxine Greene (1988) eloquently evokes the emancipatory spirit inherent in this social vision:

This is what we shall look for as we move: freedom developed by human beings who have acted to make a space for themselves in the presence of others, human beings become "challengers" ready for alternatives, alternatives that include caring and community. And we shall seek, as we go, implications for emancipatory education conducted by and for those willing to take responsibility for themselves and for each other. We want to discover how to open spaces for persons in the plurality, spaces where they can become different, where they can grow. (p. 56)

When I critically study my teaching, I reflect on such questions as:

- Who has power over whom?
- What social structures maintain this relationship of power over others?
- What effect does this persistent domination have on those who are required to submit?
- Are those who are being dominated even aware that they are submitting?
- Would they really care if they knew?
- Do they only desire to be like their masters?
- How can we interrupt and possibly transform the inequities of wealth, status, and power?
- How can those who must submit be emancipated, and how shall this emancipation be understood?

My critical engagement is inspired by meditating on the ideal of **postmodern multiculturalism**. Postmodernism refers to the point of view that there are no universal truths. Postmodernists believe that there are no rational procedures humans can follow that will enable them to stand above the reality of human differences. The postmodernist Jean-Francois Lyotard (1984) writes that we must give up the search for a "master narrative" that will lift us above diverse human interests and values. Traditional multiculturalism focuses on understanding ethnic and other human differences from the point of view of dominant American middle-class values. An example of this type of multiculturalism is the Walt Disney film *Pocahontas*. The American Indian princess Pocahontas is not portrayed as a young woman in an authentic Native American culture. She is an Indian viewed through the lens of a dominant American corporation's interpretation of beauty and goodness. Imagine the real Pocahontas getting in a time machine that takes her to the present time. What if she understood our current American English and saw the Disney film? How would the real Native American woman react to the cartoon character who is supposed to represent her?

Postmodern multiculturalism celebrates human differences without overtly or tacitly promoting dominant American middle-class values. A postmodern multiculturalist would portray Pocahontas with more cultural honesty. She wouldn't be turned into an American Indian Barbie doll who nicely fits into Walt Disney, Inc.'s theme parks. I like Kanpol's (1994) definition of postmodern multiculturalism:

This approach to multicultural education will seriously consider race, class, and gender relations of minority cultures. Within this approach, a critical pedagogue [teacher] will attempt to change stagnant or stereotypical views about ethnic groups. To do this, a critical pedagogue must first view ethnic minority family, social, value-oriented, and economic relations as different from (extrinsic to) Western culture [as currently understood]. . . . Second, a critical postmodern theory of multiculturalism will require the critical pedagogue to critique the present cultural situation that doesn't allow for extrinsic acceptance of another culture or cultures. This critique will be geared to finding ways for school clientele (students and teachers in particular) to accept others intrinsically (be they minorities, as in this case, or anyone else) as equal on the simple fact that we are all human and are all different. . . . [This critique involves] a struggle to undo the morally reprehensible acceptance of the dominant culture (white Anglo-American) as pure truth, the best or only living culture in this country (this is a blatant form of ethnocentrism). (pp. 41–42)

My passion for social justice and equity continuously inspires my teaching actions, and I enthusiastically share this passion with my students. I want them to understand what animates my contemplations, and I want them to begin to explore their social values and visions.

CONCLUSION

You have now been introduced to each teacher-character's distinct constructivist perspective as well as the preferred critical style of each. Their ideological differences are summarized in Figure 2.1. Hopefully, their contrasting points of view will help you critically examine the content of your constructivist beliefs and the process you use to clarify and refine these beliefs. Keep in mind the close relationship between content and process in human believing. Also remember the subtle distinction between critical reasoning and critical engagement. As mentioned in chapter 1, critical reasoning and critical engagement are two sides of the same coin. The purpose of these two forms of critical examination is to help you make wise educational decisions, which you will hopefully enact in a pragmatic way through the use of the decision-making cycle. Critical reasoning helps you identify "good" reasons for pragmatic action, while critical engagement helps you become attuned to "good" intuitions, feelings, and personal metaphors. Without practicing both types of reflectiveness, how could you function as an independent decision-maker and as a responsible member of a democratic learning community? Now that you have read this chapter, consider these questions:

- What are your beliefs about "good" constructivist practice? If you haven't as yet constructed such beliefs, which teacher-character perspective seems most attractive?
- How do you critically examine your beliefs? If you haven't as yet cultivated a definitive critical style, which teacher-character approach seems most appealing to you?

TEACHER–CHARACTER	CONSTRUCTIVIST PERSPECTIVE	CRITICAL STYLE	SYMBOL
Johnny Jackson	Academic meaning–making	Conceptual analysis and classical study	Open book
Amy Nelson	Facilitating thinking skills	Critical reasoning and moral–religious reflection	Personal computer
Dennis Sage	Personal meaning–making and existential growth	Aesthetic awareness of teacher–student transactions	Clasped hands
Silvia Rivera	Facilitating historical agency and sociopolitical empowerment	Social liberation analysis	Scales of justice

Figure 2.1
Teacher-Characters' Perspectives, Critical Styles, and Symbols

This chapter has been designed to help you think about these questions. There are no right or wrong answers to these inquiries, but teachers can certainly be more or less committed to the critical examination of their constructivist practices. Even though the four teacher-characters differ in their orientations, they all model a high degree of reflective commitment. Hopefully, you will set a similar study standard for yourself.

REFERENCES

Bernier, N. R. (1981). Beyond instructional context identification—Some thoughts for extending the analysis of deliberate education. In J. L. Green & C. Wallat (Eds.), *Ethnography and language in educational settings* (pp. 291–302). Norwood, NJ: Ablex.

Brophy, J. (1995). Probing the subtleties of subject-matter teaching. In A. C. Ornstein & L. S. Behar (Eds.), *Contemporary issues in curriculum* (pp. 70–76). Boston: Allyn & Bacon.

Chance, P. (1986). *Thinking in the classroom: A survey of programs*. New York: Teachers College Press.

Eisner, E. W. (1991). *The enlightened eye: Qualitative inquiry and the enhancement of educational practice*. New York: Macmillan.

Ellsworth, E., & Whatley, M. (Eds.). (1990). *The ideology of images in educational media*. New York: Teachers College Press.

Freire, P. (1971). *Pedagogy of the oppressed* (M. Bergman Ramos, Trans.). New York: Herder & Herder. (Original work published 1970)

Greene, M. (1988). *The dialectic of freedom*. New York: Teachers College Press.

Hunter, M. (1982). *Mastery teaching*. El Secundo, CA: TIP Publications.

Hutchins, R. M. (1952). *Great Books of the Western World: Vol. 1. The great conversation: The substance of a liberal education* (pp. 1–131). Chicago: Encyclopaedia Britannica.

Joyce, J. (1934). *Ulysses*. New York: Random House. (Original work published 1914)

Kanpol, B. (1994). *Critical pedagogy: An introduction*. Westport, CT: Bergin & Garvey.

Lee, K. (1993). Transcendence as an aesthetic concept: Implications for curriculum. *The Journal of Aesthetic Education*, 27(1), 75–82.

Lipman, M. (1995). Critical thinking—What can it be? In A. C. Ornstein & L. S. Behar (Eds.), *Contemporary issues in curriculum* (pp. 145–152). Boston: Allyn & Bacon.

Lyotard, J. F. (1984). *The postmodern condition: A report on knowledge* (G. Bennington & B. Massumi, Trans.). Minneapolis: University of Minnesota Press.

McLellan, D. (1986). *Ideology*. Minneapolis: University of Minneapolis Press.

Moody, W. (Ed.). (1990). *Artistic intelligences: Implications for education*. New York: Teachers College Press.

Pinar, W. F. (1994). The method of *currere*. In W. F. Pinar (Ed.), *Autobiography, politics and sexuality* (pp. 19–27). New York: Peter Lang.

Reich, R. (1991). *The work of nations: Preparing ourselves for 21st-century capitalism*. New York: Vintage Books.

Rosenshine, B., & Stevens, R. (1986). Teaching functions. In M. C. Wittrock (Ed.), *Handbook of research on teaching* (3rd ed., pp. 376–391). New York: Macmillan.

Sleeter, C. (Ed.). (1990). *Empowerment through multicultural education*. Albany, NY: State University of New York Press.

Soltis, J. F. (1978). *An introduction to the analysis of educational concepts* (2nd ed.). Reading, MA: Addison-Wesley.

van Manen, M. (1986). *The tone of teaching*. Richmond Hill, Ontario: Scholastic-TAB.

van Manen, M. (1991). *The tact of teaching: The meaning of pedagogical thoughtfulness*. Albany, NY: State University of New York Press.

S E C T I O N

2

Constructivist Practices

In this section you will be introduced to four general constructivist practices:

- Solving complex learning problems in a constructivist way
- Creating a constructivist curriculum design
- Enacting constructivist transactions
- Creating a classroom learning community

These **practices** are discussed in separate chapters, and each chapter follows the same pattern. The chapter begins with a vignette to introduce the constructivist practice under consideration. A general protocol of that practice is presented, followed by a teacher narrative to illustrate the protocol. We call the teacher narrative a *critical incident*. Next, the four teacher-characters discuss this protocol from their ideological vantage point. Finally, additional reading recommendations are offered.

As you read these four chapters on constructivist practices, keep in mind that the protocols are applications of the decision-making cycle discussed in chapter 1. Collectively, the four protocols encourage teachers to integrate curriculum and instructional decision-making.

3

Solving Complex Learning Problems in a Constructivist Way

Lindsay Duma was planning for her first year of teaching. She had just been hired to teach in a mid-sized suburban high school and knew that she would be teaching ninth-grade biology and general science.

Lindsay was particularly anxious about the two general science classes. From her teacher education classes, she had developed a dislike for ability tracking, but her new school continued the practice, as did most high schools in the state. So here she was, about to be confronted by a roomful of ninth-graders who knew they were in the low track and who did not want to be in science at all. She was about to become the teacher of students who had been categorized as either hard-to-control or unmotivated as a result of their behaviors and lack of success in previous classrooms. (She knew this was a stereotypical view of their abilities, but she still couldn't get this view out of her thoughts.)

Lindsay decided that her only hope was to plan well. She believed in constructivist learning, but, as she had learned from her experiences in student teaching, students with no previous exposure to learning in that way needed a gradual introduction. Her first decision was to start the class in a highly structured, more traditional mode to make sure she could maintain control and get a chance to learn about her students individually.

Lindsay was committed to constructivist learning. She decided that she would first try to find out about her students' learning purposes and what they already knew about science. Then she would look for ways to encourage them to take responsibility for their own learning and gain an active understanding of a few key science concepts. One "advantage" to working with lower-track students was that there would be no strong pressure from administrators or parents for coverage of content. She was a little uncertain of how to proceed, especially because of her fears about students who are unmotivated or hard to control. She talked with her favorite professor, called a few science friends from college, met with her department chair, and acquired several books that she thought might help her cause.

Finally, after many conversations and not a little reading, she came up with a plan to try in September and October. She promised herself that she would carefully observe the results of her plan and make adjustments as necessary.

Introduction

Teachers make as many as two hundred decisions every day. Most of these decisions are fairly routine and don't require much time or energy, but smooth-sailing days are rare in the classroom. Teachers must be prepared to confront challenging problems. In this chapter you will inquire into the practice of solving complex learning problems in a constructivist way. In pursuing this reflective practice, you must be able to distinguish it from technical and administrative problem solving.

Technical problem solving is fairly straightforward and automatic. You simply follow a precise procedure to solve the problem. Suppose you have learned a four-step method for diagnosing a student's learning style. You encounter a situation that requires identifying a particular student's learning style, so you use the procedure you have learned. Based on the information you have gathered, you try to solve the problem. Your actions are similar to baking a cake: you carefully follow a recipe to achieve a desired outcome. Unlike baking a cake, however, the technical procedure you use may not solve the problem. In fact, it may make the problem worse. Now what do you do? If you are limited to working with technical methods, you're stuck. You need to learn how to engage in more open-ended, deliberative, and imaginative problem solving, which is the focus of this chapter.

Administrative problem solving is guided by administrative, not educational, goals. Posner (1992) provides a concise overview of administrative goals:

Schools . . . are organizations and, as such, are concerned not just with the education of their students, but also with the maintenance and improvement of the organization. Therefore, accomplishing goals such as limiting budget increases to 10 percent, hiring more minority teachers, lengthening the school year, adding a new science laboratory, and repairing the high school's roof may indirectly improve the quality of education but are not educational objectives themselves. (p. 75)

Administrative problems are important, but they shouldn't be confused with educational problems. Solving a busing problem does not necessarily help teachers improve students' literacy.

Even when guided by educational goals, administrative problem solving can sometimes interfere with educational problem solving. If the administrative team in a particular school district engages in **micro-management** of its teachers—if it decides what students will learn and how they will be disciplined—the teachers are disempowered. This forces the teachers to focus on solving the "problem" of following administrative directions, rather than solving the very real and complex problems they confront daily. Such working conditions can cause teachers to become insensitive to students, concentrating instead on implementing organizational policies. How many uncaring, bureaucratic teachers have you encountered in your education? How often did they cite rules and procedures rather than try to solve your learning problem?

This chapter focuses on solving messy, complex learning problems. This category covers those dilemmas and predicaments that require teachers' serious attention, for example, individual student problems such as reading difficulties or school- or district-wide problems such as drug or gang involvement. If teachers don't grapple with these problems, the educational service they are providing may be at risk.

Note the emphasis that the service is at risk, not the students. Teachers who limit their deliberations to technical and administrative problem solving may be supporting unimaginative programs that are likely not to help students with their complex learning problems. However, wading into the area of complex learning problems can be a messy, confusing affair. Schön (1983) writes:

> In the varied topography of professional practice, there is a high, hard ground where practitioners can make effective use of research-based theory and technique, and there is a swampy lowland where situations are confusing "messes" incapable of technical solution. The difficulty is that the problems of the high ground, however great their technical interest, are often relatively unimportant to clients or to the larger society, while in the swamp are the problems of greatest human concern. Shall the practitioner stay on the high, hard ground where he [sic] is constrained to deal with problems of relatively little social importance? Or shall he descend to the swamp where he can engage the most important and challenging problems if he is willing to forsake technical rigor? (p. 42)

In general, solving complex learning problems in a constructivist way is an important practice in the repertoire of a reflective teacher. But it is also somewhat unnatural because many teachers may not have intuitively developed the habit of thinking in this way. In fact, learning to tackle complex learning problems in a constructivist way demands a teacher's most intelligent efforts.

A General Protocol

As Schön (1983) notes, the process of solving complex learning problems in a constructivist way cannot be defined precisely. There are no obvious technical or administrative solutions. He writes that those who "choose the swampy lowlands" of confronting messy problems "speak of experience, trial and error, intuition, and muddling through" (p. 43). Though there is no definitive procedure for solving complex problems, there is a general process that can assist the deliberative efforts. This process is an application of the decision-making cycle introduced in chapter 1 and illustrated in Figure 1.2.

Remember the three normative concepts introduced in chapter 1: Dewey's (1910/1933) analysis of pragmatic intelligence, Lewin's (1948) action research and Kolb's (1984) experiential learning. In applying pragmatic intelligence, Dewey suggests that once a problem is identified, tentative conclusions and tentative actions are in order. At this point we do not know that inferences we have necessarily made based on our past experiences will really lead to a productive solution. We are caught in a paradox in that we cannot know if our tentative efforts will be successful until we act, but it is difficult to act without knowing exactly what to do. Lewin's action research model provides a moderately straightforward approach to dealing with this paradox, yet it also acknowledges that results must be reviewed since your solution may not work. He discusses six key dimensions of good action research: analyze a problematic situation, gather additional useful information, define the problem, hypothesize a solution, act to solve the problem, and evaluate the results of your actions. Kolb reminds us that, as experiential learners, we must strike a balance between acting and observing and between participation and detachment. All three concepts support the teacher in investigating problems in a cycle of fluid planning, empowered enacting, participant observation, and pragmatic reconsideration, being ever ready to return to the planning stage when implemented solutions are not successful.

Also in chapter 1, we described the constructivist teacher as one who sees learning as a complex interaction among each student's personal purposes, past experiences, and the requirements for subject matter inquiry. (Figure 1.1 in chapter 1 illustrates this idea.) Therefore, constructivist teaching can focus on subject matter understanding, self-understanding, and/or democratic understanding.

Solving complex learning problems in a constructivist way involves four interrelated, recursive steps. The steps are interrelated in that they are closely connected to one another. Progress in one step cannot proceed too far without progress in the others. The steps are recursive in the sense that they often feed back on one another. Progress in later steps can require renewed work in earlier steps, and vice versa. Using this protocol as a guide should not be confused with following a precise technical procedure. It is a broad, metacognitive referent, not a precise "recipe" on how to act. It is scaffolding for a particular open-ended reflective practice; it provides general advice that should be discarded as warranted. The four steps are:

1. Frame the problem for constructivist learning. Decide what aspects of the problem you want to focus on—based on your inquiry teaching and in light of your students' personal purposes and past experiences. This becomes the foreground for your problem-solving efforts.
2. Brainstorm possible constructivist solutions. These are solutions that encourage students to engage actively in meaning-making. This is often done best in collaboration with others. It is also helpful to review pertinent literature for new ideas.
3. Try out one or more solutions. Observe what is or isn't working.
4. Review the situation. Determine whether further inquiry or action is appropriate, usually by asking yourself whether the situation now promotes constructivist learning.

Note that these steps incorporate the decision-making cycle described in chapter 1. Steps 1 and 2 correspond to fluid planning, step 3 includes both empowered enactment and participant observation, and step 4 is a form of pragmatic reconsideration. Keep in mind that you will need to apply these step-wise suggestions to make sense in a specific context. You may need to elaborate these four steps into seven or eight, for example, and that's perfectly all right. What's really important is the answer to the question, "Am I solving complex learning problems in a constructivist way?"

Framing the Problem

In this chapter's opening vignette, Lindsay Duma framed her problem for constructivist learning. She knew she was going to teach general science topics, and she guessed that the students' past experiences did not include constructivist learning, so she decided to move slowly. She also knew that she did not have much of an idea of the students' personal purposes, so taking time at the beginning of the school year to learn this was also part of her plan. Note that Lindsay did not frame the problem as a behavior problem or a student motivation problem or a tracking problem, although she was certainly concerned about these issues. Instead, she framed the problem so that constructivist learning was in the foreground. She wanted to find a way to help her students become active learners in science, to take responsibility for their own learning.

This type of problem solving involves numerous overlapping personal and sociocultural factors. Teachers, possessing their own beliefs, values, feelings, and goals, must interact with students, who also have their own beliefs, values, feelings, and goals. In addition, parents, administrators, other school staff, and members of the community expect teachers to consider their beliefs, values, feelings, and goals. Constructivist teachers also must consider many cultural factors, including program designs, school policies, student diversity, community values, socioeconomic patterns, and state and federal mandates.

This contextual complexity creates a foreground-background problem that teachers must address. They cannot consider all potential factors at once. They must decide which factors to highlight or place in the foreground, relegating other factors to the background. This decision, guided in part by personal beliefs, affects the definition of a problem. For example, when confronting a student drug problem, one teacher might place personal values in the foreground. This teacher thinks, "If students can acquire sufficient self-discipline to 'just say no,' the problem can be addressed. Another teacher might put family factors in the foreground. This person thinks, "The drug problem is associated with the decline of the nuclear family. We should concentrate our efforts on family values." For a third teacher, social values might come to the foreground. This individual might think, "Our society's capitalistic values encourage drug entrepreneurship. We need to help students examine their outlooks on life." Given the complexity of the drug problem, none of these teachers is entirely right or wrong. Each has decided which aspects of the problem to place in the foreground and has therefore decided on the proper focus for problem solving.

As noted, the decision on what to put in the foreground is based partly on personal beliefs. This is just as true for teachers who follow constructivist principles as for those who don't. When constructivist teachers are trying to frame a problem and decide what to foreground, they orient their thinking to the goals that concerned them most, such as helping their students' subject matter inquiry with reference to their personal purposes and past experiences.

Once the relevant factors in a complex learning problem have been identified, even a group of like-minded constructivist teachers will frame the problem in many different ways. For example, one teacher may see a student's reading difficulty as an enrichment problem, while another may regard it as a motivation problem. Both teachers might be right. They both might be wrong if their definitions of the problem do not lead to solutions. One teacher might be right, and the other wrong, and there would be reasons for this, too. Perhaps you can think of some. Whatever the case, there is no precise way to define the so-called reading problem, even among reflective, constructivist teachers.

Brainstorming for Solutions

Consider a male elementary school teacher who confronts a female student whose behavior seems hostile. Let's say he has framed the problem in psychological terms. Now he wants to try brainstorming for possible ways of solving this problem. There are many ways he could proceed with this deliberation. He could talk with teachers who have taught this student, have a conference with the student's parents, or discuss the problem with the school psychologist, and he might read a few journal articles on student hostility on his own. As he proceeds with this brainstorming activity, one or more imaginative solutions may become apparent. He may think again about his definition of the problem. After deliberating over several possible solutions to the problem, he may recognize that the student's hostility is not just psychological in nature. He may see that sociological considerations must also be brought into play or even that the psychological frame of reference must be dropped. Redefining the problem would not upset him because he knows that the four problem-solving steps are recursive, that they can feed back into one another.

Note that there are two critical components to this brainstorming activity. First, it is not done in isolation. The saying that "two heads are better than one" definitely applies here. As you try to articulate the problem to supportive colleagues, listen to their suggestions, and discuss the issues with parents, guardians, or care-givers, you will gain insights. As you consult relevant literature, you may find new approaches you hadn't thought of or lessons that others have learned from their experiences. In tackling complex learning problems, the more input you pursue, the more likely you are to hit upon an attractive, maybe even successful, solution. However, working collaboratively may not be easy if you have been socialized to work in isolation. We will have more to say about professional collaboration in chapter 8.

Second, the solutions that you come up with are filtered through your constructivist lens before they make it for final consideration. You may ask yourself, "Will this solution help this student move toward active understanding, or is it a dead-end solution?" This solution may work today, you might think, but will it serve the student's best interests in the long run? You might wonder whether the long-term result of this solution will be, in Dewey's (1938) terms, educative or miseducative? Educative solutions allow for continuing growth, while miseducative solutions lead to learning stagnation. If a solution cannot make it through your constructivist filter, if it is not consistent with your constructivist goals, it should not be considered further. This is the end of the planning stage.

Trying Out Solutions

Let's return to the example of the elementary school teacher with the hostile student. The teacher decides it is time for empowered enactment. He will try two solutions that he formulated with the help of the school psychologist. In a quiet, one-on-one setting he invites the student to talk about her feelings. He also gives her a highly desirable duty to let her know she is a valued member of the class. He asks the student to take the lunch money to the office.

Following this attempt to reduce the hostility of the student, the teacher waits and watches. He is acting as a participant observer. He expects that his initial actions may not work, so he tries to gather more information as he interacts with the student.

Reviewing the Situation

When a teacher has acted to solve a problem, according to Lewin (1948), it's time to evaluate the results of the actions. As a constructivist teacher, you would evaluate those results in reference to how well they have worked to promote constructivist learning. You would engage in a possible pragmatic reconsideration of what you know about the problem. You would be willing to alter your own beliefs, values, feelings, and goals in light of your problem-solving experience since you are dedicated to personal-professional inquiry.

Continuing with our example of the elementary school teacher with the hostile student, the teacher now reviews the situation. He must repeatedly probe the student's perceptions, deliberate, collaborate, and examine his own teaching until he finds a resolution to the difficulty. He is committed to this extensive problem solving because he is a caring and creative professional. Furthermore, he is a student of constructivist learning theory, so he knows that he must not take the student's hostile attitude personally. This hostility is dysfunctional, but it is a behavior that represents the student's reaction to the classroom environment and is undoubtedly based in part on the student's past experiences. It will not be overcome easily; perhaps it cannot be overcome at all. The teacher knows that he must be patient and that, for the sake of this student's future, he must not give up. The teacher must ask himself, "How can I help this student understand herself? And then, can I move on to help her understand the subject matter in light of her own personal purposes and past experiences?"

The following critical incident provides a context-specific illustration of this four-step problem-solving protocol.

CRITICAL INCIDENT

Solving Complex Learning Problems in a Constructivist Way

Jennifer Waldbauer and Sharon Klimm

BACKGROUND

Jennifer Waldbauer has seven years of teaching experience. She began her career in the early 1970s, teaching children in traditional third and fourth grades. She took a thirteen-year maternity leave, which she also considers her "first Master's degree," since her parenting required in-depth learning about three different subpopulations—autistic, gifted, and learning-disabled—represented by her children.

Five years ago, Jennifer resumed teaching in a rural district, where she worked for two years. She taught students who were identified as gifted in third through sixth grades. She has most recently transferred to an affluent suburban district where she teaches gifted third- and fourth-graders in a specially equipped resource room.

For the first two years of her work in this district, Jennifer functioned as many special education resource teachers do, independent of other teachers in the buildings where she worked. This year, for the first time in the history of the district, Jennifer collaborates with regular classroom teachers to offer appropriate education to students in the regular class-

room, including those identified as gifted. Jennifer writes of her experience, and subsequent reflection, from a co-teaching experience in a regular fourth-grade classroom.

THE INCIDENT

The video camera rolled, operated by a professional colleague. I stood before the group of fourth-grade students who were participating in an experimental grant project. Three of us had collaborated on the project: Mrs. Catley, the visual arts teacher; Mrs. Hildebrand, the fourth grade regular classroom teacher; and me. Our aim—to meet the needs of students gifted in the visual arts—would ultimately affect all students in the class. For now, I stood before a group that wasn't just my students. They were verbal and energetic, and I knew anything could happen. I knew it would be immortalized on videotape.

The three teachers had bonded easily through teamwork and mutual support. We had all given the time and effort needed to make this collaboration work. In the process of making arrangements for this lesson, Mrs. Hildebrand and I discussed the fit of my proposed subject matter with the fourth-grade curriculum. Every teaching moment must be used to its fullest. I knew the pressure she felt as a result of newly implemented student proficiency standards by the state department of education. For the first time ever, tests would be given to students in social studies, language arts, and math. The news media waited hungrily for the results. Mrs. Hildebrand had given me forty minutes of her precious teaching time, and my responsibility was to accomplish curricular goals.

Longitude and latitude concepts formed the meat of my lesson. To make these abstract concepts concrete, I incorporated visual, auditory, and kinesthetic learning experiences. My background in gifted education gave me unique methods and goals in higher-level thinking, which I also included.

The basketball, with which I began my lesson, caught the attention of everyone, even students we considered disinterested. As I swirled the ball around in my hand, I asked the students to determine how they might describe the location of the air hole on the ball. Students pondered the need for a directional system, and possibly, even a grid system.

"How might we find our way around on this surface? What words might we use to describe locations and directions?" The children used the questions as springboards for their own curiosities. Their analysis and synthesis of information led them to form questions of their own. Students who learned best through a hands-on approach plotted latitude and longitude on their own small Styrofoam globes.

The most difficult part of problem solving for me is deciding what the problem is. As I later reflected on my teaching and viewed the videotape, I pinpointed a moment that created dissonance for me. Melissa, an ordinarily quiet student, asked a question to which neither I nor anyone else had an answer.

"Why is the earth tilted on an axis?" she asked.

During my previous work with this class and Mrs. Hildebrand, I had learned that Melissa's father had died suddenly just three months ago. In class, this little girl seemed preoccupied and was not participating. Mrs. Hildebrand had subtly urged Melissa to focus on school and be more organized.

Now, during the lesson, Melissa's question could have led to a whole new line of inquiry and learning. She had left her private world of thoughts to enter our discussion. I wanted to take advantage of this breakthrough, but I did not have the answer for her. My immediate reaction was to praise her for her interest and good thinking. I told her how important good questions could be, apologized for not knowing the exact answer, and suggested she do some research. I hoped that by being positive, I could show Melissa that her taking a risk and joining our discussion had not been in vain. I was frustrated, however, by my inability to immediately satisfy her curiosity. It was such a good question. My discomfort stemmed from a deep-seated belief that "good teachers know the answers and stick to the subject." From my experience as a teacher of gifted children, I know this is not true. Yet a part of me wanted to tell this little girl exactly what she wanted to know.

Fortunately, my reaction did encourage Melissa to ask even more questions. In fact, Melissa's query opened a flood gate for other students' curiosities. "Why do the sun's direct rays only travel between the Tropics of Capricorn and Cancer?" "Has the earth's axis always been the same?" "Who decided where the Prime Meridian would be?"

What was the real problem here? The dissonance I felt cued me that I had hit on a problem area. I knew if I didn't take the time to determine the nature of the problem, my quick fix would not last, and I would soon feel the same disquieting feelings again. I reflected on my memories of the lesson, how I had felt, and what I had observed on the videotape.

As a member of a collaborative team, I drew upon the impressions of my fellow teachers to formulate my problem focus. Through our conversations, the theme of unanswered questions arose repeatedly. We all noticed how many students had raised their hands to ask questions but were never called upon. We also wondered how best to facilitate student inquiry into their complex and deeply felt questions. How many students had questions in mind but did not even attempt to ask them aloud?

Staring back at the problem of unanswered questions were the limitations of a short time frame of forty minutes, an outcome-focused test of student knowledge that could make or break district levy elections, a state-mandated course of study with particular curricular aims, and my own knowledge of the subject. How far could I let the questioning go before, like a good fisherman with knowledge as bait, I must reel my catch back in?

FRAMING THE PROBLEM

What were my students' needs during the latitude/longitude lesson? Could it be that some of my dissonance came from my sense that I was leaving some needs unmet? How could I better meet these needs? How might my colleagues help?

My responses to these questions on behalf of the children constituted the foreground of my problem framing.

This was not my class. I could not be sure what prior learning had occurred or what the students brought with them to the learning situation, personally and academically. I could usually rely on signals from students to engage my intuition, but these were not yet apparent to me. Without this awareness, I felt compelled in this initial lesson to lay a foundation—my foundation—of knowledge.

As I considered the more complex situation, my lack of knowledge of students' academic and personal backgrounds moved into the foreground. Mrs. Hildebrand, the children's regular classroom teacher, knew the students. Another foreground issue seemed to be time—time for students to reflect, ask questions, seek answers and reflect again. My push for a common knowledge base had led me to conduct a mostly teacher-directed lesson. Perhaps student engagement was another issue in the foreground.

For now, I chose to move the issues of proficiency test objectives, limited classroom space, and my old feelings that "good teachers should know the answers" into the background. I would not forget these elements completely, but I would not attend to them for the present. If these elements became highly relevant during any stage of my problem solving, I could pull them into the foreground and perhaps push other elements into the background.

The process of framing the problem was my attempt to focus the key elements of the problem into a workable frame for finding solutions. As I reflected, my focus on the foreground issues of student background and needs, time, and meaningful learning changed three times! The deeper I looked into myself, the students, and the incident, the more complex yet targeted my problem became.

At first, the problem appeared to be one of facilitating student question-asking. I believe the best learning occurs when students ask the questions. I initiated the question-asking to lay the foundation, and though some students asked provocative questions in addition to mine, I controlled the lesson and did not pursue their questions with them in any depth.

Then the problem appeared to be one of providing students with adequate written materials to answer their questions. This was a part of the problem, but it didn't fit with my belief that peer collaboration and students' creative problem solving are just as, or more important, than finding "correct answers" in books. I asked myself, "What experiences are important for these students in this situation?" Then I readjusted the frame of the problem: "How might I help students inquire into their questions creatively?"

The constructivist in me realized that my task was to help Melissa and the other students make sense of the questions they were asking. I used a variety of teaching approaches to reach the variety of learning styles the children preferred. My lesson was not constructivist enough, however, because it required too much teacher-directed learning and not enough student-constructed knowledge.

There had been a time during the lesson when all the students worked in small groups. They could ask questions of one another and compare their responses.

The videotape showed all students actively engaged at this point in the lesson, working with Styrofoam balls to simulate globes. Students had the means to share their questions, ideas, and knowledge. This observation helped me to focus on another problem issue: "How might we (my colleagues and I) help students inquire into their questions creatively with each other?"

I decided to increase the percentage of time for group work. To enhance this portion of the lesson, we teachers would circulate and respond to questions or challenge the students to think more deeply. During these times, students would listen to each other as we helped them formulate complex questions that they could research. We would then guide the students to find their own answers through group interaction and a review of written materials. Each student's question would be heard and would have an opportunity to be answered.

TRYING OUT SOLUTIONS AND OBSERVING RESULTS

My next lesson with Mrs. Hildebrand's class provided me with an opportunity to try out this solution. The content for this lesson combined a fourth-grade self-esteem unit with the artistic formation of an assemblage. Each child's assemblage consisted of a molded plaster mask, items of importance to the child, and descriptive words. Prior to our co-facilitated lesson, Mrs. Hildebrand worked with the students on the concepts of the origin and expression of feelings and their effects on self-esteem. Also prior to the lesson, Mrs. Catley, the visual arts teacher, guided the students' creation process of the assemblage, which incorporated elements of design.

We gave each student three cards, each depicting a positive feeling in a picture and in words. The students privately recalled situations in which they had experienced the feelings portrayed on the cards. After some thought time, class members traded one card they chose as describing themselves least well. We moved around the class to help groups of students help each other consider their own personality characteristics.

The students then searched for cards they thought were self-descriptive. The boys and girls browsed and bartered. At our direction, the students formed into groups to share the times and events when they had experienced the feelings named on the cards they had chosen. We acted mostly as observers, though we helped the group formulate and resolve group process issues as those issues arose.

By knowing themselves better, students could then reflect their personal qualities in their art work. The assemblages combined artistry and visual thinking with self-awareness and personal growth.

I watched Melissa through much of this feelings/reflection activity. She seemed to have so many feelings, good and bad, jumbled inside. She fumbled with her "feelings cards" as she tried to sort through her emotions. Perhaps she had put her grieving process into hibernation so the others around her could heal. Now she was being asked to identify her feelings. Fellow students were identifying and sharing their feelings with her. In this small and safe setting, Melissa smiled and opened up a little. She told her peers about a time she was "afraid," and once, when she was "wishful."

ENGAGING IN FURTHER INQUIRY

Melissa's problems did not disappear that day. She continues to receive counseling to help her through these difficult times. The lesson did, however, provide for the active participation of all students, including Melissa. All students had the opportunity to make their questions and comments heard and to seek answers from others. Students could also share at their own level of comfort.

As I work more with these students, I have come to know them better. It has become more possible to trust my intuition and be creative. This brings up new incidents that I reflect upon, resulting in further inquiry and changes in planning. Questions I now have include: How might we help students inquire into their own questions, creatively and with each other, in integrated content such as math and language arts? How might I help students when I do not have time allotted for co-teaching? How might we engage students in planning the learning activities with us?

For me, pragmatic reflection is an ongoing process. It does not begin at a pre-assigned moment, nor does it last a predetermined length of time. I value time with my colleagues to discuss complex situations. Our roles change as we work together. One day I may act primarily as a problem initiator. In our next collaborative planning session I may be the coordinator. My colleagues and I support each other in solving complex learning problems through our commitment to this end and to each other and through our willingness to share roles and ideas.

Teacher-Character Advice

Johnny Jackson

Students' complex academic problems should be your highest priority as a teacher. My strategy for dealing with them is generally known as **academic problem solving,** meaning that I concentrate on the underlying disciplinary structure in a particular subject.

I subscribe to the constructivist theory of learning. I believe that students "construct their own meaning of new information and ideas on the basis of their existing knowledge; learning is not a matter of passively taking up 'static' information" (Erickson & MacKinnon, 1988, p. 121). Teachers must be bridge builders. They must actively create bridges between the formal knowledge of a subject and the past experiences and personal purposes of their students.

Donald Schön (1988), a leading researcher on reflective practice, has described a four-step process for academic problem solving. Here is an adaptation of his recommendations.

1. Observe carefully what a student says and does. Understand the learning problem from the student's point of view.
2. Think of what your student says and does as a puzzle you want to solve. You must assume that somehow the student is making sense. Unfortunately this type of making sense may be unrelated to the subject matter inquiry requirements in your lesson.
3. Invent bridges between your student's understanding and the subject matter.
4. You have successfully solved the puzzle when your instructional bridges are meaningful to the student. When this occurs, you have made a connection between the student's naive knowledge and the privileged knowledge of the subject matter.

To serve as a bridge builder, of course, you must understand the academic side of the "river": you must have a thorough command of your subject matter. You must also know the other side of the river, understanding your students' pertinent past experiences and personal purposes. This takes good listening skills and empathetic understanding.

You can try your hand at academic problem solving now, even without your own class. You'll need the help of your peers and a good coach, someone who is a strong academic problem solver and a patient guide.

Let's look at how a good coach helps Jill, a social studies student teacher, practice academic problem solving. Jill has just taught her students a lesson on the relationship between propaganda and social prejudice. One student, John, was upset by the lesson. Jill's supervisor, Ms. Lincoln, helps her reflect on this problem.

> Jill: I think most of the students were fascinated by the dramatic changes in the public images of the good mother and wife that occurred after World War II. During the war, patriotic women went to work each day to help their sons and husbands defeat the enemy. Once the war was over, women were supposed to return to the home to provide a steady, loving presence, like Beaver's mother in *Leave It To Beaver*. If a woman worked she was seen as the cause of all sorts of social problems, like juvenile delinquency and divorce. I wanted the students to examine why the images of the good mother and wife had changed so quickly in 1945. Was it mainly due to men's fear that women would compete with them for scarce factory jobs? Questions like that. During the lesson, I could tell that John was getting more and more upset.
>
> Ms. Lincoln: What was upsetting him?

Jill: I wasn't sure, so I asked John if he had any reactions to the lesson. He was kind of sullen, but he did softly mutter that mothers should be at home. I didn't know what to do. I was teaching an inquiry lesson, and he was taking it so personally!

Ms. Lincoln: Did you try to have a private conversation with John after the lesson?

Jill: I thought about it, but he seemed too upset to want to talk to me.

Ms. Lincoln: Perhaps he was, but you could have extended an invitation for a private talk anyway, and then let him accept or decline the invitation. In fact, you can still make the offer. To return to the lesson, is there anything else you might have done with John's comment?

Jill: I don't know. Nothing came to mind at the time.

Ms. Lincoln: It's hard to think on your feet, but what about now? How could you get a student to explore such stereotypical phrases as "a woman's place is in the home?"

Jill: I suppose I could ask the student why he feels that way.

Ms. Lincoln: He's not the only one who feels this way.

Jill: I could get into their feelings—why people feel that women should stay at home.

Ms. Lincoln: You might want to try another approach. Once one student shares a personal image, ask the class to contribute their images of women. Get them inquiring into the metaphors they use. Instead of just focusing on one student's image, and the feelings surrounding that image, open up the dialogue. If a student gets fixated on an image, don't get fixated on him or her. Remember, you're trying to conduct an inquiry lesson. What do you think?

Jill: Maybe I was overly anxious for students to see the sexism in the changing images of women at the end of the war. Maybe I don't need to push so hard. Perhaps I can figure out some different ways students can explore the personal images they carry about women.

Ms. Lincoln: You might also want to consider ways to switch to a related topic when feelings get ruffled. What about our changing images of the Japanese and the Germans during and after World War II? Couldn't that topic also help you with your objective, which was to explore the relationship between propaganda and social prejudice?

Jill: I see your point. I'll give that some thought.

Note that the coach, Ms. Lincoln, helped Jill frame her problem and headed her in the direction of solutions that are more consistent with constructivist goals. This dialogue was inspired by a book chapter written by Erickson and

MacKinnon (1988). You might want to refer to this chapter for more examples of coaching dialogues.

Once you're familiar with the concept of academic problem solving, I recommend that you design situations in which you can receive coaching assistance. In a university classroom you can set up role-playing scenarios where you teach students with specific academic learning problems. One or more coaches, either faculty members or other students, can serve as coaches to help you define and solve the problems. After you've had sufficient role-playing experience you can move into a classroom to practice academic problem solving with the assistance of a knowledgeable and supportive coach.

Whether you are role-playing or solving learning problems in a classroom, keep an inquiring attitude. Stay open to the complexities of the learning situation and the way you have framed the problem. Maintain an experimental posture toward your solution; check to make sure that your actions are consistent with your constructivist goals and be ready to inquire further into the problem. Remember, academic problem solving is a critical part of good teaching. If you can't build meaningful bridges between your students' naive knowledge and the subject matter you are teaching, they will remain stuck on their side of the river. Please give them the opportunity to cross those bridges.

Amy Nelson

When you solve a complex learning problem, you construct judgments as to what the problem is and how it should be solved. I recommend that you continually review the quality of your judgment with the help of research on students' learning achievements. This is not a difficult way to solve problems, but you can't do it if you don't do this research. After all, other people have worked at trying to figure out a lot of the problems that teachers encounter. I do believe that every situation is unique but is usually similar to other situations reported in the research literature.

Think of your problem solving as a practical judgment that is based on either an empirically flawed or an **empirically sound argument** (Fenstermacher, 1987). An empirically sound argument is one that can be supported by evidence gathered through careful formal or informal research. For example, "If students attend class regularly and study effectively, then they will get good grades." An empirically flawed argument has one or more if-then premises that can't be supported by research. For example, "If a student fails the final exam, then he will still get an 'A' in the course."

Good educational problem solving is based on empirically sound arguments. Therefore, in brainstorming for possible constructivist solutions, it's important to make sure that the basic premises are accurate and that the proposed solutions logically follow. Consider an example adapted from a chapter written by Fenstermacher (1986). Suppose a teacher is confronted with too many distracting discipline problems. For this teacher, students are not achieving as efficiently as he would like, and their test scores are lower than they should be. The teacher makes this initial judgment: If he structures his lessons better, then he will have fewer discipline problems and his students' test scores will go up.

But then he begins to wonder whether his empirical judgment is sound. He recalls that educational research on a method known as direct instruction indicates that this teaching strategy helps minimize discipline problems. He knows that direct instruction is a highly focused type of teaching that requires students to concentrate on the task at all times. He also knows that there are numerous specific prescriptions associated with direct instruction. The teacher decides to review the research on this method and finds prescriptions such as this one:

Students should know what work they are accountable for, how to get help when they need it, and what to do when they finish. Performance should be monitored for completion and accuracy, and students should receive timely and specific feedback. (Brophy & Good, 1986, p. 364)

He then checks to make sure that these ideas match with his conception of constructivist learning. He asks himself how he can use these prescriptions to move students along the path of understanding subject matter and taking more control of their own learning. He then adapts these prescriptions to fit his situation and implements the modified direct teaching solution he has devised.

Next he carefully studies the consequences of his action. Are the distracting discipline problems occurring less frequently? Is student achievement improving? Are constructivist learning goals being promoted? Are some students rebelling against the added structure in the classroom day? He recalls educational research indicating that teachers who are too direct in their instruction inhibit student motivation. As new evidence comes in, he willingly reconsiders his decision to implement direct instruction by identifying and reviewing his empirical judgments.

Here are the problem-solving steps that this exemplary teacher followed, and that I hope you will follow:

1. Identify the learning achievement problem that you must solve.
2. Consider ways to solve this problem, consulting with supportive colleagues for additional ideas.
3. Identify the empirical judgments associated with step 2. Remember, these are if-then premises associated with students' learning achievements.
4. Determine how educational research supports, challenges, or modifies your empirical judgments.
5. Make final adjustments in your problem solving in light of step 4, referring to your concept of constructivist learning to guide you.
6. Act to solve the problem.

7. Study the consequences of your actions and, in accordance with the dictates of educational research, make any further adjustments in your problem-solving behavior.

8. Continue this cycle until you have resolved the problem in an empirically sound manner that is consistent with your constructivist principles.

You can practice the discipline of constructing your own empirically sound arguments. In a university classroom you can set up a role-playing situation in which a problem emerges. First you identify the problem and consider how to solve it. With the help of your instructor and your peers, identify the empirical arguments in your proposed solution and consider ways to verify, strengthen, modify, or refute these if-then premises. Use your understanding of constructivist practices to guide your choices. Apply your refined solution to the problem and then study the consequences of your actions. Once you become adept at analyzing the empirical soundness of your practical judgments in role-playing settings, you can move to a classroom to further practice this disciplined form of problem solving.

I agree with Johnny Jackson that you should maintain an inquiring attitude throughout your problem-solving deliberations. I like to use research on teacher effectiveness to help me frame and solve complex learning problems. But I also know that the teaching-learning transaction is extremely complex and that when you combine differences in individual student's experiences and purposes with the subject matter, your problem-solving strategies must remain tentative. You can never be certain that you have correctly diagnosed an achievement problem, so be prepared to think of different ways of framing and then solving the problem. Remember, you want your students to be winners in our society. If they are successful, our society is the real winner because the students' achievements contribute to our overall social and economic stability.

Dennis Sage

To me, solving complex learning problems is an intuitive matter between you and your students. Expressions such as "deliberating over learning problems" are too academic and formal for my taste. These phrases are too cold. Good teachers develop rapport with their students. They find a way to mesh their personalities with those of their students. Once teachers are attuned to their students, a lot of so-called problems disappear.

Teaching is about motivation. When you've got motivated students, the classroom is alive with energy. You've got to be enthusiastic about your subject matter, and you've got to want to work with your students. If they sense that you don't want to be with them, all the deliberation in the world isn't going to help you solve your teaching problems.

Teaching is a passionate love affair, and it is this passion that engages your intuitive abilities. Certainly you will encounter problems as a teacher, but just listen carefully to yourself and to your students, and appropriate solutions will begin to emerge. Studying educational research distracts you from your intuitive listening. How much of this research was conducted in passionate settings, anyway? What wisdom is discovered through carefully controlled empirical research? To be responsive, you must be connected to the teaching present—to the teaching moment. One of my favorite books is Leonard's *Education and Ecstasy* (1968). Here's how he describes the high moments in teaching, which for me are the final solution to complex learning problems.

How many of those times do you remember? *Something happens.* A delicate warmth slides into parts of your being you didn't even realize were cold. The marrow of your bones begins to thaw. You feel a little lurch as your own consciousness, the teacher's voice, the entire web of sound and silence that holds the class together, the room itself, the very flow of time all shift to a different level. . . . How many teachable days? One out of a hundred? Then you are of the favored. (pp. 8-9)

Let me ask you three questions. Do you really solve the problems in your life using an academic problem-solving or an empirically based judgment perspective? If you became more academically or empirically versed, would you be better able to solve your problems? Where is the wisdom in such formal, analytical approaches?

If these questions got you thinking, you might want to keep looking for the problem-solving style that fits you as a person. If you can't be your own person in the classroom, how in the world are you going to connect with your students? If you're not authentic, how are you going to establish rapport? And without rapport, how can you be intuitive?

I believe in **intuitive problem solving.** Open up, enjoy working with your students, and allow your intuition to come into play. Teaching is like dancing with a partner. Get into the rhythms! You can't solve all the problems of the world, but you can share the joy of learning with your students. Here are some specific recommendations on how to do this.

1. Get to know your students as unique individuals. Look for opportunities to talk to them about their past experiences, current interests, and future goals. As much as you can, get to know their family and community backgrounds. All of this information will help you contemplate the best course of action for each of your students.
2. Maintain a good, poised mood when you are at school. If you are unhappy, if you feel too much stress, your students will know it. You won't be helping them feel good about their education, and you will be limiting your intuitive capacities. An unbalanced personal-professional lifestyle may be your greatest obstacle to becoming a sensitive, inquiring teacher.
3. Allow yourself to feel your students' learning anxieties. If you were in their shoes, what would you be feeling? To be an intuitive problem solver you must be empathetic and imaginative.
4. Think about the learning problem and its solution with reference to what is best for each student. Your problem-solving referent should be an indi-

vidual student's personal aspirations, not some academic or research tradition. How can they have a happier, more fulfilled life? What is best for them in the long run?

5. Whatever solution you try out, maintain a thoughtful composure. Stay in tune with the student's feelings and your intuition. If you feel that the solution isn't right, gently move to another. Teaching and learning aren't easy because life isn't easy. The art of living is based on contemplative self-discipline, and you model this art for your students by solving their learning problems in a composed and wise way. As your students get older, they will discover their own ways to practice a contemplative discipline, and they will thank you for demonstrating this possibility to them. We can never be free from life's problems, but we can all find our paths to personal wisdom.

These recommendations are based on Goldberg's (1983) ideas. If they sound good to you, you may want to work at strengthening your intuitive abilities. This is a highly personal and passionate matter, but it never hurts to get more information on the topic. There are many good books on intuition.

In his book *The Intuitive Edge: Understanding Intuition and Applying It in Everyday Life* (1983), Goldberg recommends that you keep an intuition journal. This is a journal in which you record your spontaneous and innermost thoughts, feelings, and sensations. Goldberg describes intuitions as the sparks of our minds (p. 20). They ignite our deliberate, rational plans, our judgments about others, and our careful analyses. Our intuitions provide us with personal intimations that we can then turn into more objective information through careful educational problem solving.

An intuition journal can help you remember and work with your own personal intuitive sparks on teaching and learning matters. When you get a spontaneous thought, feeling, or sensation, write it down as soon as possible. If you have the time, describe the circumstances of your intuitive flash. Did it come to you while you were taking a shower? Was there something you were thinking about? Did you get a clear insight or just a hazy feeling? Then, when you have more reflective time, go back to your initial journal entries and give them some more thought. What do you think of your intuition now? Is it a useful idea? Does it help you get better insight into one of your problems? Can you use your intuition in your educational problem solving? Make notes of your reflections in your journal. This way you will have your authentic thoughts and feelings concerning your intuitions as well as the sparks themselves. By keeping this two-part journal you will sharpen your ability to draw on your intuitions to help you in your problem solving.

The problem-solving technique I am describing is not mechanical at all. You must first be very committed to your students; then your intuitions about their best selves will begin to emerge. You are not trying to help them get ahead in their lives, but rather to get into their lives. This metaphorical distinction is critical to understanding the advice I am offering. I hope you will give it some thought.

Silvia Rivera

Classrooms are part of a society and they reflect its particular social context. The complex learning problems that teachers face in the classroom occur within a broader sociocultural context. Therefore I recommend **socially aware problem solving.** To understand what socially aware problem solving refers to, it may help to learn about bounded and unbounded problems.

Weizenbaum (1984) clarifies the distinction between bounded and unbounded problems. A *bounded problem* is relatively clear, and its solution is readily apparent to teachers with different beliefs and habits. For example, a student has an addition problem in math because he doesn't understand the distinction between the number columns. The definition of this problem would be apparent to most informed teachers, and a good problem-solving teacher with a background in math and math methods could develop a strategy for solving it successfully. Consequently, bounded problems are like a 10-piece puzzle. Anyone with a little skill and some common sense can put it together.

An *unbounded problem* is far more complex because it is often multi-layered. There may be many different but legitimate ways to define it, or information about the problem may be incomplete. The solution for solving the problem may not be readily apparent or may not yet exist.

For example, a white elementary school teacher ponders why a black student is hostile to the teacher and to the other students, many of whom are also black. How can the teacher define this problem? Is it a psychological problem? If so, which psychological theory provides the best insight? Should the teacher turn to the school psychologist for help? Perhaps the problem is sociological. Is it a personal problem of adjustment, a problem of family breakdown, a problem related to race relations, or what? What information should the teacher collect to help define and solve the problem? Perhaps there's more than one good solution. Unbounded problems are more like a 500-piece puzzle. It takes time, effort, patience, and insight to put all the pieces in the right place.

Modern society is full of 500-piece puzzles, and sometimes the pieces get mixed up. Sometimes I need to look beyond the school, to society at large, to find the pieces I need to complete my classroom puzzles. Society's problems influence what happens in our classrooms.

Let me illustrate this broad social perspective on teaching problems with an example. When I experience a discipline problem in class, I look for sociological insight to define both the problem and its solution. Suppose I have a student who continuously disrupts a class. I ask myself, "Where did this behavior start?" Usually my answer is, "In the home environment." Then I analyze the student's home environment to determine what might be encouraging the disruptive behavior. Perhaps the student comes from a single-parent family led by a hard-working, highly stressed mother. What social forces are operating on this type of family? What caused the student's mother and father to separate? Why isn't there a better supportive network in our society to help single parents raise their children? Is the mother working in a job where she is underpaid and overly stressed? How many women in our society are led into that kind of work, and why? Why is it that men generally can find more interesting and higher-paid work?

I could go on and on with such questions, but I'm sure you get the point. Teaching problems generally are not isolated from specific social problems. Teaching takes place in a complex web of interconnected social forces. Only a naive, unaware teacher would deny this dimension of educational difficulties. I like what Beyer and Apple (1988) say about the unbounded nature of educational problems:

We need to think about education *relationally*. We need to see it as being integrally connected to the cultural, political, and economic institutions of the larger society, institutions that may be strikingly unequal by race, gender, and class. (p. 4)

Think about what Beyer and Apple are saying. If racism occurs in the private, commercial, and political sectors of your community, for example, it will inevitably have an impact on the teaching problems you face. Problems in the classroom are closely tied to problems outside the classroom. It's that simple and that complex.

I recommend that you persistently examine the social context of the problems you face. See the problems as unbounded, as involving cultural, political, and economic forces of our time. Once you have framed the problem in its social context, decide on an appropriate solution. Usually when you define a problem as broadly as I do, you discover you can't solve the problem by yourself. You will need help. Sociocultural problems generally require collaborative action.

Let's return to the problem of the student's acting-out behavior. If there is a sociological context to the problem, other teachers should also be experiencing the same or similar problems. The impact of broad social problems is rarely limited to just certain classrooms. If I find that other teachers are experiencing similar difficulties in their classes, I encourage my peers to work with me to solve the problem together. This professional collaboration might extend to other service professionals in the building—the school psychologist, the school nurse, and the school administrators. You might collaborate with other service professionals in the community, including social workers, health care providers, and police, and other responsible members of the community, such as parents, community activists, and local politicians.

My problem-solving approach has led me to recognize that a highly participative school organization is a necessary requirement for socially aware problem solving. In chapter 9 you will read more about this type of school organization.

To summarize, I recommend that you deliberate on problems as follows:

1. Identify a classroom learning problem.
2. Analyze the sociological context of the problem. How is this problem related to the cultural, political, and economic conditions of our society?
3. Seek ways to collaborate with others to solve the problem. Recognize that this type of collaboration may require the establishment of a participative school operation. The way your school is organized may be part of the problem. Can you do anything about this?
4. Implement your solution, but keep a critical eye on the consequences of your actions. Were you just treating a symptom, or did you really find a cure for the illness? Did your solution move you and your students closer to the constructivist goals you believe in?

Persistent, socially aware problem solving leads toward a particular **praxis** orientation in teaching. To me, praxis means practice informed by utopian thought. It is the attempt to facilitate needed social change through educational means. Despite what you might hear from socially unaware, image-conscious politicians and popular media, our modern society is no utopia. Inequities pervade all aspects of our lives. With the help of praxis-oriented teachers, students can gain insight into these inequities and, I hope, discover their own collaborative role in the historic challenges of creating a better society. An educator committed to a praxis orientation in teaching wrote: "Teaching . . . is a Utopian challenge to social limits on thought and feeling. I can't imagine a more optimistic way to go about education" (Shor, 1987, pp. 269–270).

I hope you will be an optimistic educational problem solver in this change-oriented spirit. Teachers can make a difference. In their own small ways, they can help alleviate the social, economic, and political inequities in our society. They can help students take charge of their learning and take charge of their lives. I hope you will ponder the link between your specific teaching problems and the societal challenges of our times.

Case Studies

As you can see from reading each teacher-character's approach, there is no single best way to solve complex learning problems in a constructivist way. Your critical thinking challenge is to find the approach that works best for you. It should fit your personality and your teaching circumstances. The best way to develop your problem-solving approach is through guided practice in classrooms, but you may want to practice on case studies first. Five case studies have been included in Appendix B. You could apply any one or a combination of the four problem-solving approaches in this chapter to these cases.

FURTHER READINGS

You can also develop your problem-solving approach through further study. The following lists are presented in three categories: books that discuss procedures for solving complex educational problems, books that describe or give suggestions about constructivist teaching and learning, and books that address action research.

The following books will help you learn more about the topic of educational problem solving.

Adams, J. L. (1974). *Conceptual blockbusting: A guide to better ideas.* San Francisco: Freeman.

Bransford, J. K., & Stein, B. S. (1984). *The IDEAL problem solver: A guide for improving thinking, learning, and creativity.* New York: Freeman.

Halpern, D. F. (1984). *Thought and knowledge: An introduction to critical thinking.* Hillsdale, NJ: Erlbaum.

Hayes, J. R. (1981). *The complete problem solver.* Philadelphia: The Franklin Institute Press.

Leithwood, K., & Steinbach, R. (1994). *Expert problem solving: Evidence from school and district leaders.* Albany, NY: SUNY Press.

Ruggiero, V. R. (1984). *The art of thinking: A guide to critical and creative thought.* New York: Harper & Row.

Sternberg, R. J., & Davidson, J. E. (Eds.) (1995). *The nature of insight.* Cambridge, MA: MIT Press.

Wakefield, J. F. (1992). *Creative thinking: Problem solving skills and the arts orientation.* Norwood, NJ: Ablex Publications.

The following books address constructivist teaching practices.

Barell, J. (1995). *Teaching for thoughtfulness: Classroom strategies to enhance intellectual development* (2nd ed.). White Plains, NY: Longman.

Brooks, J. G., & Brooks, M. G. (1993). *In search of understanding: The case for constructivist classrooms.* Alexandria, VA: Association for Supervision and Curriculum Development.

Fosnot, C. T. (1989). *Enquiring teachers, enquiring learners: A constructivist approach for teaching.* New York: Teachers College Press.

Zemelman, S., Daniels, H., & Hyde, A. (1993). *Best practice: New standards for teaching and learning in America's schools.* Portsmouth, NH: Heinemann.

These books include descriptions of action research as well as examples of action research done by teachers:

Anderson, G. L., Herr, K., & Nihlen, A. S. (1994). *Studying your own school: An educator's guide to qualitative practitioner research.* Thousand Oaks, CA: Corwin Press.

Carson, T. R., & Sumara, D. J. (Eds.). (1989). *Exploring collaborative action research.* Alberta, Canada: Canadian Association for Curriculum Studies.

Cochran-Smith, M., & Lytle, S. L. (1993). *Inside/outside: Teacher research and knowledge.* New York: Teachers College Press.

Patterson, L., Santa, C. M., Short, K. G., & Smith, K. (Eds.). (1993). *Teachers are researchers: Reflection and action.* Newark, DE: International Reading Association.

Sagor, R. (1993). *How to conduct collaborative action research.* Alexandria, VA: Association for Supervision and Curriculum Development.

REFERENCES

Beyer, L. E., & Apple, M. W. (1988). Values and politics in the curriculum. In L. E. Beyer & M. W. Apple (Eds.), *The curriculum: Problems, politics, and possibilities* (pp. 3–16). Albany, NY: State University of New York Press.

Brophy, J. E., & Good, T. L. (1986). Teacher behavior and student achievement. In M. C. Wittrock (Ed.), *Handbook of research on teaching* (3rd ed., pp. 328–375). New York: Macmillan.

Dewey, J. (1933). *How we think: A restatement of the relation of reflective thinking to the educative process* (2nd ed.). Boston: D. C. Heath. (Original work published 1910)

Dewey, J. (1938). *Experience and education.* New York: Macmillan.

Erickson, G. L., & MacKinnon, A. M. (1988). Taking Schon's ideas to a science teaching practicum. In P. P. Grimmett & G. L. Erickson (Eds.), *Reflection in teacher education* (pp. 113–137). New York: Teachers College Press.

Fenstermacher, G. D. (1986). Philosophy of research on teaching: Three aspects. In M. C. Wittrock (Ed.), *Handbook of research on teaching* (3rd ed., pp. 37–49). New York: Macmillan.

Fenstermacher, G. D. (1987). A reply to my critics. *Educational Theory, 37,* 413–421.

Goldberg, P. (1983). *The intuitive edge: Understanding intuition and applying it in everyday life.* Los Angeles: J. P. Tarcher.

Kolb, D. A. (1984). *Experiential learning: Experience as the source of learning and development.* Englewood Cliffs, NJ: P T R Prentice-Hall.

Leonard, G. B. (1968). *Education and ecstasy.* New York: Dell.

Lewin, K. (1948). *Resolving social conflicts.* New York: Harper & Brothers.

Posner, G. J. (1992). *Analyzing the curriculum.* New York: McGraw-Hill.

Schön, D. (1983). *The reflective practitioner: How professionals think in action.* New York: Basic Books.

Schön, D. (1988). Coaching reflective teaching. In P. P. Grimmett & G. L. Erickson (Eds.), *Reflection in teacher education* (pp. 21–22). New York: Teachers College Press.

Shor, I. (1987). *Critical teaching and everyday life* (2nd ed.). Chicago: University of Chicago Press.

Weizenbaum, J. (1984). Limits in the use of computer technology: Need for a man-centered science. In D. Sloan (Ed.), *Toward the recovery of wholeness: Knowledge, education, and human values* (pp. 149–158). New York: Teachers College Press.

4

Creating a Constructivist Curriculum Design

Joan Haggerty, who is a highly respected second-grade teacher in the Elmdale School District, has an extensive background in mathematics education and is active in several professional teaching associations. The new superintendent in her school district believes in teacher empowerment and school-community collaboration and is an advocate of the state's new guidelines for constructivist math. He has asked Ms. Haggerty to form a curriculum committee to create a general curriculum design or framework for the reform of math education in the school district. He has asked her to chair this committee because he knows that she is quite familiar with the state's new instructional guidelines for mathematics and because of her leadership abilities. He has told her that whenever she needs release time from classroom duties for committee work, she will get the support she needs.

At first, Ms. Haggerty wasn't sure she would accept the offer. She had to consider the personal and professional consequences of assuming this important curriculum leadership responsibility. How much would it interfere with her teaching? Would she lose valuable evening and weekend time with her husband and children? After about a week of soul searching, however, she decided to take the job. She realized she would have a unique opportunity to foster educational reform in Elmdale.

Ms. Haggerty realized that she had to select a committee that would represent the major interest groups in the school district. She decided to include a progressive building administrator from the school district's middle school; several parents who are highly visible in the community; two community leaders with local political clout, one an undertaker and the other a minister; several energetic and visionary teachers; and two high school student leaders, one who loves math and one who has despised the subject since the first grade. It took her three weeks of hard work—and some cajoling—to form the committee she envisioned.

It is now the night before the committee's first meeting, and Ms. Haggerty is sitting in her kitchen preparing the agenda. She wonders whether the committee will have any real impact on how math and related subjects are taught in the district. She has assembled an imaginative, hard-working, and critically aware group. If they can establish a common curriculum vision, decide on new materials that encourage problem solving, create some exciting new interdisciplinary programs, and build a performance-based evaluation system, their curriculum design efforts should bear fruit. She knows that she will need to work closely with all the teacher leaders in the school district, and she looks forward to this collegial collaboration. After completing the agenda, she turns off the kitchen light thinking to herself, "I feel fortunate to have this leadership opportunity, and I'm going to hope for the best. At this stage in the game, I won't let the cynics get me down. I know we can provide better constructivist learning services for our students. With a little luck, I think we can encourage significant changes in our educational programs."

Introduction

The topic in chapter 3 was the practice of solving complex learning problems in a constructivist way. In this chapter, you will inquire into a related educational practice: creating a constructivist curriculum design. You will study how teachers can contribute to the creation of a curriculum framework that supports constructivist transactions between teachers and students.

Curriculum is a complex term referring to planned educational experiences. The **curriculum design** is the general framework for an educational program. This framework can be compared to an architect's blueprint. Without this blueprint, there can be no coordinated construction project. Similarly, without a curriculum design, there can be no coordinated educational program. Henderson and Hawthorne (1995) write:

> . . . A curriculum design offers the big picture—the overall view of, and rationale for, an educational journey. It delves into the specifics only to illustrate. In addition to stating publicly what is worth learning and what kinds of learning are valuable, a curriculum design functions as a plan for planning. Accordingly, it should enhance the

. . . imaginations of teachers and other educators who "know" the specific students and school and community context. (pp. 59–60)

Given the ideological nature of education, deliberations over curriculum design can be highly divisive, collaborative, or somewhere between these two polar opposites. Curriculum design deliberations will be discussed from a collaborative point of view in this chapter. This is obviously an ideal, but it is consistent with the progressive, democratic outlook of this book. You will read more about the values and challenges of educational collaboration in chapters 8 and 9.

A collaborative approach to curriculum design involves the work of teachers, students, school administrators, parents, and community leaders. Curriculum design is viewed as a responsibility shared by the school and the community.

A General Protocol

Curriculum design activity can be directed toward either **teacher implementation** or **teacher enactment**. As Snyder, Bolin, and Zumwalt (1992) note, teacher implementation refers to top-down control. A framework created from this point of view attempts to dictate to teachers. The curriculum design states specific performance goals and perhaps even the instructional procedures for attaining these performance goals. The message to teachers is straightforward: "Your success will be evaluated in accordance with how well students successfully meet the required objectives."

An orientation of teacher enactment for curriculum design work allows for professional discretion. A curriculum design based on enactment uses open-ended statements about educational goals and procedures, treating teachers and students as equal partners who engage in their own relevant meaning-making. Snyder et al. (1992) write:

> From the enactment perspective, curriculum is viewed as the educational experiences jointly created by student and teacher. The externally created curricular materials and programmed instructional strategies . . . are seen as tools for students and teachers to use as they construct the enacted experience in the classroom. (p. 418)

Curriculum design for enactment is facilitative. The goal is to empower teachers—to give them the latitude they need to humanize their work in the context of daily constructivist transactions with students.

The Five Elements of a Curriculum Design

When creating an empowering curriculum design, teachers work with others who hold a stake in education—parents, students, educational administrators, community leaders—on five key elements:

- *Vision Statement*. The design committee formulates a general description of what is considered the best educational practice with reference to a particular social vision.
- *Critical Analysis*. The group assesses current teaching practices in light of the vision statement.
- *Content Selection*. The committee determines the type of content that will be used to support teacher-student constructivist transactions.
- *Program Organization*. This element involves creating a blueprint for coherent educational programs. This blueprint must not interfere with content organization, which is left to the professional discretion of the teachers.
- *Graduation Assessment*. This step is the establishment of procedures for determining when, and with what qualitative distinction, students are allowed to exit from a particular program. This assessment establishes the final evaluative frame of reference for a program, but it should not interfere with teachers' evaluations of courses, units, and lessons.

Each of these design elements will now be explained more fully. The four teacher-characters will then offer their distinctive opinions on a good curriculum design for constructivist enactment.

Vision Statement

A key element of curriculum design is the articulation of a school's overall educational commitment. This is not a straightforward task in complex pluralistic societies, where various interest groups may have different ideas about what constitutes an appropriate educational journey. To address this pluralism, the design committee may need to hold public forums to allow dialogue and debate over desirable human capacities and virtues. The vision statement should emerge from this democratic process. Without consensus, it will be difficult for the design committee to proceed with the rest of its work. The final vision statement is an articulation of what are considered the best educational practices with reference to a particular social vision. This statement must have relevance in the particular school-community context.

Critical Analysis

The design committee needs to assess current teaching practices in light of the vision statement. Sirotnik (1991) provides a precise way this work can occur. He argues that good critical work in education is guided by the following questions:

- What are we doing now?
- How did it come to be this way?
- Whose interests are, and are not, being served by the way things are?
- What information and knowledge do we have (or need to get) that bear upon the issues?

- Is this the way we want things to be? What are we going to do about it? (pp. 250–252)

The committee needs to collect descriptive data to answer these questions. They can gather personal narratives such as anecdotes, stories, and testimonials in formal meetings or informal conversations. They can collect other types of data through the use of prescribed data-gathering methods. There are many such procedures on the educational market, and it is beyond the scope of this book to list and describe them.[1] Once the design committee has collected data on what is currently occurring, the next task is to compare that information with the vision statement of what should be occurring. This critical analysis may create dissonance that can hopefully be resolved over time. If there is no hope for an immediate or eventual resolution, it will be exceedingly difficult for the design committee to continue its work.

Content Selection

The design committee also needs to decide what type of curriculum content should be selected to support the desired teacher-student constructivist transactions. The design committee will need to deliberate over the question of what knowledge is of most worth. Educational philosophers, curriculum theorists, and teachers have long wondered about what students should be learning. Clearly not everything can be taught in school. What, then, are the criteria by which educational content should be prioritized?

This curriculum question is even more complex than it might initially appear. It invites a series of additional questions. For example, should there be a universal curriculum for all students in a society or in an individual classroom, regardless of interests, propensities, socioeconomic background? Should content be sorted out according to disciplines and subject areas, or should student learning be comprised of trans-disciplinary content that focuses on "real world" problems? Should the curriculum completely avoid teaching content in the usual sense, instead imparting critical thinking skills that students can apply to a wide range of problems? Should students be taught the content, skills, attitudes, and behavioral norms needed to merely survive in the real world, or should they be emotionally and intellectually primed to change the world for the better? Should values and attitudes be taught at all in school? Can schools avoid teaching them? Should they be a part of the overt, "advertised" curriculum, or should schools teach them covertly, as part of a hidden curriculum?

Such questions raise the fundamental issue of where educators should look to find the legitimate source of educational content and curriculum goals that are of most worth. Should subject-matter experts hand teachers the curriculum in each

---

[1] For a good overview of selected formal data-gathering tools, see K. Acheson and M. Gall, *Techniques in the Clinical Supervision of Teachers* (3rd ed.). New York: Longman, 1992.

discipline? Or should people in the local community be surveyed to ascertain the desired curriculum content? Perhaps teachers should observe and listen to their students to derive goals from their interests and needs.

Every major subject field, such as mathematics, literacy, social studies, and the sciences, has established general content selection standards appropriate for constructivist teaching. Again, it is beyond the scope of this book to present all of these standards. For purposes of illustration, however, the following excerpt from the National Council of Teachers of Mathematics' (NCTM) policy statement, *Curriculum and Evaluation Standards for School Mathematics*, shows an example of a standard for solving problems in mathematics.

Standard 1: Mathematics as Problem Solving

In grades K–4, the study of mathematics should emphasize problem solving so that students can:
- Use problem-solving approaches to investigate and understand mathematical content.
- Formulate problems from everyday mathematical situations.
- Develop and apply strategies to solve a wide variety of problems.
- Verify and interpret results with respect to the original problem.
- Acquire confidence in using mathematics meaningfully. (1989, p. 23)

Since the curriculum design committee's responsibility is to create a guiding blueprint for instruction, they need to be aware of this type of constructivist content standard. In the United States, much of this national standard setting has been translated into specific state guidelines, which should be quite helpful to a local curriculum design committee.

Program Organization

The curriculum design committee must also create a blueprint for coherent educational programs. The goal is to organize teachers and their students in such a way as to maximize constructivist transactions. The committee must be careful not to engage in the organization of content, which should be left to the professional discretion of the teachers. Content organization, which is central to instructional planning, will be covered in chapter 5. This chapter will present a view of teaching as integrated planning, acting, and evaluating.

Program organization requires decisions about grouping of students and teachers. Students can be grouped in accordance with a wide range of criteria including age, ability, disability, motivations, and interests. Teachers can be grouped by individual classrooms, by teams, by subject areas, by interdisciplinary areas, and so on. When selecting criteria, the committee should be guided by two general considerations. Will the organizational scheme support teachers' continuing professional development, and will the organizational scheme support teacher-student constructivist transactions? If teachers are too physically or psychologically isolated in their work, they may not be inclined or encouraged to grow. Many current program designs encourage teachers to become task-oriented and efficient at disseminating knowledge rather than facilitators of constructivist learning.

The review of literature on educational program design is beyond the scope of this book. For further information on this topic, consult general curriculum texts that cover educational programming. The committee may need to study such books or hire a consultant who has such knowledge before making its decisions. The organization of Central Park East, a New York City high school, is presented as an example of how educational programs can be designed to support teachers' constructivist enactments.

Central Park East is part of the Essential School Movement in the United States. The Coalition of Essential Schools was created in 1984 through the support of foundations and professional associations. The coalition was inspired by several national studies that criticized the organization of secondary education in the United States. The most significant of these was Sizer's *Horace's Compromise: The Dilemma of the American High School* (1984). This study chronicled serious problems in the modern comprehensive high school and recommended dramatic institutional reform. The recommendations served as the basis for an alliance of approximately 45 private and public secondary schools in the United States and Canada. The common beliefs of these schools are stated as follows:

> The common principles of the Coalition . . . focus our attention on a limited number of important features of schooling: the school's purpose should be to help students learn to use their minds well; the school's goal should be that each student master a limited number of essential skills and areas of knowledge; the academic and social goals of the school should apply to all students; teaching and learning should be personalized; the student is to be the worker and the teacher more of a coach; the diploma should be rewarded on the basis of demonstrated competence; the school's norms should emphasize trust, decency, and unanxious expectation; the faculty should view themselves as generalists rather than specialists; and the budget should permit total teacher loads of no more than 80 pupils, while staff salaries remain (or become) competitive and total expenditures remain fairly constant (i.e., they are not to increase more than 10 percent beyond the current cost per pupil). (Houston, 1988, p. 110)

By operating according to these beliefs, the schools in the coalition have radically altered their institutional operations. No two coalition schools have exactly the same organizational structure, but they all share several features. The school principal functions less as an administrator and more as a member of a leadership team that includes the school faculty. This team makes all significant school-based decisions and establishes the policies for educational standards and methods of assessment (Houston, 1988, p. 110). The professional staff collaborates regularly. For example, the teachers are usually organized into four-member interdisciplinary teams that are responsible for 80 students for the entire school day. Each teacher specializes in one of the four so-called essential subjects: English, social studies, science, and mathematics. No teacher works with more than 20 students at a time, and the team members meet daily to coordinate their activities. Instruction is highly personalized. Typical high school services such as athletics, extracurricular activities, or vocational programs are cut back or eliminated if they interfere with the professional work of the teachers.

Central Park East is a member of the Coalition for Essential Schools with grades 7–12 enrollment. This teacher-run school professes the following educational philosophy: "We looked upon Dewey, perhaps more than Piaget, as our mentor. . . . We also saw schools as models of the possibilities of democratic life" (Meier, 1987, p. 36). Central Park East has created the following organizational blueprint:

- All educational professionals, including the librarian and the principal, teach.
- The educational professionals supervise one another. No outside district supervisors work at this school.
- The school is organized into "Houses" of 80 students, and each House has four teachers.
- Class size never exceeds 20 students.
- To ensure personalized educational services, teachers and students in a House stay together for two years.
- The entire school faculty has curriculum meetings twice a month.
- The teachers in each academic department have a three-hour curriculum meeting each week.
- The four-member interdisciplinary House teams take a daily 80-minute lunch together to coordinate their efforts.
- The curriculum is designed by the teachers.
- The curriculum schedule is flexible and can be altered to meet emerging instructional purposes. Administrative needs never dictate the schedule.
- Curriculum resources can be purchased from teacher-determined sources. Teachers are not bound to district-adopted texts.
- Parents meet with teachers twice a year to review portfolios of student work. (Meier, 1987, p. 37)

As you can see, the teachers at Central Park East work in an organization designed to encourage their humanistic growth as they engage in constructivist practices.

Graduation Assessment

The final task for the curriculum design committee is to decide on procedures for determining when, and with what qualitative distinction, students are allowed to exit from a particular educational program. This assessment establishes the final evaluative frame of reference for an educational program. However, this design work must be done in such a way as to guide but not interfere with teachers' course, unit, and lesson evaluations—a topic that will also be covered in chapter 5.

The design committee can choose from a wide range of options for determining standards and procedures for student graduation. The committee should be aware of these options before making a decision. Again, it is beyond the scope of this book to cover all these evaluative possibilities. The committee should consult the appropriate literature on this topic or work with a consultant who possesses this knowledge. Whatever the committee decides, a key consideration should inform their deliberations: the graduation activities should encourage and support students' constructivist learning. Are students allowed to graduate simply by accumulating a predetermined number of course credits or by passing one or more standardized proficiency tests? Do the graduation procedures encourage student inquiry? These types of questions should guide the design committee's deliberations, and there are three evaluative principles that can inform their decisions.

Evaluation that is democratic, performance-based, and authentic helps encourage and support constructivist learning. Democratic evaluation involves public, collaborative decision-making. Performance-based evaluation requires students to demonstrate their proficiency by completing complex tasks. When these evaluative tasks are related to real-world activities, the test is an example of **authentic evaluation** (Brooks & Brooks, 1993).

A widely enacted graduation assessment procedure in higher education incorporates all three of these features. Ph.D. programs in the United States are generally considered to be top-notch—the best in the world. Students do not graduate from these programs until they have successfully defended an original dissertation study. The defense takes place among a group of faculty members, who afterwards deliberate over the quality of the student's defense. They must collectively discuss and evaluate the student's performance. The student's dissertation defense is authentic because it involves peer review. Most Ph.D. work in U.S. higher education, including teaching and publication activity, is continuously subjected to peer review. Imagine K–12 teachers working to prepare their students' learning defenses in an appropriate democratic, authentic performance context. What would happen to the quality of K–12 educational practice under such an evaluative design?

Practicing the Decision-Making Cycle

The curriculum design committee has a responsibility to reflectively explore the relationships between the five elements of curriculum design and make adjustments as necessary. If they do not, their work would not be considered progressive. They would not be following the decision-making cycle introduced in chapter 1.

The curriculum design committee must continuously ask themselves a series of tough questions:

- What are teachers' and other service providers' reactions to our vision statement and the related critical analysis? Is this work relevant to them, or are we engaging in goal-setting activities that they view as meaningless? Will we be creating a mission statement that will be read and quickly forgotten?
- Do our content selection decisions support constructivist transactions in the classroom and other settings, or are we interfering with this important educational work? Are we making resource decisions that are better tackled at the direct service level? Are we purchasing the most up-to-date, imaginative, and compelling constructivist materials possible? What is the feedback from our service providers on this question?
- What feedback are teachers and other service providers giving us on the way the educational programs are organized? Do the programs need any adjustments?
- Do the teachers and other service providers value our graduation evaluation procedures? Does the community respect our graduates? Can we engage in an ongoing quality assessment of our graduates, and how could this assessment provide continuous feedback for all our design decisions?

CRITICAL INCIDENT

Creating a Constructivist Curriculum Design

Susannah Miller and Sharon Klimm

BACKGROUND

Susannah Miller has taught for 23 years. Her experience ranges from teaching in an orthodox religious school to her current position as a fifth-grade teacher in public education. Susannah's grandfather, who was a leader in character education, worked with John Dewey. Susannah attributes her love for democracy and education to the conversations held each night around the dinner table in her early family years. Her mother and father, who also were teachers, provided the space and support for this ideological sparring. "My environment encouraged thinking and debate. My education aimed to free my mind and challenged me to break the rules," Susannah remembers.

Last spring, Susannah represented her middle school in a curriculum design experience with teachers from across the district. The purpose of the forum, begun by the Curriculum Director, was to frame the district's social studies curriculum according to state-mandated outcomes and the state-approved course of study. A body of appointed educators from around the state had developed the outcomes and general scope and sequence at each grade level, based on teacher-designed national recommendations and models.

Susannah and her colleagues were to create the district social studies design for K–12. They were to base their work not on a set of textbooks, but on important topics in these categories: American heritage, people in societies, world interaction, decision making and resources, democratic processes, and citizenship rights and responsibilities. Susannah served as liaison between her colleagues, fifth- and sixth-grade teachers, and the design forum.

In her story, Susannah relates her design experience, as well as how she enacted the design in her own classroom. She organizes the incident in five sections—one for each part of the protocol but presented in a different order from the previous section of this chapter. Susannah begins her reflection of this incident with Content Selection.

CONTENT SELECTION

My design work for this project began in the spring of 1994, when grade-level representatives from my district gathered to examine the state's recommended performance objectives. We were asked to address selected themes by having students compare and contrast geographically different cultures through the use of biographies. We were strongly encouraged to use a multi-resource approach, as the state wanted to discourage the use of textbooks as primary sources.

During several meetings over the summer, I chose to compare the Maya Indians of Mexico, the Iroquois Indians of the Northeast Woodlands, and the Inuit Indians of Alaska. I envisioned a culminating activity involving all the students, their parents, and the teachers. Our learning community would hold a powwow on sacred ground—the high school football field. We would wear masks we made in art classes, perform authentic songs and dances we learned in music, and compete in foot races we'd practiced in physical education. In the regular classroom, we would learn Mayan math and study the myths and legends of Native Americans. We would demonstrate our learnings at the powwow and then trade the jewelry and weapons we had made. The evening would end around a huge campfire, where we would tell stories and celebrate our learnings. The unit design and accompanying activities met the criteria outlined by the state. I believed the program would excite parents and children alike.

VISION STATEMENT

As I look back over the curriculum design, I see my role as one of holding up a vision and calling teachers out of their adult structures and back into the world of the child. In my vision, we teachers learn side-by-side with the students. When teacher and student share the role of learner, education can truly be an awakening to any possibility.

My experience in education tells me that the creative magic in children goes far beyond what we as adults can even begin to imagine. Somehow, as we become culturally mature, we lose sight of the wonder inherent in all learning. A learning environment that promotes inquiry and experimentation, problem solving and cooperative learning is an environment that continually tests the power of the creative imaginings of children. When the teacher becomes a learner along with the students, the learning community focuses on process rather than product, involvement rather than extraction of specific information, on meaning-making.

I have always marveled that the Mayans constructed stone temples over two hundred feet tall without the use of metal or the wheel. The questions still intrigue me. Where did the stone come from? How was it transported to the construction site? How were the temples built with such precision and expertise that they still stand two thousand years later?

One young learner, Mike, became intrigued with the why and how of cultural creation as he struggled to solve the problem of building a model Mayan temple. Mike exemplified the struggle of any culture as it tries to discover ways to create those things that are essential to everyday life. He was determined to build the temple with a hinge so that burial would be possible in the tomb beneath the temple. The Mayans had no metal, so Mike chose to construct the tomb from clay.

On the first day, the clay stuck together and broke. On the second day, Mike tried again, deciding that wet clay against dry clay might work better. That hinge worked for about six hours until the wet clay dried. The third day, Mike decided that if the clay was thicker and the connecting wall was stronger, the hinge would not crack so easily. He continued to search for solutions. At the end of the allotted time he said he thought he could still find a solution and would continue to think about it.

As my students worked through their problems and creations, I saw the children individually developing their own vision toward which they were learning. While Mike focused on the development of a hinge, others experimented with bead making, weapon development, or weaving. My vision was no longer paramount as each child's motivation shifted from external to internal. The students were each guided by their own personal understanding and connection to the culture.

Creating a vision does not guarantee that others will be able to see or understand the same vision. At some point, teachers have to be asked to step forth and try new methods on faith. Adequate help and support must be provided on a daily basis. I had invested much time and energy in the design, and I desperately wanted it to work.

When I learned at one point that only about half the students planned to participate in the powwow, I visited the classes to explain the festival and encourage their involvement. After I visited each class, we had almost 100 percent participation. The excitement of the students seemed to carry the teachers through our culminating evening. After this first experience, the vision has become a common bond for us all, and staff hostility and resistance have subsided.

CRITICAL ANALYSIS

I have been doing curriculum design for nearly twenty years. I have a good grasp of what works and what doesn't. I have had the opportunity to learn through an experience-reflection model that has been used in American churches for some time. In this model, after any experience, a reflection is held in which the participants respond to questions: What happened? How did you feel? What did you learn? In this process, nothing can be a failure because the focus is always on what is learned.

As I began to see my colleagues resist the constructivist method of teaching I proposed, I began to see how difficult it is for teachers to believe that children really are capable enough to determine their own learnings. The teachers wrestled with the idea that learnings can be different for each child. The threat of relinquishing their control exacerbated the teachers' anxiety. As a result, the potential excitement and enthusiasm were lost for many of the children. The teachers faced the chaos and confusion of aimlessness. They didn't know how to continue with the unit.

The teachers reacted to this void in different ways. Some handed out printed material and gave paper-and-pencil tests on vocabulary and key concepts. Some assigned specific projects, and all students did the same ones in the same ways. Some teachers took risks, offered the students freedom, and celebrated the results.

I believe that risk-taking is a formula for surprise and success. How could I have anticipated that Mike would seek to develop the idea of a hinge? I am continually amazed that students who are engaged in constructivist learning compose and identify so many valuable concepts. I have come to understand that by letting go of control, I have become open, allowing transformation to occur and magic to blossom. We are limited by our own experience and imagination. By welcoming all learners, our own plans become better than ever expected.

PROGRAM ORGANIZATION

This curriculum design aimed to immerse the students in the lives of each of the native tribes. The immersion occurred over several weeks, through students' in- and out-of-class experiences and the staff's continuous reflection and development. The first four days in class, teachers presented and discussed information on one of the tribes. Each student considered creating projects from a list of about twenty-five possibilities, knowing they were not limited to the ideas presented. Each student then made several projects that related the life and beliefs of that tribe.

The first week of the unit in my own classroom, energy consumed the students as they engaged in lively discussion of what they might try and with whom they might work. Day after day, my desk was surrounded by students who brought their efforts in to be admired. We had show-and-tell time, and I encouraged the students to copy one another but try new and different methods. The chaos and confusion of these days stemmed from an undertone of creative productivity.

To facilitate other teachers' growth and comfort with the new curriculum design, the district design committee planned ongoing staff development, which took place over the coming year. Our first staff development session motivated the group and brought us together as adventurers. Teachers shared possible techniques and activity outlines. Some teachers expressed frustration stemming from the lack of a textbook. Several teachers hesitated about "the ambitious festival." They wondered aloud, "Perhaps the large-scale powwow activity would be best tried after several years of 'refining' the curriculum?"

As teachers returned to their classrooms to enact this curriculum design, they began to struggle with the shift away from a teacher-directed classroom to a student-directed learning environment. Some teachers verbalized anxiety that bordered on hostility. I realized my position as a peer facilitator was not going to be a comfortable one.

I felt challenged as I promoted ideas to teachers who had not had my experiences. Being a peer complicated the matter. I cringed when a colleague said, "Well, you should know, you're the expert." Our administration sensed our apprehension. They assured us that we were all learning together and we could take as much time as necessary to put programs into final form. We were encouraged to develop units together and were given time to iron out the wrinkles as they appeared. Teachers cautiously tried new activities, but only after their frustrations were heard and acknowledged.

In follow-up training sessions, teachers walked through the design step by step. Teachers continually clarified their expectations and shared their classroom successes as well as the resources they'd found helpful.

GRADUATION ASSESSMENT

Competency checks, proficiency testing, grade-level passage, and twelfth-grade graduation comprise elements of the blueprint for our district's graduation assessment. Students are continually assessed on district competencies, a list of learnings culled from the district's pupil performance objectives. Solon teachers developed this list of learnings, which they deem essential for student success in future learning. Students who do not exhibit competency in an assessed skill or concept receive intervention by the classroom teacher, and then they are re-assessed. In Solon, grade-level passage is based on mastery of grade-level competencies.

A more encompassing form of competency assessment is proficiency testing, which is administered in Ohio in grades four, six, nine, and twelve. The recently implemented proficiency tests in social studies, science, math, and language arts are state-developed and mandated. Passage of the ninth-grade test is required for a student to graduate from high school. (The student must also satisfactorily complete a high school program at an accredited high school.) Passage rates for area districts are published in newspapers and serve as a public measuring stick of school effectiveness. Proficiency testing also has had significant impact on courses of study and methods of instruction around the state.

In the case of our Native American unit, graduation assessments range from student self-assessment, in the form of writing in journals, to teacher assessment of student performance on district competencies to state-directed proficiency testing. Proficiency testing of the students' cumulative learnings in social studies will be assessed next year. The fifth-grade teachers—as well as teachers of all the lower grades—take to heart the contribution they must make to each student's meaning-making in the social sciences.

Some competency assessments and student products will be included in each student's portfolio, which is a repository of student performances. An example of one student's self-evaluative paragraph for a Native American project detailed the student's experience, amount of time spent, how the project reflected the life of the tribe, and what she had learned.

I'm going to work on social studies tonight after school. I'm going to grind corn, make clay beads, make worry dolls, do some weapons like arrows or a hatchet, grind coffee, and make a gourd into a bowl. I love social studies and it is so fun to learn about Indians. I love to know about the Indians. I told my mom about the culture and how they did sacrifices. She wanted to puke but it was fun to tell her the stuff.

"Effort and willingness to risk by trying new ideas" formed the most important competency in this unit. Misfires were as important as successes. This emphasis on learning freed students to explore and reflect as a culture would in its efforts to thrive. The success or failure of a particular project was irrelevant. Students knew the project they created could be traded or displayed at the powwow, and that parents, other students, and guests would be present to ask questions and comment on the students' work. Students knew that a project didn't have to succeed to count toward their grade.

A final, more academically structured assessment provided a view of each student's knowledge base and ability to compare the three Native American groups. Each student chose at least seven areas from a list—housing, clothing, family life, entertainment, weapons, religion, mode of travel, community life, government, art, science, food, geography, special contributions, role of women, and role of children—to discuss in the comparison.

Many students exceeded the requirements and chose to discuss ten or fifteen areas of life. Each student demonstrated a solid knowledge base and concept formation, though each child's awareness was unique. Significantly, too, each student met the standard of comparing and contrasting divergent cultures effectively.

This curriculum design enabled us to connect with people so different from us, yet like us in some ways. We shared their frustration, joy, and awe as we mirrored their culture and struggled in our projects. Our steps toward fuller intellectual and human development were measured—some by the students, some by teachers, some by the state. Ultimately, our aim is that the person who emerges from twelve years of schooling in Solon will embody the characteristics described in our district mission:

Our mission is to provide all students with the knowledge and skills to reach their potential and to become productive, ethical citizens in a changing world through effective programs, an involved community, and a responsible, caring staff.

Teacher-Character Advice

Johnny Jackson

I think curriculum design work is very important. Teachers can no longer be passive about the instructional context in which they work. They must get involved in curriculum design decisions. If teachers aren't intellectually engaged in all aspects of their work, if they are only pawns in an educational system, how can they expect to generate much love of learning in their students?

If I were a member of a curriculum design committee, I would argue for the preparation of a liberally educated citizenry. I want to support education that helps adults apply great ideas to the specifics of their lives. I am reminded of Hirsch's (1989) illustration of a worker whose problem solving was informed by a rich background in the humanities. With such a background, workers can frame the problems they encounter in a much broader historical and philosophical context. I would also want to use this academic frame of reference to critically analyze current educational programs. I want students to understand the basic conceptual structure of Western civilization, and I am critical of programs that don't prepare students in this way.

Concerning the issue of content selection, I believe that our duty as teachers is to renew for the next generation the cultural heritage that we have inherited. Acquiring this cultural heritage, the accumulated wisdom of past generations, empowers our students, for with it they need not go about reinventing the wheel, rediscovering for themselves every important skill or piece of time-tested information. The most important aspects of this heritage are embodied in the academic disciplines that are usually—and rightfully—taught in school.

Each discipline is composed of an important group of canonical works. These are the works of science, literature, art, and other disciplines that have stood the test of time and are valued by the experts in each field. As a high school English teacher, I believe students should confront classical works of literature, those which a consensus of scholars considers highly meritorious. For example, in 1984 the chairman of the National Endowment for the Humanities, William Bennett, surveyed scholars, journalists, teachers, and government leaders to determine which texts should be studied in school. The literary works cited most often included Shakespeare's *Macbeth* and *Hamlet* and Twain's *Huckleberry Finn* ("U.S. Culture," 1984). I think these are excellent choices. Most textbooks on the market are developed under the guidance of renowned scholars and are good sources of content in literature and other disciplines.

A hero of mine, R. S. Peters, has argued that education can be seen as a process in which a teacher initiates a student into the citadel of existing knowledge. Peters (1964) writes:

One technique of initiation is . . . to lure people inside the citadel by using their existing interests in the hope that, once inside, they will develop other interests which previously were never dreamed of. . . . This is, of course, a very limited conception of initiation. For it neglects the fluidity of wants. What people in fact want or are interested in is, to a large extent, a product of their previous initiation. The job of the educator is not simply to build on existing wants but to present what is worth wanting in such a way that it creates new wants and stimulates new interests. (p. 45)

Think back to your own experiences as a student in school. Who were the teachers who taught you the most about the larger culture while increasing your interest in it? Did you have an English teacher who initiated you into the splendors of Latin while engendering enthusiasm and respect for this language? Did you have a science teacher who made you want to learn more about the relationships among scientific concepts? Recall the example I cited in chapter 3 of an English teacher who introduces *Julius Caesar* by way of *Star Trek*. That teacher is a master at introducing important content in an engaging way. As he travels with his students through that story with its own internal structure, he builds a bridge between Shakespeare's ideas and his students' lives. For such a teacher, organizing the curriculum means respecting the internal structure of each discipline, but teaching in a way that makes students want to discover more about the knowledge that constitutes our cultural heritage.

I don't want to be perceived as overly European-oriented, that is, Eurocentric, in my views. I am concerned about students' multicultural literacy. Their core reading list should include classics from a variety of intellectual traditions: African-American, Native American, Hispanic, and so on. Simonson and Walker's (1988) special multicultural literacy issue of *The Grey Wolf Annual* is a good curriculum reference for this topic. This book includes selections from the works of James Baldwin, Paula Gunn Allen, Carlos Fuentes, and other great writers.

When it comes to organizing teachers and their students, I am most concerned that academic content be properly handled. As a high school teacher, I like departmental organization. By being part of an English department, I can concentrate on the structure of my discipline, and I don't have to worry about learning the structure of another discipline. I'm willing to engage in some interdepartmental collaboration, as long as this work doesn't water down the academic inquiry I want to facilitate. I tend to be an advocate of homogeneous student grouping. I find it easier to work with students who are organized by academic ability and interests. Not all students have the necessary mental equipment or motivation to take advantage of what I have to offer as a teacher. I am happy to work with these students in more remedial ways—as long as I don't have to do it all day—but I don't want to mix them in with the more academically able learners.

Finally, what about graduation assessment? I will concentrate my comments on the academically oriented students; they are the ones that particularly concern me. Our final assessments should be constructed to ascertain whether the students are liberally educated and have begun to internalize the conceptual structure of one or more academic disciplines. In order to graduate from high school, they should pass a comprehensive arts-and-sciences written examination, and they should demonstrate their inquiry proficiency in one or more academic areas by completing and defending a research project. We must take care when evaluating students that we are not merely asking them to give back the results of rote memorization. We must insist that they understand the academic traditions. It is difficult, if not impossible, to do this using objective tests with multiple-choice, matching, or true-false questions. Essay exams and research papers, on the other hand, require students to synthesize or evaluate what they have learned.

Amy Nelson

I feel it is important for teachers to get involved in curriculum design work. If educational professionals just passively accept the programs in which they work, if they are not proactive in this aspect of their work, how can they encourage their students to become proactive workers? They are not even proper role models.

I envision a society composed of achievement-oriented, collaborative problem solvers, and I strongly embrace Reich's (1991) argument that educators need to prepare a generation of symbolic analysts. I presented an overview of Reich's argument in chapter 2. I am very impressed with high-tech companies like Microsoft and Gore-Tex, where workers are encouraged to be creative users of complex information systems. As a member of a curriculum design committee, I would bring descriptions of such businesses to the meetings. I think students should be prepared to work at places like Microsoft, and I would be critical of educational programs that are still tied to the bygone manufacturing era. Educators should not be preparing docile, assembly-line workers. We have become a postindustrial, information-age society, and our education systems need to reflect this historical change.

My advice on content selection and graduation assessment will be linked together. I like problem-solving protocols, and I am very impressed with the curriculum procedures developed by J. Franklin Bobbitt and Ralph Tyler.[2] Bobbitt (1924) advises that curriculum designs should be based on three steps:

---

[2] J. Franklin Bobbitt and Ralph W. Tyler were both professors of curriculum at the University of Chicago; Bobbitt's *The Curriculum* (New York: Arno Press, 1918) is the first general curriculum text in the United States. The publication of this 1918 text is widely viewed as the beginning of the field of formal curriculum studies, an important subdivision in American education. Ralph W. Tyler was one of Bobbitt's doctoral students before he became a professor of curriculum. Tyler's *Basic Principles of Curriculum and Instruction* (1949) is generally considered to be the most influential publication in the 77-year history of U.S. curriculum studies.

analyze and categorize adult experience into broad fields such as work, citizenship, and leisure; list specific activities associated with each broad field; and create educational objectives from these activity lists. Tyler's protocol nicely begins where Bobbitt's ends. Tyler (1949) states that curriculum designers should take four steps: determine appropriate educational purposes; decide how these purposes are translated into student learning experiences; systematically organize these learning experiences; and evaluate student learning.

Based on my educational vision, I have integrated Bobbitt and Tyler's advice into the following six-step protocol:

1. Identify emerging symbolic-analytical fields.
2. Describe activities associated with these fields.
3. Form educational purposes that are focused on the preparation of students to engage in these activities.
4. Translate these purposes into behavioral objectives.
5. Use task analysis to properly sequence these objectives.
6. Use the list of behavioral objectives as a guide to develop good assessment instruments.

As a member of a curriculum design committee, I would feel fortunate that most of the work in the first three steps of this protocol has already been completed in four prestigious policy reports:

• *What Work Requires of Schools: A SCANS Report for America 2000* (1991).
• *Learning a Living: A Blueprint for High Performance* (1992).
• *America 2000: An Education Strategy* (1991).
• *Raising Standards for American Education: A Report to Congress, the Secretary of Education, the National Education Goals Panel, and the American People* (1992).[3]

Since there is no point in reinventing the wheel, we can just study and adapt their work for our school district's program design.

Because the curriculum design committee doesn't want to interfere with teachers' ongoing instructional practices—their particular planning, teaching, and evaluating—steps four, five, and six in my protocol should be left to the discretion of the educational professionals, with the exception of graduation assessment. I will have more to say about teachers' instructional responsibilities in the next chapter.

---

[3] Secretary's Commission on Achieving Necessary Skills (SCANS), (1991), *What Work Requires of Schools: A SCANS Report for America 2000*, Washington, DC: U.S. Department of Labor; Secretary's Commission on Achieving Necessary Skills (SCANS), (1992), *Learning a Living: A Blueprint for High Performance*, Washington, DC: U.S. Department of Labor; U.S. Department of Education, (1991), *America 2000: An Education Strategy*, Washington, DC: Author; National Council on Education Standards and Testing (NCEST), (1992), *Raising Standards for American Education: A Report to Congress, the Secretary of Education, the National Education Goals Panel, and the American People*, Washington, DC: Government Printing Office.

For graduation assessment, I recommend the creation of an authentic performance-based test of students' symbolic-analytical skills. This kind of instrument is called a **criterion-referenced test**. When taking such a test, students demonstrate the competencies they have had the opportunity to practice (Popham, 1987). Creating a symbolic-analytical criterion-referenced final examination requires teachers to prepare their students properly. This type of final exam allows for instructional discretion but does require teachers to remain attentive to the final learning expectations of a program. I would like to see these tests given at the end of a primary school program (K–4), a middle school program (5–8), and a high school program (9–12). In other words, before receiving a high school diploma, students will have to demonstrate their competencies on three separate occasions, in accordance with prescribed symbolic-analytical criteria.

I have some very specific ideas on how students should be organized into viable programs. I am a proponent of homogeneous student groups. Teachers have the best opportunity to maximize learning achievement when students are organized by ability and motivation. In order to best enhance athletic performance, coaches create "A" and "B" teams. Teachers should do the same. I am more flexible on the topic of teacher organization. Many of the symbolic-analytical competencies require interdisciplinary learning, so I lean toward team teaching as long as it is not distracting to teachers. I don't like schools without walls. That type of open classroom experimentation creates too much confusion. I want teachers to function in work environments that support efficient student achievement. I'm inclined to get a lot of input from the professionals on what they view as the most viable program designs for competency learning.

Dennis Sage

I enjoy the very human process of curriculum deliberation, the give-and-take of thinking about educational ends in relationship to educational means. I have willingly joined curriculum design committees in the past, and I will do so in the future. I think this school-community work is an important professional responsibility. My overall education aim is to prepare adults who are self-actualizing. According to Maslow (1954), the highest or most complex need is the need for self-actualization. Self-actualization is the attainment of one's innate potential. People are self-actualized when they become all that they can be: unique and fulfilled human beings who see their lives as meaningful.

The curriculum must aim to fulfill each student's need for self-actualization. By definition, then, the curriculum must be different for each student. Moreover, the emergence of needs and desires is an ongoing process, making them difficult to predict in advance. In addition, because a human being is a growing, changing organism, all of these needs are interrelated in a complex web, each continually affecting the others.

Because of the personal, dynamic, and holistic character of student needs, I reject the use of behavioral performance objectives in teaching. Objectives are standardized, they are formulated prior to learning engagements, and they attempt to divide learning into discrete behavioral particles. They do not reflect the true diversity of human needs. I am critical of educational programs that don't support student self-actualization.

I believe that the content that teachers use in their programs should be imaginative and holistic. Therefore, I am an advocate of **organizing centers**. Goodlad (1963) uses this concept to describe, plan, and analyze learning activities. The creation of organizing centers helps teachers integrate content with student thinking and feeling over varied "chunks" of time—a twenty-minute lesson, a five-week unit, a year-long course, or a multiyear program. An organizing center can be a broad theme, a problem, a project, or some other integrating strategy that serves four purposes:

1. Chunks of content are connected together in some coherent manner.
2. The content is inviting and accessible to students.
3. The content supports multiple learning styles.
4. The content encourages individual construction of meaning.

Project Moonbase meets these four criteria. This is a science and technology simulation developed by NASA, businesses, and schools for hundreds of high school students in Northeast Ohio. The simulation requires students to create a moonbase that supports a team of astronauts around the clock for several days. With teachers helping them, the students are responsible for planning and implementing the necessary communication, security, health, nutrition, and waste systems. The project involves a cross-section of students—not only the "best and brightest"—an interdisciplinary team of teachers, and a diverse collection of adult experts from the local community.

Project UPDATE (Todd, Hutchinson, & Doyle, 1993) is another example of the use of the organizing center strategy. Supported by the National Science Foundation (NSF), the purpose of this curriculum project is to integrate science, mathematics, and technology education from grades K–8. Students collaborate to solve problems that range from simple—for example, how to design and construct a bed for "Berry Bear"—to sophisticated—such as how to engage in interplanetary travel.

Organizing centers can stimulate the inventiveness and resourcefulness of teachers and their students. This is the type of provocative content selection I advocate. I want to see heterogeneous teams of students and teachers engaged in exciting, imaginative learning. I am opposed to schools that are organized like factories with self-contained classrooms, high ratios of students to teachers, and desks in neat rows. This rigid, compartmentalized organization makes it difficult to institute flexible programs that encourage student self-actualization. I welcome creative diversity. Schools should operate like think tanks and artistic communities. Why does education have to be so homogenized?

Finally, let me say something about evaluation. Evaluation is a vital classroom activity, but I deplore the fact that many people, both educators and noneducators, equate evaluation with testing. Like many other progressive thinkers, I believe that objective tests trivialize and dehumanize the learning process. See, for example, Roland Barth's (1972) *Open Education and the American School*. We need evaluation techniques that respect the complex, personal, dynamic nature of the curriculum process at its best. What are some alternative approaches? I suggest reading *Beyond Standardized Testing,* a booklet by Archbald and Newmann (1988). Although directed toward secondary schools, the booklet details a variety of novel, sensible techniques for evaluating academic achievement that are appropriate for most grade levels. I especially like the suggestions about exhibitions of student performances (p. 20) and portfolios of student works (pp. 29–30).

I haven't said anything specific about graduation assessment because I feel that teachers and others should be very careful about making final judgments about students' growth. I want educators to support their students' self-actualization. How can teachers conclusively evaluate something that is so open-ended? Do fair-minded critics try to provide a definitive judgment of the quality of a Shakespearean play, a great painting such as the *Mona Lisa*, or any other great work of art? Certainly, they can offer informed, critical commentary; just as certainly, teachers and perhaps other responsible professionals can offer feedback on students' constructivist learning. That is, they can engage in critical judgments on students' learning performances for the purpose of facilitating personal growth and helping improve educational programs. These judgments can be presented to students, their parents, and/or other interested parties. Just as good art critics don't pretend they have discovered the true meaning of some form of art, good educational evaluators shouldn't pretend they have achieved a final understanding of some student's growth.

Silvia Rivera

In chapter 3, I spoke of the need for a transformative education that enables students to discover their role in creating a more just, humane, democratic society. Curriculum problem solving is critical to this transformative process. A teacher should work with a curriculum design that (a) honors the possibility of a better world, (b) incorporates an understanding of how to move beyond the prevailing social/political/economic system that impedes the realization of that better world, and (c) suggests how to pass these attitudes and understandings on to students.

Therefore my answer to the question, "What knowledge is of most worth?" is this: It is that knowledge which enables individual students to move beyond a state of subjugation toward a true mastery, or empowerment, over the affairs of their own life as part of a larger communal life. A good curriculum draws its content from the skills and domains of learning that foster this movement.

I agree with Giroux (1994) that "schooling [should] be empowering rather than merely humanizing" (p. 283). He argues that politically aware cultural studies should be the referent for designing curricula. Teachers help students become politically aware by helping them study "the dynamics of those institutional and cultural inequalities that marginalize some groups, repress particular types of knowledge, and suppress critical dialogue" (p. 302). Cultural studies is a good vehicle for this type of study. Students can examine films and other social artifacts from the point of view that their culture is actually a historical creation that is always "unfinished and incomplete" (p. 303).

I can easily envision a society composed of a critically aware citizenry committed to principles of justice and the creation of a strong, viable democracy. I admire countries like Canada and Sweden that have made a good deal of progress establishing a "safety net" of social services for all citizens, and I wonder why the United States can't make similar progress. There shouldn't be great disparities of wealth in any society; such economic differences foster alienation, cynicism, and violence. I would be highly critical of any educational program that either directly or indirectly promotes social inequity.

One public school program that offers students truly important skills and content is the Community Issues Program (CIP) implemented by Newmann, Bertocci, and Landsness (1977) in Madison, Wisconsin. The sequence of courses in this program includes these:

First semester

- Community service internship
- Political-legal process course
- Communications course

Second semester

- Citizen action project
- Action in literature project
- Public message

In the first semester students in the community service internship contribute to the missions of governmental and social agencies and public interest organizations. Students volunteer in various capacities. They might assist a television news reporter, tutor young children, help elderly people, or gather data for a neighborhood organization. In the political-legal process course students examine the formal and informal structure of the political system by analyzing the institutional processes they experienced in their internship. In the communications course they practice language skills in discussions and interviews with the people in these agencies and organizations.

In the second semester students are immersed in community affairs. The citizens action project, such as lobbying for legislation or establishing special youth institutions, usually develops from the first semester's internship. Students attend clinics on political and social skills such as fund raising and canvassing techniques while developing their project. Meanwhile, for the action in literature project, students read critical works of drama, poetry, biography, and fiction by writers such as Gandhi, Thoreau, and James Baldwin. The discussions that grow out of these texts challenge students to confront issues of political struggle, civil disobedience, and the nature of the "good society." Finally, the public message course allows students to communicate their experiences and discoveries from the program to the general public.

This curriculum moves out of the sheltered, artificial, naive world of the self-contained classroom into the realities of public life. I believe that this kind of curriculum is crucial to the progressive education of future citizens. A community-based curriculum is more difficult to implement with younger children, but a transformative educational approach can also be used in an elementary school setting. Adler and Goodman (1986) offer several suggestions for activities that promote a "critical pedagogy" for teaching history for younger children:

- Students "do" history rather than "learn about" historical events. For example, "children examine history through photographs, artifacts, and oral reporting of past events" and then "attempt to portray what life might have been like during a given historical event or period of time" (p. 5). This requires that children imagine, speculate, and analyze rather than merely memorize.
- Students view slides of turn-of-the-century transportation systems and then watch demonstrations of various types of shaving razors. Students are encouraged to speculate about the "materials, design, function, and values (e.g., disposability, efficiency, safety, materialism) that played a role in the development" (p. 5) of each.
- After reading biographical sketches of life in Wisconsin between 1880 and 1940, students use various historical themes (e.g., food, clothing, housing, occupations, entertainment, social roles, families) to analyze the lives of the individuals portrayed.

Teachers must learn to see all learning as value-based, not as a set of skills or content that is taught in a moral vacuum. Even our teaching methods have half-hidden consequences, so it is unwise to think of curriculum and instruction as two separate processes. Moffett (1985), for example, decries methods of teaching reading that treat texts as meaningless word particles or isolated words rather than as potentially powerful tools. The use of phonics or programmed workbooks tends to render reading insipid. Such methods may appear to teach reading while actually crippling it, never allowing students to see "reading as a personal resource with which to do what *they* want to do" (p. 53). The whole-language approach and Freire's (1970/1971) social literacy training approach, on the other hand, help students to associate reading with an exploration of their own values and their connections with the larger world.

Educational programs should be sensitively organized to support the democratic empowerment of students and teachers. This will require heterogeneous, interdisciplinary groupings. Giroux (1994) notes: "Historically, schools . . . have been organized around either traditional subject-based studies (math education) or into larger disciplinary/administrative categories (curriculum and instruction). Within this type of intellectual division of labor, students have had few opportunities to study larger social issues" (p. 280). For at least part of the school day, I want to see teachers and their students organized into cultural study teams that allow for pluralistic social interaction and broad critical inquiry.

Likewise, evaluation strategies need to be carefully selected. We teachers must avoid giving students the sense that artificial rewards such as good grades or honor rolls are the primary reason for learning. In the Community Issues Program I described earlier in this chapter, Newmann and his colleagues (1977) recommend using evaluation as a tool for giving students critical feedback on their work and as an opportunity for assessing the meaningfulness of their projects in terms of their own lives. For only if students become interested in, and capable at, working toward a more just and peaceful world can we say that our curriculum leadership has been successful. Newmann seems to understand what education should be about. Graduation assessment should be a formal occasion for formative feedback on a student's growing critical, democratic maturity. I don't believe in summative evaluation; this type of judgment aids and abets social hierarchies. However, I would like to see students create portfolios that demonstrate the quality of their cultural study. They would receive feedback on their work from school and community representatives before being allowed to graduate.

FURTHER READINGS

The following books will help you learn more about the practice of creating a humanizing, constructivist curriculum platform. You can study these books independently or as part of a course.

Alberto, P. A., & Troutman, A. C. (1982). *Applied behavior analysis for teachers: Influencing student performance* (2nd ed.). Englewood Cliffs, NJ: Merrill/Prentice Hall.

Archbald, D. A., & Newmann, F. M. (1988). *Beyond standardized testing: Assessing authentic academic achievement in the secondary school*. Reston, VA: National Association of Secondary School Principals.

Beane, J. A., Toepfer, Jr., C. F., & Alessi, Jr., S. J. (1986). *Curriculum planning and development*. Boston: Allyn & Bacon.

Ben-Peretz, M. (1990). *The teacher-curriculum encounter: Freeing teachers from the tyranny of texts*. Albany, NY: SUNY Press.

Brooks, J. G., & Brooks, M. G. (1993). *In search of understanding: The case for constructivist classrooms*. Alexandria, VA: Association for Supervision and Curriculum Development.

Connelly, F. M., & Clandinin, D. J. (1988). *Teachers as curriculum planners: Narratives of experience*. New York: Teachers College Press.

Egan, K. (1985). *Teaching as storytelling*. Chicago: University of Chicago Press.

Eisner, E. W. (1994). *The educational imagination: On the design and evaluation of school programs* (3rd ed.). New York: Macmillan.

Elmore, R. F., & Fuhrman, S. H. (1994). *The governance of curriculum* (1994 Yearbook of the Association for Supervision and Curriculum Development). Alexandria, VA: Association for Supervision and Curriculum Development.

Gronlund, N. E. (1985). *Measurement and evaluation in teaching* (5th ed.). New York: Macmillan.

Henderson, J. G., & Hawthorne, R. D. (1995). *Transformative curriculum leadership*. Englewood Cliffs, NJ: Merrill/Prentice Hall.

Kohl, H. (1976). *On teaching*. New York: Schocken.

Mager, R. F. (1962). *Preparing instructional objectives*. Belmont, CA: Fearon.

Moffett, J. (1985). Hidden impediments to improving English teaching. *Phi Delta Kappan*, 67(1), 50–56.

Newmann, F. W., Bertocci, T., & Landsness, R. M. (1977). *Skills in citizen action: An English-social studies program for secondary schools*. Skokie, IL: National Textbook.

Ornstein, A. C., & Hunkins, F. (1993). *Curriculum: Foundations, principles, and theory* (2nd ed.). Boston: Allyn & Bacon.

Paris, C. L. (1993). *Teacher agency and curriculum making in classrooms*. New York: Teachers College Press.

Posner, G. J. (1992). *Analyzing the curriculum*. New York: McGraw-Hill.

Posner, G., & Rudnitsky, A. N. (1994). *Course design: A guide to curriculum development for teachers* (4th ed.). New York: Longman.

Schubert, W. H. (1986). *Curriculum: Perspective, paradigm, and possibility*. New York: Macmillan.

TenBrink, T. D. (1986). Writing instructional objectives. In J. M. Cooper (Ed.), *Classroom teaching skills* (pp. 67–110). Lexington, MA: D. C. Heath.

Tyler, R. W. (1949). *Basic principles of curriculum and instruction*. Chicago: University of Chicago Press.

Walker, D. F., & Soltis, J. F. (1986). *Curriculum and aims*. New York: Teachers College Press.

Wiles, J., & Bondi, J. (1989). *Curriculum development: A guide to practice*. Englewood Cliffs, NJ: Merrill/Prentice Hall.

Zais, R. S. (1976). *Curriculum: Principles and foundations*. New York: Harper & Row.

Zemelman, S., Daniels, H., & Hyde, A. (1993). *Best practice: New standards for teaching and learning in America's schools*. Portsmouth, NH: Heinemann.

REFERENCES

Adler, S., & Goodman, J. (1986). Critical theory as a foundation for methods courses. *Journal of Teacher Education*, 37, 2–8.

Archbald, D. A., & Newmann, F. M. (1988). *Beyond standardized testing: Assessing authentic academic achievement in the secondary school*. Reston, VA: National Association of Secondary School Principals.

Barth, R. S. (1972). *Open education and the American school*. New York: Schocken.

Bobbitt, J. F. (1924). *How to make a curriculum*. Boston: Houghton Mifflin.

Brooks, J. G., & Brooks, M. G. (1993). *In search of understanding: The case for constructivist classrooms*. Alexandria, VA: Association for Supervision and Curriculum Development.

Freire, P. (1971). *Pedagogy of the oppressed* (M. Bergman Ramos, Trans.). New York: Herder & Herder. (Original work published 1970)

Giroux, H. A. (1994). Doing cultural studies: Youth and the challenge of pedagogy. *Harvard Educational Review, 64*, 278–308.

Goodlad, J. I. (1963). *Planning and organizing for teaching*. Washington DC: National Educational Association.

Henderson, J. G., & Hawthorne, R. D. (1995). *Transformative curriculum leadership*. Englewood Cliffs, NJ: Merrill/Prentice Hall.

Hirsch, E. D. (1989). *The dictionary of cultural literacy: What every American needs to know*. Boston: Houghton Mifflin.

Houston, H. M. (1988). Restructuring secondary schools. In A. Lieberman (Ed.), *Building a professional culture in schools* (pp. 109–128). New York: Teachers College Press.

Maslow, A. H. (1954). *Motivation and personality*. New York: Harper & Row.

Meier, D. (1987). Success in East Harlem: How one group of teachers built a school that works. *American Educator, 11*, 34–39.

Moffett, J. (1985). Hidden impediments to improving English teaching. *Phi Delta Kappan, 67*(1), 50–56.

National Council of Teachers of Mathematics. (1989). *Curriculum and evaluation standards for school mathematics*. Reston, VA: Author.

Newmann, F. M., Bertocci, T., & Landsness, R. M. (1977). *Skills in citizen action: An English-social studies program for secondary schools*. Skokie, IL: National Textbook.

Peters, R. S. (1964). *Education as initiation*. London: Lowe & Brydone.

Popham, W. J. (1987). Instructional objectives benefit teaching and testing. *Momentum, 28*, 15–16.

Reich, R. (1991). *The work of nations: Preparing ourselves for 21st-century capitalism*. New York: Vintage Books.

Simonson, R., & Walker, S. (Eds.). 1988. Opening the American mind [Special multicultural literacy issue]. *The Grey Wolf Annual, 5*.

Sirotnik, K. A. (1991). Critical inquiry: A paradigm for praxis. In E. C. Short (Ed.), *Forms of curriculum inquiry* (pp. 243–258). Albany, NY: State University of New York Press.

Sizer, T. R. (1984). *Horace's compromise: The dilemma of the American high school*. Boston: Houghton Mifflin.

Snyder, J., Bolin, F., & Zumwalt, K. (1992). Curriculum implementation. In P. W. Jackson (Ed.), *Handbook of research on curriculum* (pp. 402–435). New York: Macmillan.

Todd, R., Hutchinson, P., & Doyle, M. (1993, June). Project update. *TIES Magazine*, 48–53.

Tyler, R. W. (1949). *Basic principles of curriculum and instruction*. Chicago: University of Chicago Press.

U.S. culture czar lists must-reads. (1984, August 12). *Cincinnati Enquirer*, p. A–8.

5

Enacting Constructivist Transactions

The classroom was a bit noisy as students in Mrs. Meyer's first-grade class debated the make-up of clouds. The students were brainstorming for different characteristics of clouds, and Mrs. Meyer wrote their words on the board. She then asked the students if they could figure out from their list of characteristics what substances might form clouds.

Takita was sure that clouds were made of cotton, and Jon added that rain was always above the clouds but only fell to earth when the cotton was soaked through. Mrs. Meyers was pleased that the children used metaphors to think about what they knew and tried to relate that knowledge to what they were hoping to understand. She knew that young children construct naive scientific explanations for natural phenomena, and she wanted them to think about how their metaphors did, yet also did not, fit clouds. What could in turn be sometimes white and fluffy, then fine and wispy, or even dark and rainy?

In planning this activity and others that would follow, Mrs. Meyer wanted to engage her students in the kinds of thinking that would help them construct valid understandings of clouds as part of a unit she was teaching on weather. She thought about her previous experiences with this class and the other classes that she taught. She thought about what she knew about clouds that might interest the children and help them move from their naive constructions of the physical world to a more truly scientific view of clouds. Mrs. Meyer was used to observing her children closely as they engaged in classroom activities and thinking carefully about their responses to her instruction. For this particular lesson, she wanted to scaffold the children's learning, to support them as they constructed new ideas from concrete activities she had designed to help them think about weather, and especially clouds, in different ways. She wanted the children to be really engaged in their thinking about clouds.

After the children finished sharing explanations and guesses, Mrs. Meyers asked some questions that she hoped would help them use what they already knew about how the physical world works. She knew this might help them focus their attention on what they were about to learn. Her questions were based on her own knowledge of weather, coupled with what she had learned about children's responses from lessons she had taught this and other classes in previous years. Mrs. Meyers helped the students remember that while it is possible to see through one layer of sheer material, it may be impossible to see through many layers of the same material. She helped the children remember how their bathrooms looked after a hot shower, and how difficult it was the week before to see out of the windows during a dense fog.

Then she conducted an experiment in a large bell jar, creating a "cloud" in a bottle. The class watched as the cloud began to "rain." Mrs. Meyers asked the children to reconsider what they thought clouds are made of and then think of ways they might test their new ideas. All the while, as she was listening to the children's responses, asking them questions, and conducting the experiment, she was also thinking about the reactions of individual children. She thought about which children were engaged in the lesson and which ones seemed to be connecting the new information in the lesson to something they already knew. She thought about which students were eagerly responding, who needed prompting, and who needed to be reminded of the class rules for taking turns and listening to others during discussions. Even while she was engaged in one part of her lesson, Mrs. Meyers was actively observing the children's responses and deciding what those responses might mean. She was also planning how to use the students' responses to create additional activities and new lessons that would further refine their understanding and help them connect aspects of her teaching to what they already knew.

Introduction

In this glimpse into Mrs. Meyers' first-grade room, we saw a scenario of a teacher putting her beliefs about teaching and learning into practice that might seem deceptively simple to an observer. Yet what might seem simple is actually an example of a highly interactive and complex cycle of planning, teaching-learning transactions, observation, and evaluation that are informed by the foundational concepts of pragmatic intelligence, action research, and experiential learning. These concepts were introduced in chapter 1.

The integration of planning, enacting constructivist transactions, observing, and evaluating is an application of pragmatic intelligence. Teachers must choose appropriate content, activities and evaluative strategies, and they must decide how they can best enact their choices in the context of a particular constructivist curriculum design. Remember that teachers are making choices based on their beliefs, not following a teacher-proof recipe for instruction. Their choices are guided by the tenets of action research as they continually monitor learning transactions, assess their students' success, and make appropriate instructional adjustments.

How teachers approach this experiential learning cycle varies, depending on their beliefs. You will see these potential differences illustrated when the four teacher-characters offer advice based on their own ideological interpretations of enacting constructivist transactions.

A General Protocol

The four formal elements of constructivist enactments are: fluid constructivist planning, constructivist learning transactions, perception-based participant observations, and authentic evaluations. These elements describe the phases teachers might use to pragmatically adapt a particular constructivist curriculum design. Each element relates directly to a step in the general decision-making cycle introduced in chapter 1.

Fluid Constructivist Planning

When teachers continuously move through the plan-act-observe-evaluate cycle guided by their own beliefs, their planning can be described as fluid in two ways. First, they are constantly adapting curriculum materials to fit their personal-professional beliefs. They don't rigidly follow textbooks and other curriculum materials. Second, they plan in an exploratory, experimental spirit. Because their overall goal is to encourage constructivist transactions, they know that they may need to make adjustments. If a particular activity doesn't facilitate their students' active meaning making, they understand that they must be flexible, that they will need to modify their plans.

May (1993) and Zahorick (1975) studied teachers' planning processes, and both found that a concern for meaningful activities rather than compliance with pre-set objectives guides teachers' planning. Whether or not this research generalization is always true, this is the planning approach that will be encouraged in this chapter. When teachers are fluid planners, they are constantly thinking about ways they can engage their students in activities that foster higher-level thinking, including analyzing, judging, synthesizing, and evaluating.

Teachers' planning deliberations are quite complex and must incorporate a host of considerations including time constraints, the use of space, available resources, school district policies, and community expectations (Posner, 1992). In the context of this decision-making complexity, constructivist teachers must select content that provides a link between a curriculum design and students' active learning. The following questions can help guide this type of planning:

What are the developmental levels of the students? What kinds of thinking are they already doing? What experiences and background knowledge do they already have?

Students come to school with varying opportunities and experiences that have an impact on how they construct meaning. As a teacher, you need to understand how your students learn as well as what they already know and can do. Students always construct understanding based on what they already know.

What do the students want and need to know? How does this relate to what the teacher knows about the curriculum?

It is not enough to interest students. Nor is it enough to create cognitive dissonance as a precursor of a planned learning activity or to focus student attention on a lesson. Teachers must also know what kinds of learning are important to construct useful knowledge that will move students along the pathway from novice to expert.

What experiences and activities will engage students in constructing meaning?

Teachers need to be aware of the relationship between what students do and what they learn. It is essential that teachers create situations that enable students to understand the important concepts in a subject, not just memorize or manipulate data. Deep understanding needs to be the goal of constructivist learning transactions in the classroom.

How do the activities help students' metacognition, their ability to understand and control their own thinking?

The hallmark of an expert learner is the ability to change learning strategies when understanding falters. Teachers need to help students know what to do when learning and understanding aren't going smoothly. Such strategies give students control over their own learning.

Are the experiences in the classroom democratic? Do they help students not only take responsibility for controlling their own learning but also value their responsibility to the learning of everyone in the classroom community?

In transmissionist classrooms, students are seen as empty vessels that receive knowledge from the teacher-as-expert. However, a classroom community should empower students as co-constructors of their own learning. Creating this type of democratic classroom will be more fully discussed in chapter 6.

> Do classroom activities take advantage of the social and collaborative nature of learning?

Vygotsky (1978) draws our attention to the "zone of proximal development." Children and adults learn more when they are coached by peers or colleagues who can guide their inquiry learning. Thus, achievement levels are conditioned by *how* we are taught as much as by *what* we are taught. An additional characteristic of constructivist classrooms is that knowledge is understood as socially constructed, rather than as residing solely in the teacher-as-expert.

These six questions do not constitute an exhaustive list. They are only illustrative of the type of inquiry that must inform constructivist teachers' planning deliberations. This questioning may not be confined to the planning phase. It could reasonably occur during enacting, observing, or evaluating. This is why teachers' planning should be flexible. However and whenever constructivist teachers engage in fluid planning, their deliberations are necessarily guided by one overall concern:

> How can I help students move toward a deep understanding of the content they are studying and away from a superficial learning of isolated facts and skills?

Enacting Constructivist Learning Transactions

This step entails translating beliefs into practice by creating opportunities for learning that keep the students thoughtfully engaged. Properly conceived, constructivist transactions are neither teacher-centered nor student-centered, but rather centered on active understanding. The planned organizing centers are not imposed or implemented by the teacher. Instead, the curriculum is enacted in the context of the learning needs of the students as the teacher understands those needs. This complexity provides a sharp contrast to more traditional ways of thinking about teaching wherein teachers simply choose content and deliver it unchanged to students. In transactional classrooms, both teacher and students concentrate on meaning and how meaning is understood. This focus on individual meaning-making rather than standardized delivery requires teachers to be quite flexible in their enactments.

You may be most familiar with the kind of classroom that is organized according to a model other than constructivist teaching and learning principles. In the past, classrooms with the teacher as expert, giving knowledge to students in the form of facts and discrete skills, were the norm. The model for such classrooms is the transmission model: teachers attempting to pour unreconstructed knowledge into students' heads. Freire (1970/1971) likened this model to banking. Teachers hold knowledge as a banker holds funds; students have to come to the teacher and withdraw the knowledge from the teacher's bank. The knowledge exists separately from teacher and students as something they possess, not as something they construct through experience. Memorization, recitation, and fill-in-the-blanks exercises reflect this transmission view of teaching and learning.

A constructivist understanding of teaching, on the other hand, views knowledge as created in the process of constructing meaning. Teachers choose activities that foster students' meaning-making, preventing their teaching from being transmissional rather than transactional. These activities have certain characteristics in common:

- Teachers encourage students to do most of the talking in the classroom. They structure activities so that students are engaged in authentic meaning-making activities. Activities are authentic when they are perceived as connected to the "real" world and are not just contrived classroom exercises.
- Teachers ask rather than tell. Questions are carefully worded to scaffold students' responses so they can construct meaning. Students' own ideas and questions become the framework for structuring learning transactions.
- Teachers ask questions that help students focus on the relationship between what they already know—their prior knowledge—and what they are learning. They help students move from an initially vague understanding toward ownership of concepts and ideas. Students develop the ability to work with the concepts and strategies they already have to gain deeper understandings of new concepts and ideas.
- Teachers help students form a classroom community where meaning is constructed and examined in a social, collaborative, and supportive setting. Listening to how others frame questions and responses helps both teacher and students form deeper understandings of the content at hand.
- Teachers affirm student responses and celebrate approximations of expert knowing. The use of invented spelling in the primary grades is a good example. As children learn to associate print with sounds, they move through stages of spelling that come closer and closer to conventional spelling. Yet as they learn more and more conventional spellings, they are engaged in a process of writing about ideas and events that are important to them without having to know exactly how to spell every word in their speaking vocabularies. For older students, cognitive dissonance can energize learning, and making mistakes can initiate a rethinking of learning strategies.
- Teachers guide students to recognize, understand, and control their own thinking processes and thus learn how to take responsibility for their own learning.

The first phase of the cycle is planning, but plans need to be monitored as they are enacted. NASA engineers, for example, constantly monitor computer-generated information about the course of a space shuttle flight, determine how that information relates to the planned flight path, and make frequent and minute course corrections to make sure the planned path of the spacecraft is the actual path traveled. Teachers make the same kinds of constant adjustments in their planning as they observe the results of their enactments. They center their classrooms on constructivist transactions, adjusting away from transmission and towards student construction of meaning in each activity.

Beginning teachers often find that, in spite of their best intentions, their lessons are more transmissional than transactional. Recalling his first year as an eighth-grade social studies teacher, an imaginary teacher named Jason illustrates this point:

> Trying to make sure I did what I had planned to do; attempting to explain it to the kids so that they had some idea of what I expected, yet still had some freedom to create and discover; trying to make sure Bryan and Adam didn't play with trading cards or that Patty and Kayla didn't pass notes back and forth while we were supposed to be doing cooperative learning—I was exhausted! But even with all the effort I put into it, I couldn't be sure that I was doing what I set out to do, or that my students were doing any constructive learning. I was too busy with what *I* was trying to do to watch my students. And I was too unsure of what a good learning transaction might look like to know the meaning of what I did observe. Was it okay if they talked and *giggled* during group work? Could I ever tell them what to do, or did they have to discover *everything*?

Beginning teachers will find they have to focus initially on the more basic elements of teaching—for example, noticing who is talking out loud and who isn't. It is not until some of the basics of teaching become second nature and the options exist for structuring activities and instruction that teachers have the necessary energy to make sure that learning is proceeding in a transactional, rather than transmissional, mode. Even veteran teachers may find that teaching a new grade level or a new subject means that their teaching occasionally slips into a transmissional mode.

Perception-Based Participant Observation

The concept of learning about people by participating in their activities while observing them comes from qualitative research traditions that are well established in anthropology and sociology and currently used in many field-based educational research studies. A participant-observer stance is useful to a teacher who wishes to understand how students are constructing meaning as well as what kinds of meaning they are constructing.

The teacher engaging in this type of observation is attempting to identify and understand student perceptions. This is why the participative observation is called *perception-based*.[1] The teacher is looking for overt behavior, verbal expressions, or more subtle indicators of how students are thinking and feeling.

---

[1] In more formal philosophical language, this observing phase could be called *phenomenological participant observation*.

How are the students responding to directions? Do they moan and groan but then move off and do pretty much as the teacher expects? How much time do they spend focused on a task? Do they ask, "When do we get to have hands-on math? Can we have writing workshops? When can we have social studies debates?" When students work in groups, which groups seem to be productive? The teacher pursues these types of observational questions to determine the status of students' meaning-making.

To solve the tension between teaching and observing, many teachers have developed ways to be "kid-watchers." Writing anecdotal records, short yet detailed notes, about each student helps teachers organize what happens during lessons. To illustrate this point, an imaginary teacher named Beth explains how she has developed a system for keeping track of how and what her ninth-grade history students are learning in a thematic unit on conflict.

> How to keep track of kids who are using several textbooks, CD-ROM and source books from the media center, and piles of tradebooks from the classroom library, all examining different aspects of conflict in history! I decided to keep little "sticky" notepads in my pocket. I wrote down things that I thought I needed to remember as I helped students choose books and sources for their projects. I made notes about what I was doing when they were working the best, who got it, who really took off and made some project on their own. I wrote down specific notes: the kid's name, what he did (read 20 pages or consulted three sources or asked a classmate to collaborate on a large chart), what I was doing, and why I thought that particular piece of information was important to know about that particular kid. Did he usually not read? Did he ever use graphic organizers to explain his learning? Stuff that was somehow meaningful to me. Then I'd take the stickies and put them on my seating chart. I eventually figured out to make each space on my seating chart the size of a sticky—smart, huh? Anyway, I'd go back later and look at who was doing what and when and how. I changed my observation slightly to adapt to the questions I had about my teaching. And I still do that. Sometimes as I go over a week's worth of notes, I'll wonder why I didn't write anything down for some student, or I'll think of a related question that will lead me to look for other things. But mostly, what I see helps me decide what's working. And what's working—and as much as I hate to admit it, what isn't working—helps me plan other concepts I need to teach and other activities that will help students learn.

Authentic Evaluation

To evaluate is to judge something according to values. Evaluation is something that people must do every minute of every day. What in our environment do we decide is noise that we tune out and ignore? What do we evaluate as information that we pay attention to and use? Our senses are keen and our brains complex; evaluating the input from our environment is a necessary process that keeps us focused and on track. It is so natural that we tend to ignore the underlying values we use to screen sensory information.

Yet we use values to screen all the information we perceive. In this book we ask you to consciously examine your own teaching beliefs. A key aspect of your beliefs lies in the values you use, which act as a screen to filter the judgments you make about teaching and learning. Inquiring into your own teaching can help you decide why you value certain aspects of teaching and learning. Your values help you decide about the usefulness and goodness of specific teaching-learning activities.

Reflective teachers put personal and professional values in the foreground of their decision-making, rather than in the background hidden behind their behaviors. They use their values to judge how well a teaching-learning transaction is progressing and to decide how students are constructing knowledge. This is not an anything-goes way of teaching, however. Not all teaching practices are equally valid in helping students understand. Not all are equally elegant in creating opportunities for active meaning-making. Not all value students as individuals and as members of a cohesive classroom community. For students, not all their constructions of meaning are useful either. The research literature about teaching is full of examples describing attitudes, abilities, and ideas that students have that are counterproductive to the ideals of disciplinary inquiry, self-understanding, and democratic understanding.

The kinds of evaluation practices that actually help teachers plan teaching-learning transactions and monitor student progress and help students understand and control their learning are very different from the typical evaluative tools used in school. The ubiquitous standardized achievement tests, which measure knowledge as if it consists solely of the kinds of questions that can be answered by darkening a circle on a computer-scored answer sheet, drive curriculum in some schools. Teachers give frequent tests and quizzes with the idea that a lot of feedback will assist students in learning. Instead, they simply measure students' ability to remember discrete bits of information rather than finding out how students are processing the deep and connected knowing of a subject. Teachers must instead identify assessment vehicles that require students to use the deep understandings they have gained to solve problems, test solutions, or create prototypes. The relationship between standardized test scores and socioeconomic levels is well documented (Oakes, 1985), yet the educational system continues to insist on using evaluation methods that foster social and economic class distinctions rather than on methods that enhance constructivist learning and an understanding of student thinking.

The concept of authentic evaluation was introduced in chapter 4. Evaluation activities are authentic in the same way learning activities are authentic: teachers *and* students perceive them to be connected to the "real" world. They don't see them as "contrived" exercises. Marsh and Willis (1995) write:

> "Authentic assessment" or, sometimes, the assessment of "authentic learning" are two names that have become popularized in the 1990s for educational evaluation encompassing far more than what students learn, as measured by standardized tests or even

by the ordinary teacher-made tests. Authenticity arises from assessing what is most important, not from assessing what is most convenient. Fundamentally, then, authentic assessment is a reaction against narrowness in education and a return toward the kind of education that connects feeling, thinking, and doing, as advocated by John Dewey and other progressives early in the twentieth century. (p. 356)

Authentic evaluation is both ongoing, or formative, and summative, or final. **Formative evaluation** helps teachers and students monitor the quality of the teaching-learning transactions. Adjustments can then be made to ensure successful constructivist learning. **Summative evaluation** helps teachers, students, and other educational stake-holders—parents and administrators, for example—determine the kinds of understanding that students have developed.

Summative evaluation can occur in three ways: at the completion of a lesson, a unit, or a course. Altogether, authentic evaluation possesses four components: the teacher's formative evaluations, the students' formative evaluations, periodic lesson and unit evaluations, and final course evaluations.

Formative Teacher Evaluations.   Teachers can use anecdotal notes of observations, checklists, student-teacher conferences, conversations, questionnaires, informal and reflective student writing samples, and samples of completed student work and work-in-progress.

Formative Student Evaluations.   Students can be responsible for monitoring some of their own progress. Conferring with peers and keeping portfolios of work-in-progress can help them take responsibility for the progress of their learning.

Periodic Lesson and Unit Evaluations.   Teachers must decide how and when to monitor students' progress as they learn. It is necessary for assessment tasks to mirror and extend the learning activities. In a writing class, assessment should consist of writing; in a mathematics class, assessment should consist of problem solving. Portfolio assessment, once used only in art classes, allows students and teachers to choose the best examples of authentic work in response to student learning. Portfolios may include projects, activities, research, and writing samples. Some of these contributions may be the students' own assessment of what and how they learned. This is an important consideration because students' insights and understandings are the aim of constructivist classrooms.

Final Course Evaluations.   Just as an author is judged when a book is published and offered to the public, or a manufacturer is evaluated when a product becomes available to the market, the final course evaluation of learning should also be public. Students need to be helped to find appropriate avenues for public and polished presentations of their learning. This final evaluation should come only after opportunities for practice and refinement. Teachers need to carefully integrate instruction and final course evaluation so that students do the kind of work that demonstrates their learning. Students don't learn about reading; they read. They don't learn about writing; they write books and poems. Students don't learn about mathematical thinking; they use it to solve real problems.

Final course evaluation should consist of many sources of data so that teachers are basing their judgments on a holistic view of their students. Viechnicki and her colleagues (1993) describe the transformation of teaching practices in a group of teachers who used multiple data sources for evaluating students. These included observing students many times throughout the day to "catch" students at work, conducting peer interviews, eliciting comments and concerns from the students' parents, and collecting unusual and creative student work that may not have a place in the curriculum. This kind of data collection mirrors the work of an ethnographer collecting data for cultural study: observation, interviews, artifacts.

As teachers and their students practice various types of formative and summative evaluation, they should be mindful of their school or school district's graduation policies. (The topic of graduation assessment was covered in chapter 4.) Review the experienced teacher's narrative in chapter 4. You will notice the way she carefully links her specific evaluative practices to her school district's graduation procedures. If your school or school district has not yet engaged in graduation assessment deliberations, this may be a fruitful area for future curriculum leadership.

Authentic evaluation is an extremely important process for fostering constructivist teaching and learning. Yet it remains rare in classrooms. The task is not impossible. Excellent books are available on authentic assessment for constructivist classrooms in each subject area. A short bibliography is included at the end of this chapter.

CONCLUSION

The plan-act-observe-evaluate cycle is based on a long tradition of teacher-empowerment research. It is a useful protocol for putting beliefs into practice, making daily adjustments, and evaluating the success of constructivist teaching-learning.

Beginning teachers may find it difficult to integrate planning, acting, observing, and evaluating. The complexity of this type of teaching may seem overwhelming at first. However, as they grow with experience, they should be better able to recognize the relationships among the elements of the cycle. As novice teachers develop into reflective practitioners, the various pieces of their work will gradually become more integrated.

The plan-act-observe-evaluate cycle serves as the referent for this chapter's discussion of enacting constructivist transactions. The different ways that teachers use this general protocol will depend on their understanding of the cycle in light of their teaching beliefs.

The following critical incident, which is based on an experienced teacher's autobiographical reflection, illustrates one professional's interpretation of the plan-act-observe-evaluate cycle.

CRITICAL INCIDENT

Enacting Constructivist Transactions

Jon Secaur

BACKGROUND

Jon Secaur has taught physics and other sciences to high school and college students for the last 22 years. Jon recently earned a Ph.D. in Educational Foundations at Kent State University. He says his graduate work greatly affects his teaching. Dr. Secaur's perspective on constructivism originated in his doctoral study of Michael Polanyi's work. Dr. Secaur also serves on Kent Roosevelt High School's active School Improvement Team. The team just received a major grant from the Ohio Department of Education to restructure education at his school. Jon is an active proponent of reflective teaching as scaffolded in this book. He believes that teachers should become career-long students of their constructivist practice.

THE INCIDENT

"Luke, you will find that many of the truths we cling to depend greatly on our point of view."

So said Obi-Wan Kanobi to Luke Skywalker, the young Jedi knight in George Lucas's film *The Return of the Jedi*. As he completed his training as a Jedi master, Luke was to find what good teachers have always known, that the same set of particulars may generate different understandings from different perspectives. In other words, meaning is found in the whole, not in the parts. The meaning one draws from the parts is intimately tied to one's perspective. Let's look in on my class one day to see the process at work.

So, you see, gravitation affects everything and decreases with the square of the distance. That was the point I wanted to make to the class. It was an important point, since Newton's law of gravitation precipitated the most profound change ever in our understanding of the universe. I wanted my students to get a sense of the way that the gravitational pull between celestial objects diminishes with distance. I asked the class to consider two identical planets orbiting a hypothetical star, one twice as far from the star as the other. Since gravitation falls off with the square of the distance, I explained, the attraction on the twice-distant star would be only one-fourth as much as on the nearer planet. An appropriate flourish of mathematics proved the point, at least to my satisfaction.

"But what difference does that make?" asked Diane. What difference, I thought—all the difference in the world! Her question seemed sincere. It was not one of those why-do-we-hafta-know-this questions. My explanation, therefore, must have been at fault. Perhaps another example: think about the earth and Venus, I asked her. Twin planets, practically, in terms of size and mass, yet Venus is two-thirds as far from the sun as is the earth. So, if it's only two-thirds as far, the pull on Venus from the sun would be. . . . I paused and looked in Diane's direction, hoping she would finish my thought.

"Nine-fourths as great," someone else volunteered.

Yes, that's it, someone understands. I nodded and acknowledged a correct response. But Diane was unmoved.

"But how do we know that?" she asked, more intensely than before. And I realized that I didn't understand her question any more than she understood my answer. I had been working from, thinking with, the perspective of a spectator out in space, measuring out the distances in the picture in my mind. That was the whole that I was assuming, working to lead my students to that same end. I wanted them to hold that same image, watching the worlds turn from that neutral and removed point of view. Instead, I felt that image crumble. Diane was seeing from a radically different perspective, but I had no idea what it was. I needed to see the problem from her point of view, and so I went looking for some parts from which we could reconstruct a new whole.

"Can you ask your question again?" I asked her.

"Okay," she said, "what I want to know is, what would be different, if you were standing there?"

"On the planet?"

"Yes, yes, on Venus."

In a flash, I understood—not only her question, but, more importantly, the perspective from which her question came. I had been watching the solar system from a remote perspective, thinking of gravitation in the more abstract sense as the force that binds planets to stars. She had imagined gravitation in the more immediate and personal sense, as that which holds us to the earth. What effects could she feel, could she experience, as a consequence of greater or weaker gravitational forces from the sun? How did my abstract lesson, the mathematics of which she understood, have meaning in her context?

By drawing on our mass media experience of watching astronauts apparently weightless in orbit, I was able to help her to see the answer to her question. I'll spare the reader the rest of the scientific details. The point is that I was able to visit with her in her perspective. More importantly, I was able to help her move to a new and larger viewpoint. This time, I knew she was there with me.

I doubt that my teaching style was so flexible at the beginning of my career. I see that I now interpret students' questions at two levels at once: I listen for the explicit content, of course, but I also find myself listening for the implicit context. The perspective from which a question is posed is at least as important as the question itself. An answer or an activity that addresses only the content may seem perfectly appropriate to me but miss the student's point entirely. I realize that my undergraduate preparation in both science and education did not prepare me to operate on those two levels.

In my science courses, for example, I learned the subjects quite well because I was able to find my place in what Thomas Kuhn (1962) calls the *disciplinary matrix*, which is the structure and logic of the subjects and the world view of a scientist. Now I can see that my professors were not only teaching me physics and chemistry; they were also teaching me how a practitioner of those disciplines sees the world, what questions are appropriate to ask, and what answers are appropriate to give.

To put it another way, we have all had experience with professors who certainly seemed to know their subjects. I say "seemed to know" because they were never able to clearly communicate it to us. They knew their subjects, but not how to teach them. In my undergraduate science courses I learned the content of science that a future scientist would need. What I have learned since is how to frame that content with a context for understanding. No one could teach me how to do that—or I should say, no one particular person has taught me. The best teachers I remember from my past experience taught me by their example, and all my students continually teach me to develop the context for the content, if only I will listen and learn from them. In the story I have related, Diane was helping me to understand context while I was helping her to learn content.

Reflective teachers begin, I believe, from a sense of collegiality with students. Certainly my students are not my peers, but they are fellow workers in the classroom. Reflective teachers identify their own perspective, teasing apart the context of the topic or activity at hand to become aware of the structure of assumptions, ideological biases, and past experience that support them in that perspective. They imagine other interactions of these parts, which might produce other perspectives in the students.

This ability to shift perspectives, to be able to see from another's point of view, is a valuable experience for our students as well. Teachers can not only model this shift but also explicitly describe it, on occasion, as they use it. For example, I might have said to the class, "You see, I was answering Diane's question as an observer hanging out in space, watching the solar system run, but she was asking from the surface of a planet."

Going further, teachers may encourage students to assemble similar parts into differing wholes through writing assignments. I routinely ask students to write about both sides of an issue, requiring them to consider the valid points they could make from either perspective based on the same data. Limiting students to writing only on the position of their choice further galvanizes them in their opinions, which runs counter to the broader purposes of education.

The type of writing assignment I described also affords an opportunity to critique students on their ability to develop logical positions and evaluate them. Indeed, the reflective process I am describing coordinates well with the current emphasis on authentic evaluation. Awareness of context—both the teacher's and the students'—provides a new window through which a teacher can make ongoing reviews of teaching and learning.

Evaluation in science classes has traditionally involved determining if a student knows something, which often reduces to whether a student can reflexively give the correct response to a prompt. Constructivism enables a more powerful metaphor, such as that of a building inspector evaluating the quality and character of a student's construction project. How well has the student followed the building codes of the discipline? How sturdy is the construction, how solid the foundation? Perhaps a more positive example would be that of master crafts workers at a shop, guiding apprentice artisans in their work, offering suggestions, showing other methods, and sometimes rejecting one product and leading apprentices to start again.

Practically, this approach to evaluation is sensitive to the students' context as well as to their content. In an essay question or a mathematical exercise, experienced teachers learn to discern how students arrived at a particular conclusion or result. Even in a multiple choice test, the students' constructions are the main consideration in the formulation of questions.

The extent to which teachers can quickly detect a student's perspective and adapt to it is one indicator of their success. Teachers can use that understanding of a student's perspective to help the student make connections within content, enlarge the student's perspective, and provide bridges to other disciplines. The very real and contributory nature of such information makes this formative evaluation of value to teachers.

Students can and should actively participate in summative evaluation. The extent to which students are able to identify their own conceptual frameworks and move beyond them is a genuine measure of student success. I believe that once students come to see the connection between this self-evaluation and their ability to learn, they value and create these connections.

Education in general and constructivism in particular are not about simply providing opportunities for inquiries and active learning. They are also for enriching students' stores of images, ideas, and experiences, furnishing students with a rich variety of experiences and insights from which they may construct their own understandings. In this sense a teacher is an extravagant litterbug, providing connections not only with the practical and the useful, but the wonderful and beautiful as well.

When I was a kid and happened to be blocking someone's view of the television, I remember being told that I made a better door than a window. It now occurs to me that two different approaches to teaching are reflected in the images of that metaphor. I would like to be a good door for my students, so that they might enter into the world of professional science through me, without my obstructing their passage. But even more, I would like to be a wide, broad window through which many perspectives are possible. I want to be a good, clear window through which all of my students might see the essential beauty of the universe and of the discipline of physics, and in seeing for themselves, come to know and understand.

Teacher-Character Advice

Johnny Jackson

Even with the help of a thoughtful curriculum design, which was the topic in chapter 4, teachers need to make careful decisions about how to adapt a general curriculum blueprint to their specific classes. Separating planning from either content or pedagogy means that teachers are acting as curriculum managers or passive implementers rather than as curriculum enactors. No matter what the subject or the age of the student, I believe that it is essential for teachers to understand both the structure of their academic discipline and their students' developmental needs in order for successful learning to take place. Shulman (1987) calls this *pedagogical content knowledge*. To me, it means that teachers are much more than masters of a subject that they teach. They also understand how the subject is organized so that they can help students construct meaningful and valid understandings of the subject as well.

In English classes, for example, the great themes and ideas in classic literary works are natural starting places for planning at both the course and the lesson level. I see my role as guiding my students toward a full and sophisticated reading experience using the great works of world literature. I agree with Arnold (1971) that students should be guided to understand the consummate products of their cultural heritage.

However, the great ideas of literature are available only if students are fully engaged in reading. My planning must then incorporate ways to engage them meaningfully with the text on a deep conceptual level. This is a difficult task for many students, even the brighter ones, in these times of television and short attention spans. I want students to focus on great ideas, but not in a superficial way. I want them to acquire deep understanding, because such understanding is necessary if they are to come to love and value great literature.

Teachers in each discipline need to think about what deep-level understanding means for their particular subject. What are the big ideas? Lampert (1986) detailed the foundational concepts of mathematics, for example. Students need to understand these ideas—that multiplication can be done in any order, that quantities are composed of other quantities, and that problems can be recomposed into sub-problems that are more easily solved, and so forth. In English, I know that when readers are fully engaged with the literature they read, they construct meaning on several levels—affectively, cognitively, and aesthetically. An astute teacher not only recognizes response to literature but also helps students recognize and move through various levels of engagement and response.

I recommend that teachers decide on these types of foundational ideas in their own discipline. What must students understand in order to construct meaning? What kind of learning will move students beyond rote work to true engagement with big ideas? Then teachers must decide how students can best work with these big ideas. A teacher must know how to build bridges so that students can connect the big picture with what they already know.

In my classroom, I make sure that students are engaged in thinking about literature because I know that is the only way they can construct meaning from the books we read. Yet I also know I need to scaffold their thinking. By providing short, informal writing assignments that guide students as they think about the text they are reading, I can engage students in constructing meaning. At the same time I monitor how successfully they are progressing in their levels of understanding. In this manner, both the students and I have a chance for continual review of their understanding.

Writing to learn is a strategy I first tried after reading suggestions in Fulweiler's *The Journal Book* (1987). It has become an important vehicle that helps students try out ideas and gain writing practice for the formal end-of-course research paper. It also provides me an opportunity to decide the kinds of prereading activities and postreading discussion questions I can structure to help students grapple with essential ideas and themes in the literature. In *Expanding Response Journals*, Parson (1994) offers additional suggestions for implementing and integrating writing to learn in all subject areas.

Some teachers might judge a student as a successful reader when that student's interpretation matches the teacher's. But I understand that reading is a transactional process. Rosenblatt (1983) has been influential in broadening our understandings of literature as transaction. I am interested in students not trying to think my thoughts but developing their own. I require students to gather evidence from the text to support their assertions and arguments. We often have engaging and thoughtful classroom discussions as students wrestle with the ideas in our readings. In my classroom there can be many good responses, but responses are clearly wrong when they are not supported or reasoned through. After all, this literature is great because it has prompted such a wide range of responses in so many people.

It is appropriate for all teachers to think about how students can be encouraged to wrestle with the big ideas in their discipline. Evaluation needs to suit this kind of learning. Fill-in-the-blank tests just won't suffice. Thoughtfully designed essay questions on end-of-unit tests help students use their knowledge and extend their thinking. For the students in my classes, a research paper moves them to thorough investigation and reasoned analysis and synthesis. This paper forms their final course evaluation. In other content areas, a problem-solving project may offer the same benefits. As I have said before, teachers must know their discipline inside out to structure the kinds of learning activities that enable students to construct the deep understandings these kinds of projects require. As Prawatt (1992) noted, "An idea-oriented curriculum places more of a burden on teachers" (p. 388). Teachers need to keep in mind that the elements of planning, enacting, observing, and evaluating form an interactive cycle. Many kinds of knowledge must be integrated for this kind of teaching to pay off with increased student meaning-making.

Amy Nelson

Teachers need to be crystal clear about what it is students are to learn and how the teacher will proceed with instruction and evaluation. So for me, planning is the essential element of the cycle of planning, enacting, observing, and evaluating. I believe well-stated but flexibly enacted goals are the necessary first step when moving from the constructivist curriculum design to the classroom. In fact, courses, units, and lessons should all be conceptualized in this way.

Teachers must (a) decide on the most appropriate learning outcomes, (b) carefully formulate instructional objectives, and (c) share these with students as a device for organizing the learning activity in advance, so that all students know precisely where they are headed. Teachers shouldn't be rigid about the enactment of their instructional objectives; rather, they should use them as a clear target for the teaching-learning transactions.

Where do the objectives come from? Each teacher should decide from the constructivist curriculum design what objectives are appropriate in scope and sequence. These objectives may be in the form of a graded course of study or a course outline provided by a school district or state or provincial board of education. Objectives are closely related to the learning outcomes that teachers plan for students.

In gathering or composing a list of outcomes, I believe that it is important to pay attention to both *form* and *task analysis*. The form that the objectives take will determine the probability of instructors successfully communicating instructional intent to the students. Objectives must be stated meaningfully because outcomes should be student-oriented, not teacher-directed. After all, it would be sad commentary indeed if any classroom had a lot of teaching and no learning going on. Clear objectives ensure that a lesson focuses on what students need to learn rather than on extraneous stuff that may be interesting but only adds confusion or wastes valuable instructional time. Task analysis means breaking down complex tasks into simpler, carefully sequenced steps. A task analysis ensures that objectives and outcomes are coherently related. Let me explain the concepts of well-formed objectives and task analysis in more detail.

Mager (1962) set out a way to create objectives that I have found useful. However, Mager was describing programmed learning, a way of learning that I am coming to understand as leaving out an essential aspect of learning—the students' cognitive processes. Nonetheless, keeping in mind that objectives should serve to help teachers structure teaching, not to substitute for teaching, I like Mager's approach to forming objectives:

1. Identify the behavioral performance that will show the student has achieved the objective.

2. Define the desired behavior further by describing the important conditions under which the behavior will be expected to occur.
3. Specify the criteria of acceptable performance by describing how well the learner must perform to be considered acceptable. (1962, p. 12)

From a more constructivist standpoint, I would rephrase Mager's (1962) three-step approach as follows:

1. Identify the behavioral performance that will indicate that the student has engaged in active meaning-making.
2. Describe the conditions under which the behavioral performance will occur.
3. Specify the criteria for an acceptable student performance of active meaning-making.

The following excerpt is an example of a clear behavioral performance statement:

> When asked to write a short paper on why there is a teen-age drug problem, the student should identify six or more probable causes. The source for this short paper will be a unit on teen-age drug use.

In this example, the desired student performance is the written articulation of probable causes for teen-age drug use. The condition for the desired performance is a unit that culminates in a short essay. The acceptable performance criterion is the identification of six or more probable causes.

Once you formulate your list of objectives, you need to sequence them effectively. Task analysis is a useful approach to sequencing objectives. It is a process that breaks down complex learning behaviors into component parts. The teacher analyzes a task to describe precisely the steps or links in the "behavioral chain" and their proper sequence (Alberto & Troutman, 1982). In a constructivist classroom, however, I use task analysis with a slightly different purpose. I want to make sure the activities I ask my students to engage in are useful for the kind of learning I hope will occur in my class. If I want them to write an essay that presents their point of view on some controversial subject, I need to be clear about what they must do to reach this goal. Some people might say that they need to practice writing correct sentences first. But if I analyze writing from a constructivist point of view, I find instead that my students need to understand ideological controversy, what makes writing interesting to read, and how to recognize that they can find a subject they consider to be worth writing about. I need not design practice in sentence writing before I assign an essay, but rather give students meaningful opportunities to explore controversial ideas and the conventions for expressing them in writing.

In a useful task analysis, each step should be simple enough for students to master without great difficulty. You can write steps in the form of objectives, and then you should place them in a logical sequence from basic to complex.

After one level of content has been mastered, the learner proceeds to the next, more complex level of performance. Task analysis is thus a part of a teaching-learning approach in which students gradually master, one at a time, a set of increasingly challenging objectives or intended learning outcomes. However, a great danger of task analysis is that teachers will design activities that do not have any real connection to the eventual learning outcome. Using my earlier example about writing instruction, identifying nouns and verbs on a worksheet might help the students identify nouns and verbs. But will that help them to explore controversy? I think not. Task analysis must not stray from the outcomes you hope to produce.

It is essential that teachers constantly monitor their teaching, and that students constantly monitor their learning. Teachers must incorporate into their teaching a check for understanding, a way to determine how students are making sense of the activities and learning objectives that a teacher has designed. Teachers might have each student write down a response, tell each student to think of an answer and then call on a student at random, or ask students to give hand signals. These steps show the teacher that each child is engaged and also help the teacher monitor each child's understanding. But the students are also monitoring their own understanding. I often pair students in learning teams. Instead of asking students the ubiquitous but useless question, "Do you have any questions?" I ask students a question based on my learning objectives and have them share their response first with their partner and then with me. That way I know whether or not students understand the lesson.

At the culmination of a unit, teachers need to give a test that explicitly relates what is being measured to what has been taught. This kind of test is called a **criterion-referenced test**. In answering specific items on such a test, students get "relevant, on-target practice in the skills or knowledge being taught" (Popham, 1987, p. 16). For example, to evaluate writing, a teacher needs to have students engaged in writing, not in filling in the blanks or copying sentences from the board. This enables the teacher to identify and record precisely which skills each student has and has not mastered.

Constructing good tests is a complex process that needs more explanation than I can provide here. I suggest you take a course or workshop in your preservice program on how to become a good test-maker. A useful source to consult is Gronlund (1985), who offers helpful advice on evaluation and test-making. But I do feel compelled to talk about the standardized achievement tests that seem to drive so much of the instructional decision-making in classrooms today. Teachers do not need to be afraid of such tests. Working together, teachers and students can align themselves to work toward understanding how to do well on such tests without having them overshadow other necessary aspects of formative and summative evaluation. I teach my students how to take such tests, how to think about the questions and come up with systems for figuring out the answers.

Doing well on standardized tests is an educational reality. I want to ensure that my students can use what they know in many ways, creatively as well as on our district's standardized measures. I would be miscreant in my teaching responsibility not to do so. But I also incorporate other kinds of evaluation that are not one-time-only scores, as the criterion-referenced tests seem to be. I also ask my students to show what they can do in meaningful ways, by creating a product that demonstrates a learning outcome.

Dennis Sage

I am interested in learning environments that nurture students and help them achieve their potential rather than environments structured to control student learning. I believe that a teacher must begin where students are and that planning should focus on long-term learning rather than short-term goals and objectives. As I plan for teaching and learning I constantly ask myself, how will this activity facilitate student growth? I like to work with broad themes. I find the use of precise goals restricts my teaching style.

Since I believe that children learn through engagement in meaningful activities and meaningful communication, I plan activities that take advantage of students' natural curiosity about the world and how it functions. Even children as young as my students in kindergarten can pursue investigations into science and history when they see a connection with their own questions and the answers such learning provides. Teachers must take special care when planning to structure activities to allow students to discover what they need and are ready to know. I feel more secure in my ability to appropriately structure discovery learning now, but when I first began this kind of classroom exploration I followed the structure recommended by Taba (1966). She identifies three thinking tasks that help students construct understanding: concept formation, interpretation of data, and application of principles.

Concept formation involves identifying key attributes of data, grouping the attributes, and developing labels and categories. In my classroom, students work at learning centers on concept formation. At one center children find many examples of seeds and sprouts, in a unit focused on the organizing center of plants and growing.

The students work in pairs to list or draw all the features of the seeds and then group them according to size, shape, color, texture, and degrees of softness and firmness. The children argue about categories, which shows me that they are thinking carefully about ways to arrange the seeds. I make an effort to write down some observation that I make about each student's talk as they are learning. How are acorns categorized? Dried corn kernels? Tiny radish seeds? Pumpkin seeds? Of course, at this age it is essential that I help them determine how to categorize. But if I scaffold for them what constitutes an essential attribute, even kindergartners can learn that seeds can be relatively large or small and still be seeds.

This kind of teaching requires careful planning to ensure students' active meaning-making. The teacher must also constantly monitor student progress. I have found that the strategies for nondirective teaching, as described by Rogers (1951/1971, 1982) and outlined by Joyce and Weil (1986), allow me to continuously review how students are constructing meaning and help students assess their understanding.

In nondirective teaching, responses to feelings as well as ideas form the basis of an interview with students designed to explore how those ideas and feelings relate to learning as the students see them. Teachers may sometimes respond to student feelings by accepting, reflecting, or paraphrasing them. They may take the lead in an interview by asking direct questions, forcing students to make a choice, asking leading and open-ended questions, or encouraging students to express their ideas and feelings more fully. This process has five phases for students: defining the situation that requires teacher help, exploring the problem, constructing a plan of action, observing the results of this plan, and reporting any personal insights. All five phases require clarification and acceptance by the teacher. This facilitative teaching approach is another application of the decision-making cycle that is being used as a blueprint in this book.

This complex interaction between teacher and student is designed not only to promote short-term understanding, but to help students develop insight, independence, and confidence. This is why I worked hard to increase my sophistication with a type of teaching that requires a great deal of teaching artistry. Although it has a specific sequence, it has no clear-cut boundaries or outcomes. As Joyce and Weil (1986) conclude:

Since nondirective teaching assumes that every student, every situation, and every teacher are unique, the specific events in a nondirective interview situation cannot be anticipated. To master nondirective teaching, teachers learn general principles, work to increase their sensitivity to others, master the nondirective skills, and then practice making contact with students and responding to them, using skills drawn from a repertoire of nondirective counseling techniques. (p. 151)

I evaluate my students as I teach. When I was a teen, there was a popular song I liked about being a "girl-watcher." Now I'm a kid-watcher! I incorporate my daily anecdotal observations into portfolios, which serve as the final evaluation for a unit or an activity in my classroom. Each portfolio is a purposefully organized collection of a student's work that the student and I select to show evidence of growth in learning. Always included in portfolios are the students' own reports on their learning. In my classes, such reports may be oral, and I may transcribe certain key comments students make. Or students may draw a representation of what they understand. In upper grades, as students become more proficient at expressing themselves in writing, their own evaluation of their learning—both insights and plans for future actions—are an essential component of their final portfolios. If you are interested in learning more about portfolio assessment, Graves and Sunstein (1992) and Tierney (1991) are good sources. Stenmark (1991) has an excellent guide to alternative assessments in mathematics instruction and Hein and Price (1994) offer a guide for authentic science assessment. Teachers need to make their evaluation as child-centered, insightful, and meaningful as their instruction.

Silvia Rivera

The manner in which a teacher interprets the curriculum design depends on a teacher's beliefs. The consequences of our teaching methods, even our classroom organization scheme (which will be discussed further in the next chapter) have profound influences on what students can and will learn. A teacher's planning must involve thinking about the manner in which teaching and learning are embedded in a broader social context.

I believe we must constantly entice students to make connections among the content of the curriculum and associations with their own lives. Additionally, I want to foster a democratic ideal. I want students to work together, value diversity, and understand that the voice of one must never silence the voice of another. Projects that require cooperative learning help students appreciate the complexity of democratic social life. In my classroom we have periodic community meetings, where we share our concerns about our classroom life and conceive workable solutions for coping with them. This interaction helps us live and productively work together, celebrating our differences rather than fearing them.

There are more structured ways to bring a collaborative community spirit to the classroom. Note the strategy used in the CIP program outlined in chapter 4. In the first semester students become acquainted with an intrinsically interesting community-based activity and acquire communications skills within this real-world context. The second semester is designed to increase student mastery of knowledge and skills. Seizing on their students' enthusiasm for the citizen action projects, the curriculum leaders provide access to relevant readings and discussions. The individual teachers then facilitate students' making connections between their coursework and struggles for social liberation.

Dewey (1916) believes that students learn to live in a democratic society when their educational experiences provide them with the skills of democratic decision-making and problem solving. Thelen's (1960) group investigation model gives teachers a way in which to structure activities that lead students to grapple with the study and subsequent improvement of a troubling social issue. Sharan (1980) adapted the group investigation technique so that students could participate in all levels of planning and problem solving. This technique can be adapted as follows. The teacher and the students have a brainstorming session where they collectively define a social problem or issue, decide on methods of investigation, and determine appropriate inquiry products. They then enact their plans as critically oriented social scientists.

Teachers must constantly monitor student groups to make sure that the goals of such activities focus on respect and dignity for all participants. They must also ensure that the activities are helping students develop ways to gather reasonable evidence to support or reject claims of knowledge. I find that in such classrooms, knowledge is not authority-based or teacher-based, but is socially constructed by my students and me as we negotiate together through data, evidence, assumptions, and claims. I must constantly help students understand the requirements of critically informed, democratic inquiry.

Although ongoing assessment of learning is an integral part of this kind of classroom, final evaluation of an investigation project is also necessary. It helps students analyze how their inquiry relates to their own lives. I agree with Dennis Sage that portfolio assessment is a valid tool to help students understand and articulate their constructivist learning. However, documents and artifacts do not need to be the only components of a portfolio. Posters, videotapes and audiotapes, and transcripts of speeches can also be used to document growth. In the CIP program, Newmann, Bertocci, and Landsness (1977) recommend using evaluation as a tool for giving students critical feedback on their work and an opportunity for assessing the project's impact on their own lives. For only if students become interested in and capable of working toward a more just and peaceful world can we say that our curriculum leadership has been successful. Newmann and his colleagues seem to understand what education should be about. I envision my classroom as a small but vital link in helping students understand that they can help transform an unjust world.

FURTHER READINGS

Ennis, C. D. (1994). Knowledge and beliefs underlying curricular expertise. *Quest, 46,* 164–175.

Ertmer, P. A. (1993). Behaviorism, cognitivism, constructivism: Comparing critical features from a design perspective. *Performance Improvement Quarterly, 6,* 50–72.

Fischer, H. E. (1993). Framework for conducting empirical observations of learning processes. *Science Education, 77,* 131–151.

Gil-Perez, D. (1994). Bringing pupils' learning closer to a scientific construction of knowledge: A permanent feature in innovations in science teaching. *Science Education, 78,* 310–305.

Holmes. G. A. (1993). Evaluating learning from a constructivist paradigm. *Performance and Instruction, 32,* 28–30.

Johnson, D. W., Johnson, R. T., Holubec, E., & Roy, P. (1991). *Cooperation in the classroom.* Edina, MN: Interaction.

Kehr, C. (1993). Assessment theory and research for classrooms: From "taxonomies" to construction meaning in context. *Educational Measurement: Issues and Practice, 12,* 13–19.

King, A. (1993). Effects of guided cooperative questioning on children's knowledge construction. *Journal of Experimental Education, 61,* 127–148.

Loughlin, K. A. (1994). Centered knowing and its influence in emancipatory learning. *International Journal of Lifelong Education, 13,* 349–360.

Riley, M. K. (1993). Walking the talk: Putting constructivist thinking into practice in classrooms. *Educational Horizons, 71,* 187–196.

Slavin, R., Schlomo, S., Spencer, K., Webb, C., & Schmuck, R. (1985). *Learning to cooperate, cooperating to learn.* New York: Plenum Press.

Tippins, D. J. (1993). Ethical decisions at the heart of teaching: Making sense from a constructivist perspective. *Journal of Moral Education, 22,* 221–240.

Zemelman, S., Daniels, H., & Hyde, A. (1993). *Best practice: New standards for teaching and learning in America's schools.* Portsmouth, NH: Heinemann.

REFERENCES

Alberto, P. A., & Troutman, A. C. (1982). *Applied behavior analysis for teachers: Influencing student performance* (2nd ed.). Englewood Cliffs, NJ: Merrill/Prentice Hall.

Arnold, M. (1971). The function of criticism at the present time. In H. Adams (Ed.), *Critical theory since Plato* (pp. 583–595). New York: Harcourt, Brace, Jovanovich.

Dewey, J. (1916). *Democracy and education.* New York: Macmillan.

Freire, P. (1971). *Pedagogy of the oppressed.* New York: Herder & Herder. (Original work published 1970)

Fulweiler, T. (Ed.). (1987). *The journal book.* Portsmouth, NH: Heinemann.

Graves, D. H., & Sunstein, B. S. (Eds.). (1992). *Portfolio portraits.* Porstmouth, NH: Heinemann.

Gronlund, N. E . (1985). *Measurement and evaluation in teaching* (5th ed.). New York: Macmillan.

Hein, G. E. & Price, S. (1994). *Active assessment for active science: A guide for elementary school teachers.* Portsmouth, NH: Heinemann.

Joyce, B., & Weil, M. (1986). *Models of Teaching* (3rd ed.). Boston: Allyn & Bacon.

Kuhn, T. S. (1962). *The structure of scientific revolutions.* Chicago: University of Chicago Press.

Lampert, H. (1986). Knowing, doing, and teaching multiplication. *Cognition and Instruction 3*(4), 305–342.

Mager, R. F. (1962). *Planning instructional objectives.* Palo Alto, CA: Fearon.

Marsh, C. & Willis, G. (1995). *Curriculum: Alternative approaches, ongoing issues.* Englewood Cliffs, NJ: Merrill/Prentice-Hall.

May, W. T. (1993). Teaching as a work of art in the medium of curriculum. *Theory into Practice, 32,* 210–218.

Newmann, F. W., Bertocci, T., & Landsness, R. M. (1977). *Skills in citizen action: An English-social studies program for secondary schools.* Skokie, IL: National Textbook.

Oakes, J. (1985). *Keeping track: How schools structure inequality.* New Haven, CT: Yale University Press.

Parson, L. (1994). *Expanding response journals.* Portsmouth, NH: Heinemann.

Popham, W. J. (1987). Instructional objectives benefit teaching and testing. *Momentum, 28,* 15–16.

Posner, G. J. (1992). *Analyzing the curriculum.* New York: McGraw-Hill.

Prawatt, R. S. (1992). Teacher's beliefs about teaching and learning: A constructivist perspective. *American Journal of Education, 100*(3), 354–395.

Rogers, C. (1971). *Client centered therapy*. Boston, MA: Houghton Mifflin. (Original work published 1951)

Rogers, C. (1982). *Freedom to learn for the eighties*. Englewood Cliffs, NJ: Merrill/Prentice Hall.

Rosenblatt, L. M. (1983). *Literature as exploration* (4th ed.). New York: Modern Language Association.

Sharan, S. (1980). Cooperative learning in small groups: Recent methods and effects on achievement, attitudes, and ethnic relations. *Review of Educational Research, 50,* 241–271.

Shulman, L. S. (1987). Knowledge and teaching: Foundations of the new reform. *Harvard Educational Review, 57,* 473–482.

Stenmark, J. K. (1991). *Mathematics assessment*. Reston, VA: National Council of Teachers of Mathematics.

Taba, H. (1966). *Teaching strategies and cognitive functioning in elementary school children (Cooperative Research Project 2404)*. San Francisco: San Francisco State College.

Thelen, H. (1960). *Education and the human quest*. New York: Harper & Row.

Tierney, R. (Ed.). (1991). *Portfolio assessment in the reading-writing classroom*. Norwood, MA: Christopher Gordon.

Viechnicki, K. J., Barbour, N., Shaklee, B., Rohrer, J., & Ambrose, R. (1993). The impact of portfolio assessment on teacher classroom activities. *Journal of Teacher Education, 44*(5), 371–377.

Vygotsky, L. S. (1978). *Mind in society: The development of higher psychological process* (M. Cole, V. John-Steiner, S. Scribner, & E. Souberman, Eds. and Trans.). Cambridge, MA: Harvard University Press.

Zahorick, J. A. (1975). Teacher's planning models. *Educational Leadership, 33,* 134–139.

6

Creating a Classroom Learning Community

After eighteen years of teaching high school English, Carol Miller knew that no part of her teaching would ever be solidified. Her way of teaching creative writing, composition, literary analysis, and vocabulary development had evolved over time. The opportunity to observe language instruction from kindergarten through twelfth grade in her school system as a part-time mentor teacher for the past five years allowed Carol to grow and develop in collaboration with peers. These observations and collaborations affected her classroom management style as well. Carol noted that in all classrooms students naturally moved and talked. She observed elementary teachers posting the same rules that she regularly issued at the high school. Third-graders were told to bring materials to class and listen when the teacher talked, just as ninth-graders were. If these same rules were in order all these years, why were her students still ignoring them? Carol decided this year to align her classroom management style with her emerging constructivist teaching style. Her teaching of writing, for instance, had for years been patterned after her own experiences in learning to write. Grammar instruction, like literary analysis and vocabulary development, was a separate unit of instruction and textbook-driven. Lately, however, Carol had learned about whole-language approaches from elementary teachers and had been working on a writing workshop approach in her own classroom. The difference in student enthusiasm and quality of writing was impressive. "Why not take similar approaches in how I manage student behavior?" she wondered.

Taking a cue from constructivism, Carol began her first classes with an inquiry designed to make students think about their own behaviors. She posed questions to her students. What do you want to get out of this English class? What grade do you want to achieve? What skills do you want to develop? What do you want to learn? What can you do to get what you want in this class? What can I do to help you get what you want? After hearing these questions, the students initially were quiet and even appeared uncomfortable. A few brave souls volunteered that they wanted to pass the state proficiency tests or that they would be satisfied with a "C" in the course. As for what they had to do to achieve these goals, the students arrived at a list of five guidelines: Be on time. Bring all necessary materials to class. Attend class. Pay attention to the teacher. Turn in homework on time. Carol asked a student to copy these rules and informed the class that they would receive typed copies the next day.

That evening as Carol prepared to type what she termed her *student-created rules*, her heart sank. "These rules are meaningless, regardless of who spoke them," she realized. Her own son had come home from his first day in fourth grade with a similar list of rules. Carol copied that list instead and entered the second day of school buoyed by a growing confidence. "These rules are from my son's fourth-grade classroom," she informed her ninth-graders. "These are not new to him and they certainly are not new to any of you. Let's throw them out and start all over with just one rule: In this classroom, we will be good to one another. As we work together and get to know each other, we will continue talking about what it means to 'be good to each other.' For today, let's just talk about what happens if Jeff here didn't bring a pencil to class. What would being good to him look like?"

What ensued was a brief discussion about sharing and how, ultimately, students were responsible for their own material. "OK, you handle that from now on. I'm not managing your materials, and I know you are each capable of managing your own behaviors."

On the third day, Carol had to stop a lesson to discuss how three students' talking was interfering with her presentation. Some students offered solutions. One recommended sending the talkers into the hallway. Another student countered that then they would not learn the lesson. Another student explained to the three "offenders" how their behavior was affecting the entire class. That two-minute dialogue resulted in a very quiet, calm learning environment. Carol walked out of her room that day realizing that discipline involves teaching and learning for both teacher and students.

Introduction

Carol Miller demonstrates in both her teaching and her management style the emerging quality of professional growth. What has evolved from her years of experience is a growing awareness of what really works, what makes sense in the classroom. This opening vignette gives you a glimpse into a classroom where self-control and caring are emphasized, two qualities of a **learning community**.

This chapter highlights the practice of building a classroom community. The notion of creating a classroom learning community suggests a different sort of setting. When a classroom becomes a community it "changes from a secular organization to a sacred organization, from a mere instrument designed to achieve certain ends to a virtuous enterprise" (Sergiovanni, 1992, p. 102). As Glasser (1992) notes, the purpose of this type of learning community is to support responsible autonomy.

The Value of This Constructivist Practice

To belong to a community of learners is every student's right. It is every teacher's responsibility to help create that community. This understanding of classroom leadership requires rethinking issues of power: who has power, how power is used, and how power is negotiated. In a traditional classroom, power is viewed and used in the sense of **power-over** (Kreisberg, 1992). This concept of power is characterized by command, control, and competition for scarce goods like "A" and "B" grades, teacher approval, and other rewards. Moreover, the power-over relationship "cuts off human communication and creates barriers to human empathy and understanding. This . . . powerless[ness] creates the space in which domination is exerted and thrives" (p. 47). Teachers must shift from a view and a use of power as power-over to power that allows for empowerment. Kreisberg (1992) echoes this thinking in his explanation of the connection of **power-with** to the process of empowerment:

> Power with is manifest in relationships of co-agency. These relationships are characterized by people finding ways to satisfy their desires and to fulfill their interests without imposing on one another. The relationship of co-agency is one in which there is equality: situations in which individuals and groups fulfill their desires by acting together. It is jointly developing capacity. The possibility for power with lies in the reality of human inter-connectedness within communities. . . . (pp. 85–86)

What encourages this interconnectedness in the classroom is a common sense of humanity between teacher and students. Imagine the following classroom learning community:

Teachers and students would mutually respect one another. In the context of constructivist transactions, the students' autonomy and initiative would be encouraged; and instructional strategies and content would be altered to meet student needs. Creative teaching and learning would be evident in the teacher's and students' flexible and imaginative behaviors. The teacher would also encourage the students to ask such critical questions as: "Why are we acting the way we are acting? Is what we are doing getting us what we need/want?" Taking the time both to ask such questions and to respond to them would not be viewed as offtask behaviors. In other words, the teacher's lesson plan would not be the sole driving force of what is learned in the classroom. How people learn would be given due credence as well. Teacher and student critical engagement would be viewed as a life-long pursuit, fostered by authentic, open communication.

A General Protocol

To turn this vision of a humanistic classroom learning community into a reality will require a teacher's best pragmatic (Dewey, 1910/1933) and action research (Lewin, 1948) abilities. The following four-step community-building protocol has been designed to support this type of work.

Fluid Planning for Community-Building

Building a community in the classroom cannot be mandated. Indeed, it cannot be overly orchestrated because to do so would be to work against the very essence of community. Any attempt at building that which is sacred and virtuous must begin with the self. Planning for community is, in part, an exercise in critical engagement. Teachers must come to an awareness of their beliefs about classroom management by responding to questions like the following:

1. What are my reactions to top-down management in my life? In my profession?
2. When have I felt empowered in my life? In my profession?
3. What are some experiences of community-building in my life? How did the sense of community evolve? What roles appeared in this community? How were conflicts solved?
4. What experiences of professional collaboration have I had during my career? How have I felt when I collaborated with another educator?
5. What is important in my classroom?
6. How do I know when students are learning in my classroom?
7. How do these reflections inform me about my own classroom management?

8. What do I now do in terms of classroom management that helps build community?

9. What changes could I make to enhance the sense of community in this classroom?

Enacting Community-Building

There are five parts to the enactment phase: establishing a collaborative ethos, articulating the classroom's core values, establishing a classroom covenant, maintaining the co-constructed covenant, and reviewing the classroom covenant. We begin with a discussion of how teachers can establish a collaborative ethos between themselves and their students, between their students, between themselves and their students' parents, and between themselves and their colleagues.

Establishing a Collaborative Ethos.   Building community implies collaboration between teacher and students, between students, between teacher and parents, and between teachers.

   1.   **Teacher-student collaboration**.   Activities that build a sense of community between teacher and students can include:
   • Ask students to discuss what kinds of student and teacher behaviors help them learn. The following examples can initiate a community-building conversation between teacher and students. "What can you be doing right now to help all of us learn this material? What else can I do to help you learn this material?" "This is the homework assignment I have come up with and these are the reasons why. I want you to be able to _____. Can you think of another homework activity that can accomplish these goals?" "I don't talk to you that way. Can you come up with another way to share your feelings with me?"
   • Give students opportunities to record their thoughts and feelings about the classroom climate in private journals and then share them with the class.

   2.   **Collaboration between students**.   Encouraging students to work in pairs or small groups increases a sense of community and cooperation. Recent work by Johnson, Johnson, and Holubec (1984) in cooperative learning is a valuable resource for building student collaboration. Other suggestions for this form of classroom community-building include:
   • Observe other teachers who utilize small-group instruction. Ask them what works and what problems they have encountered.
   • Talk with students about their perception of cooperative learning groups.
   • During a lesson, invite suggestions about what would work better—for example, individual or small-group learning.
   • Ask students to figure out a way to solve problems or answer a question by working with each other.

3.   Teacher-parent collaboration.   Parents rarely begin their child's schooling with a desire to be unencumbered by school communication. After a series of letters and phone calls about how their child has cried again on the playground, loitered in the rest room, or forgotten another library book, parents can easily begin to equate the teacher's voice with bad news. Furthermore, since many parents do not have happy memories of their own school days, the teacher-parent link is often tenuous at best. Building a relationship between parents and teachers means that they must articulate a shared caring for the child, despite any feelings of distrust and fear. Ways to include parents in the learning community can include:

- Make initial phone calls to each student's home within the first few weeks of school. Introduce yourself and discuss with each parent one genuinely positive observation about the child.
- Continue making these phone calls with positive messages throughout the school year.
- Try to attend co-curricular activities, like drama presentations or sporting events, where you know your students will be performing. Seeing you at their child's activity will go a long way toward building rapport with parents.
- When a problem does arise, approach parents with an attitude that says, "We both care about this child. What can we do to work through this problem?"
- Involve parents in classroom projects. Invite them to the classroom for special events like book fairs or drama readings.
- Parents do not necessarily stop caring about what their children are doing in school when the students leave elementary school. Keep the junior high and high school doors open to them.

4.   Collaboration between teachers.   That teachers teach in isolation is no surprise. Many educators have responded to the trend of work teams by establishing cooperative learning experiences for their students, yet seldom do they work collaboratively. In an article about teachers becoming team learners, Isaacson and Bamburg (1992) write:

> We are accustomed to defining "learning as an individual phenomenon." The result? Most schools include neither time, structural arrangements, cultural norms, nor a language to promote team learning, and most staff development programs only support the learning of individuals. Beginning teachers are left alone to learn the ropes. Teachers are perceived as really working only when they are supervising students. (p. 43)

When teachers talk to one another about their community-building endeavors, they can better examine and expand their thinking and behavior. Such teacher-to-teacher collaborative activities can include:

- Establish brown-bag lunch sessions. Over lunch work with a small group of fellow teachers who are interested in creating learning communities. Share ideas and concerns. Engage in problem solving. Support one another's ideas.

- Use journal writing as an extension of your group collaboration. Perhaps you and a cohort could focus on community-building in your classrooms and describe in journal entries what is happening as you go about this change in classroom management. Teaching is complex, dynamic, and volatile. Reflective journal writing can freeze this complicated work "long enough to reflect on it and to begin to understand and direct" (Holly, 1989, p. 78).
- Form a study group. Members of such groups usually meet once or twice a month and share articles, books, and videotapes about common interests. Consider using the works of Glasser, Sergiovanni, and others mentioned in this chapter.

Articulating the Classroom's Core Values.   If our classroom management practices are to go through the motions of re-enacting how we were treated as students, what we are doing is worse than a bad habit. How can we expect students to gain meaning from the content we pose when our own behaviors are, at times, meaningless? Centered teachers, as noted in the first chapter, strive for congruency between their beliefs and their values. Achieving this congruency in terms of community-building requires deliberation over core values and the classroom practices that emerge from these values. Such deliberation can evolve from questions like:

- What is important in this classroom? Is it important that students not wear hats? Is it important that all students read the same book? Is it important that a student has a clean desk? Is it important that they want to change seats?
- Is a particular rule really important? Three principles can guide your responses to this question: (a) never set a limit or condition unless you can explain why it is important; (b) overcontrolling a child's behavior results in blind obedience; and (c) an overmonitored child tunes out the teacher.
- What are some mission statements for this classroom? For example, the teacher might say, "This is a place where people help each other."

Establishing a Classroom Covenant.   Creating a community of learners does not occur by imposing rules on a group of strangers. Taking the time to collaborate and communicate about core values leads to agreements among community members. **Covenants** are "solemn and binding agreements between two or more parties that provide reciprocal rights, duties, and obligations on the one hand, and guidelines for action, on the other" (Sergiovanni, 1992, p. 103). The reciprocal rights, duties, and obligations are the core values deliberated early on in the community-building stages. Guidelines on action become the agreed-upon ways of establishing a humanistic environment, i.e., a classroom in which constructivist learning qualities can flourish. Establishing a classroom covenant, then, is really articulating aloud and on paper how the community's core values will be demonstrated. Some possible elements of a classroom covenant are:

- It makes sense to ask for help.
- We can each learn at our own rates.

Maintaining the Co-Constructed Covenant.   Maintaining the classroom-community covenant may involve new learning for the students, and, quite possibly, for the teacher. As in all new learning, mistakes will be made and the temptation to return to old ways will be great. What will you do in your learning community when an argument breaks out between two students or when a student behaves rudely to you? Some recommendations for maintaining the covenant come from Sergiovanni (1992):

- *Say it*. Communicate the community's core values clearly and often to inside and outside constituencies.
- *Model it*. Act on these core values. When it comes time to make tough choices and consider trade-offs, make it clear that the core values drive the final decisions.
- *Organize for it*. Put in resources to support the core values. Organize incentives and rewards for students whose actions exemplify a commitment to core values.
- *Support it*. Provide additional resources that promote core values. For instance, when mapping out a curriculum, base decisions on which core values to leave in and which to leave out.
- *Enforce it and commend practices that exemplify core values*. Embody core values in student evaluations.
- *Express outrage when practices violate the core values*. Outrage is a powerful form of communication. Outrage tells people what is important. (p. 74)

Reviewing the Classroom Covenant.   Master teachers know that returning to past lessons helps ensure student mastery. Known as *intermittent scheduling* or *spiral teaching*, this process means that old learnings are often incorporated into new lessons or even stand on their own critical reviews. Reviewing the classroom covenant can take several forms:

- Ask students to keep a response journal on their experiences with the classroom covenant. Guiding questions for this journal assignment could be: "How is the covenant article about cooperation working for you in our classroom?" and "In what ways could our class improve on its agreement about open communication?"
- Videotape the classroom often enough so students and you are comfortable with the camera running. Show occasional clips of a class session and invite comments about how the covenant is working or not working.
- Use surveys. Ask students to comment about parts of the covenant. Encourage honesty and suggestions.

Observing Community-Building

As a classroom of learners evolves into a community, a number of changes will occur, some subtle and some not so subtle. In the same way a teacher can observe the academic development of a child or group of children, the teacher can observe the development of community-building behaviors and attitudes. Critical observation requires conscious attention. Ways to focus attention on behaviors and attitudes that promote and denote community-building can include:

1.   Honestly assess who is involved in the learning process. Invite a peer to observe a lesson and record evidence of student participation (e.g., using tally marks to note running dialogue between students or indications of nonverbal engagement).

Ask students to complete a one-minute summary of the lesson. For one minute, students write down what they learned in the lesson or how they felt about the lesson or even how they performed during the lesson.

Analyze a videotape of your lesson. Look for student involvement, amount of teacher talk, and student-to-student interactions.

2.   At regular intervals, stop teaching content so you can discuss the classroom environment. Invite students to respond to these questions: What is working in our classroom? Who is in control here? How are we changing? Is what we are doing here different? In what ways?

3.   During a management predicament, such as an argument among students or a conflict between teacher and student, try to focus on both intervention strategies and student involvement. Watch to see if other students involve themselves in a positive way to diffuse the situation. Do other students try to calm down a classmate who is upset? Do any students try to calm you down? Does the event result in a power-over situation or a power-with situation?

4.   At regular intervals ask students to write down their reflections on the development of their self-control. Student writing can be a good indication of growth and help you determine not only their mastery of content matter and writing skills but changes in attitudes as well.

5.   Talk with the students' parents about your questions and concerns as well as about your positive insights. Parents can provide valuable information about the students in your classroom.

Reflecting on Community-Building

Observing and reflecting on the community-building protocol are not two distinct steps in a process. Observation leads to reflection when teachers internalize what they have observed. Many classroom teachers utilize both formal and informal means of reflection.

Formal Reflection Activities.   Some examples of formal activities you may use to reflect on your teaching are:

- *Journals*. Start a journal to record your insights, concerns, and questions about the classroom community, the covenant, and individual students. Focusing on the singular aspect of classroom community can lead to a greater sense of clarity and direction.
- *Shared journals*. You and a fellow teacher in your school may have a common interest in the classroom community. Sharing your reflections by reading each other's journals can be most insightful.
- *Teacher support groups*. Teachers need support as they struggle with any new practice. Form a group where you have a setting of mutual support to share your reflections as your classroom becomes a community of learners.

Informal Reflection Activities.   Typical questions that float through teachers' heads as they enter the classroom can include:

How shall I set this lesson? How many students did their homework? What should I do if a certain student is absent today?

Teachers may instead want to center their thinking and feeling on the sense of community in the classroom. Questions that can guide the teacher to a position of centeredness may include:

How would I like this classroom to feel today? What parts of the lesson may lead to confusion or frustration for the students? What do I know about various students that can help them work peacefully today?

CRITICAL INCIDENT

Creating a Classroom Learning Community

Janice Hutchison

BACKGROUND

Teaching teenagers has been part of Janice Kridler's life for nearly twenty years. For the first few years of her career, she was a Title I reading teacher in a state institution for incarcerated young men. During that time, what crystallized for this young educator was the belief that teaching is both a science and an art. According to Janice, the science of teaching is "more or less the intellectual aspect of teaching children. I would never discount the many lessons I have learned both in university courses and from my own readings. However, I've seen too many teachers, especially at the secondary level, who confuse knowledge of subject matter with good teaching." Janice feels that teachers can and should achieve a balance between the science of teaching, or the technical aspects of instructional design, and delivery by having an aesthetic sense of what good teaching is about. Asked how a class-

room teacher develops artistry, Janice responded, "By listening to her heart." The critical incident that follows focuses on this teacher doing just that—displaying a mastery of techniques and listening to her heart while she builds a classroom learning community in a public high school English class.

THE INCIDENT

My freshman English classes have an intriguing mix of teen-agers. The majority of my students are ninth-graders who have been identified by the school psychologist and the middle school staff as "at-risk." I realize that this designation offends some people. At times, particularly as I get to know these adolescents, I am also offended by such a description. I've also come to believe that a risk for all students is being badgered by a system that seldom tries to connect with them.

I decided several years ago to use the term *at-risk* as a course opener. During our first few days together in the fall, for example, I usually tell the students that they have been identified as being at-risk. We talk about that label in terms of "at-risk of what." Usually the students fill in the blank with phrases like "dropping out of school," "failing," and "getting in trouble."

I don't like to hide behind smoke screens. I help students understand from the beginning that watering down the curriculum and padding grades are practices that can defeat them. From the first week on, part of our conversations will focus on how to reduce the risk of their not doing quality work.

About three-fourths of the students enrolled in my classes are those at-risk ninth-graders. The rest of the students are mainstream special education students and older students who previously failed the course. The special education students have Individual Education Plans with a variety of labels—learning disability, developmental handicap, severe-behavior handicap. The school psychologist and the special education teachers request student placement in my classroom. The main reason for this tradition is the reputation of my classes as "places where people belong."

The fact that I began my teaching career in a prison setting is definitely unusual and probably contributes to the kind of classroom manager I am today. I learned early not to take student behavior personally. In my current position I work as a mentor to beginning teachers, and I notice how common it is for these novices to personalize the negative behaviors of students. I think that attachment to external forces is emotionally and spiritually draining. In my own classroom, I try to stay centered and calm. When a student erupts in anger, for instance, I strive to stay detached. I believe very deeply that two very strong emotions are present in human behavior—love and fear. I do not like to contribute to student fear nor do I like to increase the anxiety level in the classroom by "losing it."

Recently, a new freshman, Summer, came into my classroom midway through the school year. She had been enrolled in another English class and had failed the entire semester. She turned in little, if any, work and became increasingly disruptive in that class and verbally abusive to the teacher. School administrators told her that my class was "a last-ditch effort."

My plan for Summer's inclusion in the classroom is typical of most of my community-building plans. I tend to let students select their own seating and work partners. I don't give a list of rules. Instead, I watch and listen. I try to focus on new students to get to know their moods, comments, interests. I watch really closely for nonverbal cues.

The first few weeks in the class were Summer's honeymoon period. By that I mean that she stayed calm and turned in her work regularly. The only disruption during our first month together occurred when I called on her to define a new vocabulary word. She curtly responded, "I didn't have my hand up."

Teacher:	Neither did I. That's the beauty if it. You never know when the spotlight will be on you.
Summer:	I have the right not to participate.
Teacher:	Good point. Let's talk about the rights of people in this room. Any comments? Summer is responding to my calling on her without her hand up and has expressed that she has the right not to participate.
Patrick:	You probably feel like Mrs. K. put you on the spot. I used to feel like that, but that's not what this is about. Yeah, you got the right not to participate but you also have a responsibility to try.
Shanna:	Yeah. It's not like most classes, here. If you're wrong, at least you're trying. People will help you.

Summer ended the dialogue with a classic student comment: "You're weird, Mrs. K."

By the sixth week of the term, the quantity and quality of Summer's work had diminished noticeably. I regularly begin each class by taking attendance and reminding each student what assignments are due. One day I commented to Summer that she had not completed several assignments, and I asked if she needed a little help with organization.

Summer:	No. I need a little help with my housework.
Teacher:	I'd like to have a talk with you about it when you're ready.
Summer:	Yeah, right.
Anita:	Oh, go ahead, Summer. You can tell her.
Summer:	Two weeks ago my Mom got busted for selling crack. She's in jail now, and I'm having to do all the grocery shopping, cooking, cleaning, laundry, and I can't get my head right.
Teacher:	That's a lot of work, Summer. I wish I could lighten your load at home but I can't. I am willing to work out a deal with you, though. When it comes to your English assignment, what can I do to help you?
Summer:	I can't keep track of the assignments. It's like my head's swimming all the time.
Teacher:	Okay. I can make a list of just your assignments in English. I can't let you off doing the work.
Summer:	I'll do it. For another week, though, till my older brother gets out of jail, can I turn in my assignments late—like no more than three days?

> Teacher: Yes, that'll work. Use my mailbox after your study hall so you don't lose any papers.

That negotiation worked out well. Summer completed every assignment and did a bonus project. I have noticed recently how quickly she detects subtle nuances of humor in class literature, too.

I wanted to gather a little more information about Summer's development so I contacted her uncle, the only adult who maintains personal contact with her and her siblings. He shared with me that his main concern about Summer was her need for a female adult in her life. In considering that need, I decided to extend my contact time with Summer. We began to meet occasionally during my planning time and her study hall to talk about clothes, her friends, and my family.

Recently I asked Summer to explain in her journal why she has succeeded in our classroom after she failed or was removed from her other classes. This is what she wrote:

> The reason I'm succeeding so well in your English class is because you don't act like you don't have time to know me as a person and not just a student. When a teacher who doesn't know me gives me some bad vibes, I give them right back, and that was the problem with Miss R. When I got into your class you didn't do that to me. You gave me a chance and I thank you for that.
>
> A lot of kids in our class have changed their behavior because we're not only students or classmates but everyone in our English class has a bond. We all relate to each other's problems, and that is what keeps us going.

After observing Summer, observing myself, and gathering her uncle's and her own observations about her immersion in the classroom, I came to see a person in fuller dimensions. Too often students can remain flat figures to us. If I expect students to make connections in the classroom, connect past learning with new learning, connect with each other, and connect with me, I have to pry open some doors.

Teacher-Character Advice

Johnny Jackson

I think this model of classroom community-building is ideal. It makes students self-disciplined and moves them toward the goal of uncovering the natural world order. Being able to articulate core values and having opportunities to collaborate will help students—and teachers too—see how community is possible. I am excited about the possibilities. Let me elaborate.

There is a structure underlying each classroom subject that can help counteract the disorder prevalent in many children's lives. Through a classroom community, students can follow an academic order necessary for a good learning environment. All children need to have a place where they can find the peace and tranquility necessary for learning and thinking.

It is essential that our modern youngsters become grounded in our cultural heritage and begin to use great people and great ideas as their models for self-discipline. The mental challenge of deep intellectual pursuit immerses students of all ages in the universal activities that constitute our humanity. This is especially important in a community that practices the ethic of caring and values the humanness of colleagues.

This mental challenge must be developmentally facilitated. Teachers can turn to Piaget for guidance in helping students construct moral knowledge for themselves. This great philosopher identified the stages of intellectual and moral growth. He hypothesized that our mental structures grow step-by-step through the complex processes of assimilation and accommodation. Teachers facilitate these processes by providing students with concrete experiences. When we talk about classroom management—even the term *management* sounds too impersonal and mechanistic—we are really talking about how students progressively learn to work with and get along with others. Teachers have to design the classroom to encourage students to construct their own knowledge about what it takes to live ethically in society. The only way to get to higher levels of both knowledge and moral action is to actively engage in learning and the pursuit of knowledge. Likewise, to reach higher levels of moral reasoning, students must have opportunities to interact with others in ways that are more advanced morally.

How do I envision this happening in a classroom? The answer is through a developmentally aware, discipline-based curriculum. Content areas such as literature and social studies offer wonderful opportunities to exercise moral reasoning. A great literary work such as Shakespeare's *Julius Caesar* can stimulate discussion about correct behavior, set behavior goals, and model the purest and best ways to act. The character of Atticus Finch in the novel *To Kill a Mockingbird* can teach a student a lot about having respect for other human beings and acting in moral and courageous ways. Adler's (1981) *Six Great Ideas* deals directly with the concepts of democracy and justice. Of course, the curriculum has to be set up to engage students and allow them to develop cognitively, expand their horizons, see other perspectives, and be critically aware. Playing a board game can help students see other points of view and practice critical thinking skills as they interpret and apply rules and develop playing strategies. Finding and using different means to help students actively confront their moral and intellectual growth is an imaginative challenge for the classroom teacher.

Modeling encourages students' developmental processes. If you engage in problem solving as the teacher, encourage students to do the same. Make it part of every activity. Teachers have to read about and have respect for our traditions. The values underlying a classroom covenant must include love of knowledge and respect for beauty and culture. Some recitation and memorization may be necessary, but problem solving and thoughtfulness should predominate. Griffin (1989) advises teachers to establish "expectations for learning that lead to problem solving rather than recall and recitation as disposition and habit" (p. 280). Those expectations must be built into the classroom covenant. For example, if students are coming into class late, tell them, "We have a problem here. What can we do about it?" Give them the chance to work with complex problems and come up with different solutions. Point out situations in which students can practice problem-solving skills with your assistance.

As I stated in the beginning of my discourse, biographies of people like Thomas Jefferson help students appreciate the importance of the democratic tradition, both throughout our history and right now in our classroom. High school students need to read and discuss biographies of great and famous people, such as Frank Lloyd Wright or Franklin D. Roosevelt. Discuss how they developed their talents, how they affected people, and what kinds of contributions they have made to our society. Help students construct knowledge not only about the world but also about how they will act in it and upon it.

I'm going to illustrate how I would use the four-phase process for community-building. Let's say that two students begin to fight in the classroom. I know right away that this behavior violates the core values of the community. I would take immediate action to stop it and remind the students of the expectation that they should not hurt anyone in the classroom. I would then take time to collaborate with the two students on how this fighting problem should be handled. As part of this teacher-student collaboration, I would ask the students to prepare a report on a great person who has exhibited self-control during his or her life. These reports would be presented orally in class as part of a general discussion on the value of self-control. After the class discussions, I would meet privately with both students to review what they have learned from this disciplinary exercise.

Amy Nelson

I like this model of classroom community-building because it recognizes the importance of self-discipline. The emphasis on identifying core values is a good example of how to set priorities for success. To be effective you must plan ahead, anticipate possible dangers, and act before students are negatively impacted.

At a workshop on classroom management with Dr. Madeline Hunter, I heard her say that the best way to prevent discipline problems is to teach masterfully. This is no mystery. The goal of the classroom should be to have students learning, being "on task." We have all seen enough chaotic classrooms to know that learning and democracy require a well-ordered environment.

To use a business metaphor, the classroom is a dynamic management system that requires the teacher's full-time attention. Many factors enter into the complex picture, including the teacher's role, the student's role, lesson content, and classroom arrangement. Students can have input, but the teacher is responsible for enforcing rules and consequences. Effective leaders set and communicate clear expectations and standards. This furthers democratic values. The norms for our society are presented in a way that students, our future citizens, can understand and follow.

Teachers need to plan for and anticipate behavior problems just as they plan for lessons. They should consider students' abilities, content, grouping, and other factors that affect learning when making the daily schedule. Experienced teachers know that the first three weeks of the school year are the crucial times for teaching students how to conform to classroom rules and regulations. As much as possible, students should be taught the classroom community's rules and values through positive reinforcement. At intermittent times when an individual student, group of students, or the entire class is behaving correctly, the teacher can congratulate them on their good conduct. The teacher should create as positive and trusting an environment as possible. Only when rules are broken, and only after clearly stated warnings, should teachers resort to punishments. These punishments should be selected primarily for their instructional value. Remember, the overall goal is to provide classroom community leadership to immature citizens, not to control wayward students.

For example, if a student is continuously talking out of turn, the teacher might ask a parent to help teach the child a lesson by taking away a half hour of television-viewing time when the child interrupts a family member. The teacher might take away five minutes of recess time when the infraction occurs in school. Once the behavior improves, the punishment is stopped. The child has learned a valuable lesson about human communication—perhaps more valuable than a successfully completed reading or math exercise.

The teacher is responsible for overseeing the socialization of students into the system and being aware of how all the components work together to establish a positive and effective learning environment. The role of the teacher as a dynamic classroom leader is really about being an efficient classroom manager. The classroom can be a mini-democracy, but the focus should be on those factors that research has proven effective in promoting students' learning achievements and their ability to make empirically based judgments. Unless students achieve, are literate, and practice self-control, our democracy has no future.

I would like to use this chapter's protocol to outline how I would deal with the problem Johnny talked about, a fight in the classroom between two students. I agree that this behavior violates classroom values and must be stopped immediately. But I view the cause as something else. These two kids are not on task; if they were, they probably wouldn't be fighting. The issue is getting them to do their work and clarifying expectations. I would act by walking around the room more often to monitor their work. I might place one of these students close to my desk. Periodically, I would ask the class questions about the work to make sure they understand it well enough to be able to do it independently at home. From time to time, I would also remind the class of our covenant to be an efficient learning community. I might enforce the rule for no disruptions—and this fighting example is such a disruption—by calling the two students' parents to tell them that conflict is not tolerated in my room under any circumstances. I might tell them that the next violation of this value would require a face-to-face conference. In my teaching I practice what Madeline Hunter termed *monitor and adjust*: I often stop to reflect on what and how my students are learning and make changes accordingly. I am beginning to apply the same principle to classroom management.

My view of the classroom seems quite popular, and there are many good books about classroom management. Most books about classroom discipline, especially books about assertive discipline and effective teaching practices, will also help you learn more about the management approach to classroom community-building.

Dennis Sage

This model of classroom community-building works because it addresses people's basic need for recognition of their individuality while showing them the importance of mutual respect and care. Although I tend to reject protocols, the openendedness of this approach allows me to use the ideas that make sense to me, reflecting my own personal values.

Let me begin by stating what I think is important. The best life is the contemplative life in which one constantly considers democratic values and how to treat other human beings with respect. I am not surprised that so many students are hyperactive in the classroom. The pace is unbearable. Students have no time to just sit and think and be alone. Young people seem like they are so wound up that they are on the verge of breaking apart. You have to calm down, slow down, and tune in to your feelings and other's feelings. Ignoring the contemplative nature of human beings is courting disaster. I just hate the feelings of tension, stress, and anxiety I get when I walk into most classrooms. If you take the time to notice, you can feel it.

In a healthy classroom a flow or an energy moves the teacher and the students to the teachable moment when there is that click of understanding. Everyone has experienced it. When that happens, it makes the job of teaching totally worthwhile. It's what a teacher works for. That's what classroom management is all about: getting to that moment.

How do you get control of kids? Your whole being is there with them. You are present in a real way. There is no pretend acting, and you tune in to the real kids in front of you. You encourage them to be there for you and for each other as well. You need to make time for students to think, be alone, be concerned and caring for each other. Give them time to simply talk about what's important to them, to encourage sharing with and even expressing love for each other.

A teacher needs a certain kind of wisdom to know about children and young adults, to know about content, and to capture all the elements that create a positive environment conducive to learning. When students come to trust the adult in the classroom, they no longer have to act out to get attention. They get into the flow, the rhythm of the group.

The school itself presents the greatest obstructions to establishing a positive learning community. So much time and energy are lost for paperwork and frequent interruptions, time and energy a teacher desperately needs to establish relationships with young people and with other adults in the building as well. We have to look at teaching and discipline holistically. van Manen (1991) notes that the term *discipline* comes from the word *disciple*, which means someone who follows a great teacher. Teachers must be able to inspire their students. Through sensitive, caring interactions the teacher models what it is like to be a member of a trusting social community. When students feel a desire to be like their teacher, whom they see as kind and concerned about others, then the teacher has succeeded in establishing a positive leadership presence. Then the students are learning appropriate conduct in the most concrete way, through positive adult example.

As a professional you need to develop your most nurturing, loving skills to have a significant impact on students of every age. You have to be thoughtful and caring. You have to be in touch with yourself through meditation, support groups, or perhaps through a relationship with nature. Find these qualities of empathy, sympathy, kindness, patience, and love of young people, and continue to develop them. This can only happen in a free, open classroom in which students and teacher make important decisions together democratically.

Using the example of a classroom disruption that Johnny and Amy talked about, I would like to explain how I would handle the situation. If two students were fighting in class, I would, of course, consider this a violation of the classroom covenant and stop it immediately. But then I might determine that the cause for this altercation is the frenzied pace of the school day and the tremendous pressure children feel to produce. That would lead me to give the student quiet "meditation breaks" to collect their thoughts and reduce their anxiety levels. Maybe I would have students gather in small support groups so they could talk to one another about their problems and renew their commitment to the classroom covenant—with perhaps some revisions. I would not see this as taking time away from their studies. Instead I would expect the experience to enhance their studies. Finally, I would remind students of their ongoing responsibility to be the very best people they can be.

Silvia Rivera

Although I generally find protocols to be simplistic and naive, I like this approach to classroom community-building because it recognizes and respects the fact that schools and classrooms don't exist in a vacuum. Rather they are set in a complex social context where attempting to find easy solutions to complicated problems is ethically untenable.

Problems in the classroom are tied to problems outside in the community. Unfairness and injustice are rampant in our world. Just using external control to get kids to blindly follow authority doesn't work in the long run. Look at totalitarian governments. You can't control people forever. That goes for school as well as society. As Kohn (1990) says, "There aren't enough M&Ms to keep people on track, to manipulate behavior once they leave the high-surveillance school setting" (p. 53).

The aim of education is to encourage students to be proactive, to change society, to make a difference. They need to know about discrimination in terms of class, race, gender, socioeconomic status, and religion. We should regard schooling as preparation not merely for living in the existing social order, but for taking action to improve the social order. Wood (1988) notes that "primary to any sense of democratic life is the notion that individuals are free to remake the social order in ways that best suit collective needs" (p. 166). In other words, we live in a fluid society; how and what changes are made are determined by its citizens. The task before the school is to empower these future citizens, these future change-makers. That is another reason why I think this leadership model based on a democratic society is right on target.

The curriculum, what we teach and how we teach it, is laden with values. Did you ever think about who decides what's important to teach? There is no list of right things to teach. Decisions about the curriculum are made by teachers, and we teachers must constantly consider how we can make the classroom promote democracy.

One way is to have students become empowered decision-makers in the classroom. Wood (1988) says, "When individuals participate in decisions that directly affect them, they both develop the confidence that such action is possible as well as the desire to participate in even broader public debates" (p. 180). What kinds of decisions can students make? Choosing reading materials, room decorations, or room management are a few examples. Right now certain views of discipline prohibit students from becoming empowered decision-makers. In behavior modification, for example, the teacher stipulates rules and punishments, and the students follow blindly.

The notion of lifelong learning has to become part of the world view of teachers and students. The walls of the school classroom vanish as we see education as a part of daily living. I never let school get in the way of education. We have to be constantly aware that academic goals, such as learning to read and write, also help students participate in the larger society, both during their school years and after they leave.

The classroom needs to offer students both personal power and the skills necessary to participate in a collaborative and cooperative environment. In a real way students of all ages can take responsibility for doing relevant, useful work and for deciding on the consequences for not doing it. Students can investigate books in all content areas to check for racist, sexist, and other biased language. Contemporary social problems provide a wealth of opportunities for discussion and problem solving. Students can address injustice and inequity within the school and work on projects that involve the greater good of society as a whole. All this encourages students to become and remain dedicated opponents of injustice and inequity.

I would like to comment on how I would respond to the problem of two students fighting in the classroom. I have to agree with my colleagues in recognizing this as a problem and stopping it before someone gets hurt. But I believe the cause of the problem lies elsewhere. The lives of these two students probably seem very unrelated to the classroom. The way they solve problems in their own lives is probably closer to fighting than to the norms of the classroom community. People respond in ways that are familiar, not necessarily in ways that are the most reasonable. I would have the class meet as a decision-making body to deal directly with the problem of fighting in the classroom. What would they suggest be done? I would let them determine the consequences. Then I would feel responsible for setting up an environment that is safe enough for these young people to take intellectual, emotional, and physical chances. I would reconsider how I could provide a safe haven for students so they could really internalize these norms and work on self-discipline.

FURTHER READINGS

Brandt, R. S. (Ed.). (1990). Student success [Special issue]. *Educational Leadership*, *48*(1), pp. 3–77. (This special issue on "student success" describes several community-building practices.)

Glasser, W. (1993). *The quality school teacher: A companion volume to the quality school.* New York: Harper Perennial.

Gossen, D. C. (1993). *Restitution: Restructuring school discipline.* Chapel Hill: New View.

Peck, M. S. (1993). *A world waiting to be born: Civility rediscovered.* New York: Bantam Books.

Pilon, G. H. (1991). *The workshop way.* New Orleans: The Workshop Way.

Senge, P. (1990). *The fifth discipline: The art and practice of the learning organization.* New York: Doubleday Currency.

Sergiovanni, T. J. (1994). *Building communities in schools.* San Francisco: Jossey-Bass.

REFERENCES

Adler, M. (1981). *Six great ideas.* New York: Macmillan.

Dewey, J. (1933). *How we think: A restatement of the relation of reflective thinking to the educative process* (2nd ed.). Boston: D. C. Heath. (Original work published 1910)

Glasser, W. (1992). *The quality schools managing students without coercion.* New York: Harper Perennial.

Griffin, G. (1989). Coda: The knowledge-driven school. In M. C. Reynolds (Ed.), *Knowledge base for the beginning teacher* (pp. 277–286). Oxford: Pergamon Press.

Holly, M. L. (1989). Reflective writing and the spirit of inquiry. *Cambridge Journal of Education*, *19*, 71–80.

Isaacson, N., & Bamburg, J. (1992). Can schools become learning organizations? *Educational Leadership*, *50*, 42–44.

Johnson, D., Johnson, R., & Holubec, E. J. (1984). Circles of learning. Edina, MN: Interaction.

Kohn, A. (1990). The ABC's of caring. *Teacher*, *1*(4), 52–58.

Kreisberg, S. (1992). *Transforming power: Domination, empowerment, and education*. Albany: SUNY Press.

Lewin, K. (1948). *Resolving social conflicts*. New York: Harper and Brothers.

Sergiovanni, T. J. (1992). *Moral leadership: Getting to the heart of school improvement*. San Francisco: Jossey-Bass.

van Manen, M. (1991). *The tact of teaching: The meaning of pedagogical thoughtfulness*. Albany, NY: State University of New York Press.

Wood, G. H. (1988). Democracy and education. In L. E. Beyer & M. W. Apple (Eds.), *The curriculum: Problems, politics, and possibilities* (pp. 166–185). Albany, NY: State University of New York Press.

3

Fundamental Topics

This section will introduce three fundamental topics related to the career-long study of your constructivist practices. Chapter 7 provides an elaboration on the four teaching virtues associated with educational constructivism that we introduced in chapter 1. The teacher-characters provide ideological commentary on each virtue, and two experienced teachers use the four virtues to critically examine their teaching. Chapter 8 presents a discussion of five forms of collaboration that teachers can employ to support one another's personal-professional development. Chapter 9, the final chapter of the book, offers a vision of a professional future where transformative teacher leaders help schools become learning communities. The key characteristics of transformative teacher leadership are discussed. Teachers who are successful in this new informal, collaborative role will have provided an important service. They will have assisted in the creation of schools as centers of inquiry.

4C Scaffolding: A Critical Examination of Constructivist Practices

In this chapter, you will have the opportunity to further refine your understanding of the study method in this book. In chapter 1, you read that this method involves three types of reflection: pragmatic reconsideration, critical reasoning, and critical engagement. The general protocols in chapters 3–6, which are applications of the decision-making cycle, are designed to facilitate your pragmatic reflection. The teacher-character commentary that follows each protocol is created to assist your critical reasoning and critical engagement. You will now learn how to reflect on your constructivist practices from a particular value-based or normative point of view: *constructivist teaching is a Calling and is Creative, Caring, and Centered work*. Since the four descriptors in this italicized statement all begin with the letter "C," they are called the 4C virtues. The guide to professional inquiry that we present in this chapter based on these virtues is called **4C scaffolding**. In effect, this scaffolding provides a particular type of metacognitive guidance for the critical examination of constructivist practices.

This chapter's metacognitive guidance will be presented in the following way. The rationale for creating the 4C scaffolding is presented first, followed by a general description of each normative referent. The teacher-characters will then comment on the four teaching virtues. After a brief introduction to autobiographical reflection, you will read the professional developmental stories of two experienced teachers who have used the 4C scaffolding to study their evolving constructivist practices. Finally, you will receive advice on how you can use the scaffolding to reflect on your personal-professional development.

Why the 4C Scaffolding Was Created

The 4C virtues are important referents for the study of your constructivist practices. Think for a moment about this type of educational service. If teachers approach their work as just an "eight-to-three job with summers off," will they be willing to assume the challenges associated with teaching for active understanding? Why should they bother with the cultivation of a constructivist repertoire? Why should they become accomplished at the four practices covered in chapters 3–6? After all, it is demanding work to solve complex problems in a constructivist way, create a constructivist curriculum design, enact constructivist transactions, and create a classroom learning community. To reflect on teaching as a **calling** is to contemplate the personal issues of motivation that are germane to the practice of educational constructivism.

Educational constructivism, however, requires more than dedicated work. This type of educational service challenges teachers to function as **caring** professionals. If teachers don't care about their students as unique individuals, how can they understand them well enough to provide constructivist services? How can they discover links between their students' prior knowledge and dispositions, their personal purposes, and the requirements for subject matter inquiry?

Educational constructivism also challenges teachers to be **creative** professionals. Reflect again on the four practices covered in chapters 3 through 6. They are not simple technical procedures; they can't be followed in a step-by-step, paint-by-number fashion. They must be enacted with imagination.

Finally, consider what happens to teachers who consistently reflect on their work. By continuously engaging in the decision-making cycle, they become seasoned pragmatic learners. Through the consistent critical examination of their teaching decisions, they consolidate and refine the justifications and inspirations that guide their educational work. They come to know themselves as professional educators. In short, they become **centered** teachers.

A General Description of the 4C Referents

To facilitate your own personalized understanding of teaching as a Calling and as Caring, Creative, and Centered work, a general description of each value-laden term will now be presented. The four teacher-characters will then offer distinctive commentary on the 4Cs.

Calling

Many teachers approach their work as a calling, not as a job. Ayers (1993) notes that present and future teachers are often asked why they have chosen such a low-paying, low-status occupation: "Teachers are asked hundreds, perhaps thousands of times why they chose teaching. The question often means: 'Why teach, when you could do something more profitable?' 'Why teach, since teaching is beneath your skill and intelligence?'" (p. 5). He lists many practical reasons for such skeptical questions: teachers are poorly paid, they are disempowered, they work under stressful conditions. Ayers celebrates the fact that, despite these vocational drawbacks, many teachers persist in perceiving their work as a calling:

> Teaching is still a powerful calling for many people, and powerful for the same reasons that it has always been so. There are still young people who need a thoughtful, caring adult in their lives; someone who can nurture and challenge them, who can coach and guide, understand and care about them. There are still injustices and deficiencies in society, in even more desperate need of repair. There are still worlds to change—including specific, individual worlds. (p. 8)

Garman (1986) adds to Ayers' list of inspirations for choosing to be a teacher with an eloquent description of the educational profession:

> Teaching is the most venerable practice we have universally experienced. Beyond our experiential worlds we harbor mysterious remnants of mythic teachers (Plato, Socrates, Jesus, Buddha). There are aspects of teaching which can be thought of as consecrated—made hallow by the ancient belief that teaching embodies devotion to service. Those who serve are reverently dedicated to their charge, and are themselves to be regarded with reverence. (p. 10)

Teachers can feel inspired about their chosen profession in diverse ways. Whatever form it takes, teachers who possess a sense of calling about their chosen career are hard-working, dedicated professionals. Their work ethic is an important prerequisite for undertaking the challenges of educational constructivism.

Caring

To care as a teacher is to be ethically bound to understand one's students. Noddings (1984) writes that when a caring teacher "asks a question in class and a student responds, she [sic] receives not just the 'response' but the student. What he [sic] says matters, whether it is right or wrong, and she probes gently for clarification, interpretation, contribution" (p. 176).

Noddings (1984) presents three important features of an ethic of caring: confirmation, dialogue, and cooperative practice. She writes:

> When we attribute the best possible motive consonant with reality to the cared-for, we confirm him [sic]; that is, we reveal to him an attainable image of himself that is lovelier than that manifested in his present acts. (p. 193)

> Confirmation, the loveliest of human functions, depends upon and interacts with dialogue and practice. I cannot confirm a child unless I talk with him and engage in cooperative practice with him. (p. 196)

When confirming a student, the teacher sees "the cared-for as he is and as he might be—as he envisions his best self" (Noddings, 1984, p. 67). To become sensitive to the "best self" of each student, a teacher must take time to listen carefully to each student's innermost yearnings. One student may want to become a mathematician, another an auto mechanic, and a third a writer of Hollywood movie scripts. The caring teacher takes the time to help all students discover their individual inclinations and capitalize on them.

Dialogue is the second feature of an ethic of caring. Teachers can't confirm their students if they don't take time to talk to them. They must seek opportunities to engage in open and honest communication.

Caring teachers must also be cooperative educators. Teachers guided by an ethic of caring understand that they can't practice personal confirmation and honest dialogue unless they work cooperatively with their students as well as the students' parents. Caring teachers must think of themselves as facilitators of learning, as "counselors and advisors in their subject fields and not just as imparters of knowledge" (Noddings, 1984, p. 187).

Creativity

Creativity refers to a teacher's flexible, imaginative, and intuitive capabilities. Creative teachers constantly seek new ways to motivate their students. They want their lessons to be aesthetically enjoyable, provocative, and meaningful. Eisner (1994) writes:

> Teaching can be done as badly as anything else. It can be wooden, mechanical, mindless, and wholly unimaginative. But when it is sensitive, intelligent, and creative—those qualities that confer upon it the status of an art—it should, in my view, not be regarded, as it so often is by some, as an expression of unfathomable talent or luck but as an example of humans exercising the highest levels of their intelligence. (p. 156)

Based on extensive interviews with teachers on the topic of creative teaching, Jagla (1994) stresses the importance of imagination and intuition in creative work:

> The use of one's imagination and the use of one's intuition overlap to a great extent. However, I feel that it is . . . imagination that one uses to plan curriculum for the classroom, and it is . . . intuition that one uses to implement the curriculum. (p. 20)

> [One of the teachers I interviewed stated:] "Intuition is what we use that enables us to trust what our imagination dishes up for us. Intuition is the enabler. Imagination is what is enabled." (p. 39)

Jagla (1994) refines this discussion by identifying a complex tapestry of themes woven into the fabric of imaginative and intuitive teaching. Creative teachers are spontaneous, open, confident, empathetic, knowledgeable, resourceful, flexible, highly interactive, good storytellers, and emotive.

Centered

Centered teachers are not people who rigidly cling to beliefs. They operate instead on the basis of deliberate moral choice. They willingly question their own opinions. Through continuous pragmatic reflection and critical examination, they cultivate a solid framework for their actions. Their teaching decisions are carefully informed and thoughtfully enacted.

Centered teachers are authentic. They have learned "to love the questions, as they come to realize that there are no final agreements, no final commensurability" (Greene, 1988, p. 134). They welcome civil argument and debate, and they understand that people often possess conflicting opinions on a complex issue. Therefore, they are not interested in playing one-upmanship social games. They believe that no one has cornered the market on truth. They welcome clarification and reject obfuscation. They prefer open dialogue, and they find concealment and manipulation—qualities associated with all melodramas—to be distasteful.

Centered teachers strive for congruency between the justifications and inspirations for their actions. They are aware of the foundational sources of their practices. Because they continuously engage in the critical examination of their teaching, they are assertive individuals who invite others to be equally assertive.

Teacher-Character Commentary

Johnny Jackson

I feel that I do have a calling for teaching, and I am saddened by many of my colleagues who think of their work as an eight-to-three job. I love what I do, and I constantly strive to improve myself. I feel fortunate that I have chosen a profession that allows me to be idealistic, not money-grubbing. My mother had a calling for teaching, but she never became a teacher. This always frustrated her. She was a house maid for affluent families in Chicago's Hyde Park neighborhood, and I bet she knew more about the paintings and sculptures she dusted than did many of the owners of these art objects. Whenever I feel frustrated about some educational problem, I remember that I get paid for what my mother could only do voluntarily.

I think caring is an important developmental referent in teaching. However, this concept must be interpreted in the context of subject matter instruction. Teachers are hired to impart content to their students. Therefore, their caring practices must be linked to the specific academic disciplines that ground their work. For high school teachers, these are the subjects they teach. From middle school on down, teachers should be focusing on the prerequisite understandings, skills, and attitudes that prepare their students for future discipline-based learning. A similar argument could be made for other types of professional work. Doctors and nurses care, but their caring must be linked to good health services. Lawyers care, but their caring must be linked to good legal services. And so on. I'm a subject-matter specialist, and I don't believe in child-centered learning that is not disciplined by the structure of academic traditions.

I think instructional creativity is quite important. Teachers confront a TV generation of children who have little exposure to significant intellectual artifacts. While Spanish and French children often take after-school and weekend field trips to learn more about their country's cultural heritage, many American children are "vegging out" in front of their home's omnipresent "tube." They are passive passengers on a trip through superficial television scripts. It takes imagination to find ways to reach them. While introducing myself, I mentioned the English teacher who taught *Julius Caesar* by relating it to a *Star Trek* episode. This is the type of imaginative teaching that I respect. I understand teacher creativity as the ability to establish meaningful links between students' everyday, prosaic worlds and the noble ideas and projects that sustain a civilized, cultured life. I want my students to realize that they can contribute to the creation of a great American civilization.

I strongly believe that teachers and their students should know themselves. They should understand their place as historical participants in Western civilization's Great Conversation. Their home, their "center," is their cultural heritage. Have you ever visited another culture? If you have, you know the feeling of "cultural shock" that comes from confronting alien ways of being. I struggle to be civilized—to not be alienated from the historical foundations of my being, and I do this by reading great books and by attending cultural events. This is the sense of centering that I try to pass on to my students.

Amy Nelson

I am strongly drawn to teaching, and I have discussed my sense of calling with several of our school district's athletic coaches. They derive great satisfaction from helping their athletes learn the value of self-discipline and the joy of personal accomplishment. This is how I approach my work. Just as I take pride in becoming an excellent teacher, I want my students to feel good about their achievements. I've promised myself that if I ever find myself counting down the minutes to the end of a school day, I'll seek out a new career. I'll look for new mountains to climb.

I am a skeptic when it comes to talk about teacher caring. Most teachers will say they care about their students, but what do they mean by that? How do they behave when they say they care? My father has a saying that goes with this skeptical question: "What you are doing is so loud, I can't hear what you're saying!" I am particularly concerned about students' learning achievement. Therefore, when teachers say they care, I want to know how their talk translates into specific student accomplishments. In other words, how do they "walk their talk"? Are they helping their students become successful, hard-working Americans?

I'm a strong advocate of teacher creativity. It takes imagination to design lessons that motivate students to achieve. I don't believe in dull, boring skill workbooks, and I have worked hard to create hands-on activities that are linked to precise performance objectives. I am quite impressed with the ways personal computers can facilitate student achievement, and I continuously struggle to stay current with the new innovations in instructional technology. In fact, I wonder sometimes if I shouldn't take some graduate course work in this field at a local university.

I know myself as a competent professional, and I want my students to be similarly centered. I am at home in my achievements, and I am always proud to share—in a humble manner—what I have accomplished. I take pride in my teaching skill, which results from years of hard work. I feel that too many people have low self-esteem when it comes to what they can achieve. They live lives of quiet desperation because they are on the sidelines; they are mere spectators of others' success. These individuals didn't get the help they needed from caring parents, teachers, and others. I don't want to make a similar mistake, so I do whatever I can to support my students' proactive approach toward life.

Dennis Sage

I am "called" to be with my students—to be attuned to their educational needs. I'm inspired by Aoki's (1992) description of the caring teacher:

All of these scientific and technical understandings of teaching emerge from our interest in intellectual and manipulative grasp and control. But in so understanding, we must be attuned to the fact that while those understandings that can be grasped are uncannily correct, the essence of teaching still eludes our grasp. What we need to do is to break away from the attitude of grasping and seek to be more properly oriented to what teaching is, so we can attune ourselves to the call of what teaching is. . . . I find that teaching so understood is attuned to the place where care dwells, a place of ingathering and belonging, where the in-dwelling of teachers and students is made possible by the presence of care that each has for the other. (pp. 20–21)

As you can see, my understanding of caring teaching is linked to my sense of professional calling. I grow as a caring teacher as I cultivate empathy for my students. When I really feel my students' joys and pains, then I know that I am deepening myself as an educator. If they cry over some educational experience, and I feel their tears, then I know I am learning to care. If I don't have this sense of empathetic connection, I reflect on my lack of sensitivity. Why don't I have more rapport with a particular student? Am I taking the time to get to know this unique soul that is under my educational care? As the old saying goes, am I "walking a mile in that person's shoes"? Have I gotten too task-oriented, too caught up in the business of the day? If so, what can I do to re-center myself as one who cares?

To be connected with my students in a caring way requires a great deal of creativity. Not only must I continuously imagine what they are thinking and feeling, I must envision interesting ways to respond to their existential worlds. Think for a moment about what I just said. Have you ever had a teacher who helped you understand and actualize your educational passions—your purposes for growing as a human being? This is a challenging way to teach and requires flexibility and imagination.

I know myself through my connectedness to others and to the planet that we all call home. When I feel lost or alienated, it is because I have lost my sense of inner union, my sense of oneness. My feeling for being centered is so deep and silent that I don't know exactly how to discuss this quality. Perhaps the best way is to quote Henry David Thoreau. He expresses so poetically what I feel about centering:

But alone in distant woods or fields, in unpretending sproutlands or pastures tracked by rabbits, even in a bleak and, to most, cheerless day, like this, I once more feel myself grandly related. . . . (Sierra Club, 1962, p. 154)

This is the sense of centering that I try to share with my students and others.

Silvia Rivera

My calling as a teacher is to provide a liberating educational service. Greene (1988) evokes my sense of calling:

This is what we shall look for as we move: freedom developed by human beings who have acted to make a space for themselves in the presence of others, human beings become "challengers" ready for alternatives, alternatives that include caring and community. And we shall seek, as we go, implications for emancipatory education conducted by and for those willing to take responsibility for themselves and for each other. We want to discover how to open spaces for persons in the plurality, spaces where they can become different, where they can grow. (p. 56)

I am called to be an educator who promotes such open, pluralistic spaces in my classroom. My passion for social justice and equity is my passion for life, and I enthusiastically share this passion with my students.

I want to grow as a caring teacher—as someone who is concerned about her students' growing sense of empowerment. I want to understand all the ways that my students feel disempowered. If they are struggling with poor self-confidence or with alienation, I want them to know that I care about their situation and will try to help them. In the spirit of people like Dr. Martin Luther King, I want them to feel that no problem is too big to handle. I want them to understand that when people work together, they can handle incredible adversity.

I want to develop myself as a creative teacher—as someone who designs imaginative ways to practice Freire's (1970/1971) problem-posing education, which I discussed in chapter 2. To create interesting and inviting lessons around social problems requires my constant resourcefulness. I'm always looking for new, exciting ways to address pressing critical issues. I read newspapers and watch television news like a hawk, ready to pounce on any meaningful event! I have folders and folders filled with newspaper and magazine clippings. Whenever feasible, I try to design provocative field trips. I want my students to have face-to-face encounters with the social problems they are studying.

I center myself as a socially aware educator. I am at home when my educational practice is a praxis, that is, when my teaching is full of ethical and visionary thought. Because I want my students to discover the emancipatory possibilities in their lives, I want them to understand that centered people avoid false consciousness. They don't pursue goals that work against an agenda of social liberation. When young girls are raised to be meek, cute little housewives or cupcake beauty queens, their false consciousness is being fostered. No one is helping them become centered as proactive, responsible agents of their own destiny. I try to be a model of this type of agency. I am centered in my own sense of professional empowerment, and I want my students to discover how they are centered as empowered **historical agents**.

Teachers' Autobiographical Reflections

How did you decide to become a teacher? What factors and what people helped shape your decision? What challenges are you encountering along the way? How are you resolving these challenges? Why are you continuing this developmental journey in spite of these challenges? These are the types of questions that guide teachers' **autobiographical reflections**.

Numerous scholars are aware of the benefits of examining our lives and our choice to teach. Zeichner (1993) notes a relationship between the improvement of our craft and this type of examination: "The process of understanding and improving one's teaching must start with reflection upon one's experiences" (p. 5). Apple (1993) espouses similar sentiments in his belief that "thoughtful educators remind us that curriculum and teaching always end in a personal knowing" (p. 14). O'Loughlin (1992) relates the importance of giving students a voice and being active participants in their own learning: "The most fundamental building block in a pedagogy of learning is acknowledgment of life experiences and the voices of our students" (p. 338). Greene (1978) discusses the importance of personal centeredness. She observes that "it is my view that persons are more likely to ask their own questions and seek their own transcendence when they feel themselves grounded in their personal histories, their lived experiences" (p. 2).

The following two experienced teachers reflected on their teaching careers in their own unique ways.

AUTOBIOGRAPHICAL REFLECTION

Charlene's Story

Charlene Newman

The fabric of becoming a career-long student of my constructivist practices has beautiful, rich colors that dance in front of my eyes. When I examine it, I begin to notice the dominant fibers that define and reshape the fabric. Without them, the fabric would be threadbare and weak. With them, the fabric has substance, body, and strength.

The more I examine the fabric, the more I realize the hard work involved in weaving such an exquisite fabric. Why spend the time and effort? What is the purpose?

Just as a weaver can stand back and admire the results of long hours and hard work, I feel a great deal of satisfaction about being a career-long student of my constructivist practices. I feel excited before I teach, confident and flexible while I teach, and critical and contemplative after I teach. Because I have planned carefully prior to teaching and remain open while I am teaching, I can use the information that I learn continuously to refine my lessons and make wiser educational decisions in the future. All of this reflective work allows me to feel a deep sense of satisfaction.

In addition to feeling satisfied, the decision-making cycle of planning, enacting, observing, and reflecting gives me a great deal of clarity about what I am teaching. Planning allows me to understand the content of what I teach as well as the philosophical foundations. Planning also directs the way I enact, opening the door to a myriad of possibilities for the material. Observing gives me the opportunity to look at the way my students respond to the material, the way I deal with their questions, and the way in which they respond to my responses. Reflecting helps me understand which aspects of planning and enacting have worked well and which need to be refined.

If the material is clear to me, it can also be clear for my students. This clarity can help guide their opportunity to become constructivist learners. They can cultivate their own critical reasoning and engagement.

Please know that I did not begin to think this way when I began to teach. The idea of becoming a career-long student of my constructivist practices was a concept that few people, if any, entertained at the time. The weaving of this fabric occurred over many years. Sometimes I was the sole weaver, and other times I had the chance to work with other master weavers. It was clear to me from the beginning that no one was weaving a fabric that was similar to mine, and I felt very lonely about that at first. Let me share with you the threads and fibers that are part of my fabric.

As I reflect now on the fabric of my constructivist teaching practices at the start of my career, my fabric looked very different from how it appears today. Dominant threads included a passionate enthusiasm for teaching, an intense fear of the students I was teaching, a strong need to control my classes, a false sense of arrogance about my abilities, and a burning desire to make school better for my students than it had been for me. Strands of one of the 4C virtues—centeredness—were barely visible. Of the other virtues, being creative and caring were more apparent. Let me describe my sense of calling to you.

I always knew.

These three words, more than any others, describe the thread of calling that I felt to become a teacher. I knew from the time I was in seventh grade, and my knowing came from a deep conviction that resided in the pit of my stomach. My decision felt right. Every time I would think of myself as a teacher, I would smile.

My sense of calling drew me to two areas in education: teaching Spanish to high school students as a full-time position, and teaching religion to junior high school students as a part-time position. I felt a powerful connection to both of these subject matter areas, and I honored that connection by teaching Spanish during the week and religion on the weekends. These two areas came to represent a certain tension in my fabric between secular and religious education which played an important part in some of my career choices. Let us now take a look at my first full-time job so that you can see the picture of that teaching position.

When I began teaching Spanish at a local high school, I was filled with a mixture of enthusiasm and fear. I couldn't wait to have my own classes, try out the ideas I had learned, and inspire students to love a foreign language. I used my natural energies and combined them with a strong desire to succeed.

What provided a pivotal contrast to my enthusiasm was the intense fear of the students in my classes. A myriad of questions went through my mind: Would I ever be able to control these students? Would my age and height—just 21 years old and 5 feet tall—hinder my ability to take charge? How could I balance having control over the students with showing respect for them? These were very real dilemmas that threatened to destroy my fabric even before I had begun to weave it.

I had been able to use my enthusiasm to fuel the creative thread through games, comic books, class dinners, and the like, but it was much more challenging to deal with my fear. What seemed logical was to focus on control. As long as my students were quiet, I thought that I would feel all right.

And so I taught for seven years with the threads of enthusiasm and fear dominating the picture. Another fiber started to appear with greater frequency: the fiber of caring. I began to notice that as I began to feel less fearful, I became more caring. Several examples come to mind.

In my early years of teaching I met Elise, a lovely and quiet student who did excellent work. In spite of her success in class, she seemed pitifully unhappy. She would talk with me from time to time, telling me about her experiences at home.

She lived with her mother and abusive stepfather. I will never forget the day she came to school visibly shaken. When I inquired, she showed me a chipped front tooth and told me that her stepfather had been violent. I was horrified and vowed to get her some help. No one else in the school may have known, but Elise chose to confide in me.

Nathan was another student who let me into his world. A fine young man with a quiet personality, Nathan was troublesome in his other classes. In my class, he was a serious student. He too would share a variety of information with me—not only his interests but also his propensity for having accidents. On one occasion he had broken a bone, took himself to the hospital, suffered excruciating pain, and chose not to miss my class. When I inquired about the mishap, he told me the entire story. In fact, I found out about what happened before his parents did.

In spite of the satisfaction that I derived from caring about my students and planning creative lessons, I felt something was missing from my teaching. A new thread was woven into my fabric: the thread of change. I had begun to lose my enthusiasm for teaching Spanish full-time. What replaced it were two desires. I wanted to be an administrator in a private religious school, and I wanted to become a mother.

Being a mother meant that I would be working part-time instead of full-time. I pursued administrative positions in private religious schools that would honor this request and was fortunate in securing two administrative posts that looked ideal.

The reality that I learned much later was that instead of following my heart as I had with teaching, I followed my head when it came to administration. After reflecting on my choices, I came to realize that I wanted to be a principal so that I could feel important. This realization triggered the need for me to begin to weave the thread of critical engagement into my fabric.

I started becoming cognizant of questions that would strengthen this thread. From what did I derive my energies? How could I best serve the educational community? In what direction was I being guided? How did I feel about this direction?

Gradually, I began to pay careful attention to my heart. I surrounded myself with caring, supportive friends who encouraged me to follow my heart. I gave myself time to reflect on my past and consider a variety of options.

Magically, the threads started coming together. They did so slowly at first and then with greater frequency. Let me explain the process to you.

Some of the fibers grew out of conversations I had with a special friend who was finishing her undergraduate degree. She would speak with me about her challenges with a Spanish class and with the professor who was teaching the class. Each time she spoke to me on this subject, I felt a surge of energy. I found it exciting to talk about education.

I did not pay particular attention to my responses to my friend until another special friend began to talk with me about returning to college. As she made her decision and started her first class, we spoke frequently. Each time we talked about her classes, I felt adrenaline flowing through me. It became clear to me that I was being called again to teach, this time with adults.

By honoring the calling to teach adults and spending time with supportive friends, I feel a satisfaction today that is both genuine and deep. The energy that I feel teaching adults confirms for me that I am doing exactly what I need to do.

Because I have been cognizant of my calling and actively involved in critical engagement, the current fabric of my constructivist practices hardly resembles that of my early career. Let me illustrate with a few examples.

Last year I had the pleasure of supervising six student teachers, all of whom were women. I noticed that several of them had very quiet, shy personalities. Curiously, they were paired with very outgoing cooperating teachers. When I would meet with the student teachers and cooperating teachers, I sensed the need to encourage each student teacher to honor her own personality. I didn't want her to think that she had to become a clone of her cooperating teacher. I fully accepted each student teacher as she was.

At the same time, several of my quiet, soft-spoken graduate students raised questions about being assertive in the classroom, especially about handling a very challenging group of students they were teaching. I saw this question as an opportunity to confirm to these students that they could be assertive. Based on my observations of them in my class, I felt certain that they could assert themselves in their own unique ways.

I posed the following scenario and asked them to respond. Pretend that you are in the express line at a supermarket. It has been a long, tiring day, and you're in a hurry. A person cuts in front of you to check out. What will you do?

The students responded quickly and energetically that they would gently confront the person who cut in front of them. Their responses proved to me that they could be assertive, and we discussed its application to their group of students.

In both cases, I fully accepted the students as they were in their own growth. My purpose was not to make them into someone that they weren't. Rather, I wanted them to be the best teachers that they could be.

In addition to fostering a "best-self" ideal with my students, my teaching practice today encourages me to be cognizant of the physical cues that I get from my body, especially those gut feelings that I have. In this regard I openly and actively confront issues today that I chose to ignore earlier in my career, even though I knew they were troubling me. One such example is the issue of racial relationships in the classroom. For example, when African-American students are placed in predominantly white schools during their field experience or student teaching, I ask them to talk to me about their experiences. My position, which I have woven into my fabric over many years and through exposure to diverse groups, is to continually inquire into the way that different racial and ethnic groups of people work with one another. I welcome dialogue on this issue because I feel at ease with the idea of diversity in the classroom. The thread of being centered allows me to openly confront issues that I consciously ignored earlier in my career. It also gives me the willingness to hear criticism in a much more positive way. In the early years of my teaching practice, the mildest suggestion given to me would unleash a flurry of rage and erect a wall of denial. Today I can listen to those words of criticism with interest and generally not take the information personally. The goal I have for myself in this regard is to reflect on what is being said so that I can uncover how I will use the information. In the process, I ask myself some key questions. What do I need to learn from this situation? Because of this information, how will I act differently next time? In the event that I find myself feeling uncomfortable with the way I respond to criticism, I take time to examine the reasons why I am responding in this particular way.

I hope this discussion of criticism will let you know that my teaching practice is neither perfect nor finished. In spite of careful planning, my encounters in the classroom as both teacher and supervisor are far from perfect. Sometimes I make incorrect assumptions about my students. At other times, I cannot predict how every single person will respond to what I say and do. I never know exactly what others will say or do.

What is clear to me today is that this weaving of my fabric is all about the process. Being a career-long student of my constructivist practice means that I pay careful attention to the weaving process. I reflect on my practice on a regular basis by myself, in journals, and with colleagues. It is the process that I celebrate today—recognition of and attention to all the threads in my fabric. The process guides, supports, and refines my teaching practice.

AUTOBIOGRAPHICAL REFLECTION

Jo's Narrative

Mary Jo Marksz

I'd like to invite you to take a retrospective look with me at my constructivist teaching repertoire. First, you must recognize two significant notions that have served as my personal scaffolding throughout my professional journey.

Teaching for me is challenging, life-long development. It is informed by past experiences, rooted in my present situation, and inspired by the awareness of what could be, and should be, quality educational and human services for learners.

I also believe in taking a proactive approach—making the most favorable of all possible decisions through enactment and review of my current teaching practices. I reflect on the experiences and creatively fine-tune my teaching practices. The cultivation of these teaching sensibilities promotes the ongoing creation of my "best self" as a teacher.

When I consider the study of my teaching in light of the 4C virtues, I recognize that this particular type of metacognitive guidance would have been helpful in my earlier personal-professional reflections. I didn't reflect so systematically then, but I can now; and so I begin with the virtue of calling.

MY SENSE OF CALLING

For as far back as I can remember, I have always had a strong desire to become a teacher. Thinking of that yearning now, it seems odd because I recall my own schooling as a stale experience in general. Ideally, I would acknowledge a significant person that nurtured my interest in teaching or perhaps a critical incident that inspired and attracted me to the profession. Sadly I cannot.

So where did this sense of calling originate? From a child's sense of wonder. I understood and accepted that school was a tidy, orderly place where quiet children were held in high regard by their teachers. I played along, because I wanted to do the right things. For instance, during a science experiment I would sit in dutiful attention, passively watching the teacher conduct the procedures. In my mind's classroom, however, I exchanged questions and predictions with the other student scientists on my team. We conducted the experiment and recorded our observations, and we discussed our interpretations and formed our conclusions. Sometimes, I rehearsed an appeal to my mom so she'd help me do this experiment for myself when I got home. I disliked the extra-practice homework, but I did need an excuse so I could take my book home and tell her I really needed to learn this important stuff.

On one occasion, I recall writing an evening newscast for my younger brother about the mysterious bacteria cultivated from fingernail scrapings of an unfortunate fifth-grade girl in Akron, Ohio. This great, hairy glob was in my test tube in the science cupboard. Surely this was something my class would explore. Watch tomorrow's news for the latest on the glob! The dangerous gelatin was sent to scientists in Washington, D.C. for further analysis. The teacher threw our experiment away, so we missed an opportunity to examine it with a hand lens or microscope and discover microorganisms.

My attitude changed by high school. By now I was determined to have some say in my learning beyond making a class schedule for the very courses everyone took anyway. I felt oppressed by the utilitarian nature of schooling, but I still had a sense of responsibility to do the right thing. However, this notion of the right thing became subject to a very broad interpretation of appropriateness. When I had to do a research report for college prep writing, my challenge was the topic. I selected the pros and cons of marijuana. The teacher never flinched. Near the end of my senior year, though, she offered some stinging advice, "You'll never be a teacher; you'll probably never even finish college. You ask too many questions, and you can't live by rules." I was deeply hurt.

BECOMING A CARING TEACHER

My first teaching assignment was in the heart of a declining urban area. The school neighborhood was a conglomeration of vacant trash-filled lots, tenement houses, several taverns, and a notorious hourly-rate motel. This neighborhood was only four miles from my home. I was ashamed to admit I had lived nearby my entire life and yet remained ignorant of the desperate poverty and social conditions in this part of town.

For the first few months I was in culture shock. I assumed caring meant focusing on my students' daily needs. Bringing peanut butter crackers for those without breakfast. Mending worn clothing with students in an after-school sewing class. Providing crayons, pencils, and folders at my own expense for all students so everyone could have the same school supplies. Referrals for clothing and shoe vouchers became routine. I burdened myself trying to mitigate the out-of-school factors that my students faced daily and that worked against an even chance for them to learn. Certainly these services made school a more comfortable place to spend the day. However, I soon realized my responses were of limited help. It became apparent to me that I, too, was part of the problem. In focusing on the immediate social conditions, I had inadvertently placed student learning in a secondary role. I realized that caring for my students meant offering the best quality educational service I could provide.

To understand my students' educational needs, it was essential that I get to know each of them on a more personal level. We started a lunch club. Each week I invited a few students to join me for lunch in our classroom. Their appearance was strictly voluntary, although I admit I did bake cookies for dessert as an enticement. This was a wonderful way to get to know them as unique individuals. Through our conversations I gained an appreciation for the students' family situations. I came to understand that lack of education had severely limited the employment potential of most parents. Few had completed high school. It was not uncommon for a child whose parent had a full-time job to qualify for the federally subsidized school lunch program. I had to develop a plan to address the first-grade curriculum within the realities of the educational inequities in this setting.

CREATIVITY IN CONSTRUCTIVIST TEACHING

The first-grade curriculum emphasized learning to read and write. The only books in my classroom were basal readers. Children should have real books. My first challenge was convincing the school librarian that the children were responsible enough to check out books. The library policy was that kindergartners and first-graders could look at books but not borrow them. Worse yet, there was a limit to the number of books I could borrow for use in my classroom. I wanted every child to have a book for personal use. The children worked cooperatively and planned ways they could cultivate their library manners, such as washing their hands before using books. I discussed this outrageous situation with my principal and faculty council. It was a dead end. The librarian had complete control of the collection and believed that children did not understand how to take care of books. Our initial negotiations were rocky, and for a while I declined the invitation to "come and look at books" in the library. Instead I borrowed plenty of books from the local public library. They had a teacher-friendly policy with one-month loan periods. My first-graders found pleasure in their books as they learned to take proper care of them.

Eventually we reached a compromise. The first-graders could check out books, but only for use in the classroom. It was a start. The following school year, first-grade students were also permitted to take their books home.

Unlike reading, writing was solely my responsibility to develop—I did not have to rely on the library. I wanted to include everyone, regardless of their ability to read. This raised more questions than answers. How could everyone participate when some children could read independently, while others were just beginning to learn alphabet letters, letter-sound associations, or basic sight words? How could I teach writing without attracting attention to differences between those who could read and those who were still trying to figure out this stuff called reading? Would the students who could not read even show any interest in writing?

I decided to use a strategy called *language experience*. I guided student discussions of an event or experience, and then we generated a class story. This enabled everyone to cultivate their speaking skills and participate in the construction of a story. Recording the children's spoken words on chart paper modeled the creation of a story from the class dictation, as well as connecting spoken and written words. We read our stories aloud as a group. Individual students could read the stories for their personal enjoyment or to classmates or any available adult, including the principal and a visiting firefighter. Our collection of stories grew. I tried having the children write or copy along with me. It was awkward from their seats. A child suggested some students might like to sit on the floor and use a lap-size chalkboard like a desk. It was wonderful. They could practice letter formation at their seats. Stories worked best when children sat in the most comfortable spot, usually the floor.

Then we moved on to the next phase in individual writing. How could I incorporate the students' own writing into the fabric of life in the classroom? Could I provide a situation that enabled children to correspond with one another and their teacher? I asked a family friend to collect discarded copy paper at work for my classroom, since we were allocated very small amounts of paper in the school budget. We installed jumbo cardboard tubes on a set of bookshelves, giving everyone their own mailbox.

BECOMING CENTERED THROUGH CRITICAL CONTEMPLATIVE STUDY

My teaching repertoire was dominated by clever learning activities, learning centers, and games for practicing skills. It seemed I had become one of the very teachers I wondered about as a child, providing basic knowledge to my students. The structure of my classroom and the organization of my teaching restrained the inquisitive nature of children. Occasionally a child would choose to read for pleasure. It was uncommon for a student to find a note from a classmate in a mail tube. Notes from the teacher encouraged conversation but few written responses. I came to the realization that these first-graders understood reading and writing merely as subjects in school. This was not my intention. My narrow understanding of how children made meanings restricted my ability to teach for understanding. Yet my vision of quality educational service incorporated students who would become actively involved in their own learning. I wanted to capitalize on their curiosity, integrate their questions into the curriculum, and facilitate their inquiry. I had no sense of how to connect that desire with a curriculum guide.

My co-teachers were essentially teaching by the book. I couldn't articulate for them why I wanted my students to participate in planning for learning. I felt I had the potential to learn new ways of thinking about teaching and learning, and I needed to find an educational setting to encourage my personal-professional growth. I discovered a school in my own system that was designed for team teaching, and I joined the staff. From a distance this seemed the ideal solution: having co-workers with whom to plan and study teaching. At first, the teaming centered on how we could organize the curriculum to best meet the needs of five classes of first-graders. We shared teaching resources freely. We had weekly meetings to discuss the ins and outs of our everyday teaching. Our meetings matured into discussions of classroom activities, materials, and strategies that were unsuccessful, and we openly discussed other teaching methods that might enhance the learning of our students. We laughed about our goof-ups and encouraged each other through continuous reflection about the situations at hand.

Working in cooperation with four other teachers had many benefits for me. I developed the capacity to plan thematic instructional units and make long-range plans. I learned more efficient techniques for keeping records and for testing children with emerging reading skills in science, social studies, and health. Most importantly for my personal-professional growth, I learned to talk honestly about my own teaching, ask public questions about it, seek support and advice, and reconsider my own views as well as the views of my colleagues.

Our team decided to study the value of the amount of time spent on testing for achievement levels in our reading program. We wondered if all this testing was providing information that enhanced our planning and teaching. We believed we lost valuable instructional time testing our students so frequently. We decided to make predictions about our students' likely test results from their ongoing class-work and compare them with the actual results of achievement tests. Our predictions were reliable enough to convince the principal that we could limit the use of unit testing to individual cases in which we needed further information. We decided to place less emphasis on testing and more emphasis on the continuous process of learning to read. Our aim was to focus on learning to read for pleasure and information. The shift in emphasis provided more time for using children's literature and lessened our dependence on basal readers, which contained stories contrived to teach a particular body of vocabulary. We were keenly aware of the community's expectation for student achievement accountability, so we continued to administer the end-of-book testing mandated by the system for this purpose.

My initial venture into constructivist teaching occurred in mathematics. I had completed graduate studies in an elementary school mathematics program. The program emphasized understanding developmental phases in the learning of mathematics as well as teaching math for students' understanding. One strategy we used was to interview children about what they knew, what they needed to know, and how they thought they could learn that. I used this strategy in a remedial mathematics classroom. With only ten students in each class, I was able to meet weekly with each child to discuss individual progress. Through these interviews I gained clear images of what each child understood and what areas needed further attention. From these insights I wrote an individual lesson plan for each student. As children finished their plans, we would meet again. This time I asked children to talk about which learning activities had been most meaningful to them. We discussed why they thought this was so. I recorded their ideas and comments on file cards. Through critical examination of these collections of student comments, a picture began to emerge of which materials and resources the students considered worthwhile.

I began to notice that these students were becoming more adept at describing their mathematical thinking, which led to another teaching exploration. If students were able to clearly articulate their understanding to a teacher, would they gain even more from discussing or possibly teaching this to a classmate? I asked several students to have discussions about their understanding. I also asked them to tape-record the conversations for me to listen to. It was remarkable how carefully they discussed their understanding and how clearly they stated their thinking. Their exchange of questions and understandings was very powerful, almost liberating to several students. One child explained that math was just a lot of work until we started to talk about it. Being able to think about it aloud helped him learn it better. Another thought, however, nagged at my sense of responsibility as their teacher. Was I abdicating my responsibilities as teacher by encouraging these student dialogues? I hadn't discussed this strategy with any other teachers or read about it in a journal. Was it valid? Because of the enthusiastic response of some students, we continued taping the discussions. I listened to them for insight and potential misunderstandings and then recorded notes in their individual assignment books.

The next challenge for me was to incorporate this interview strategy into an elementary classroom where I had many more than ten students, ranging from twenty-five to thirty, and responsibility for all areas of the curriculum. We began keeping weekly math journals. I asked students to write detailed responses explaining their understanding of a particular mathematical situation or scenario. It seemed a bit strange to them at first to be writing in math class, and it took them a while to accept this as a way of documenting their learning without receiving a grade. It also took a while for me to become comfortable with the amount of time required to respond and share. We had captivating class discussions, as students voluntarily shared their thinking about a particular mathematical connection. Eventually the journals became their personal math resource—a tool to confirm a hunch about a particular algorithm, review for a quiz, or explain to their parents what was going on at school.

Journals gave me new insights into the students' mathematical questions and their learning needs. Now I was willing to go beyond supplementing the textbook. I began to view the text simply as one of many resources at my disposal for teaching mathematics. I studied this math class and the development of the curriculum through a process of planning, enacting, and reviewing. I spent the summer critically evaluating my materials and determining what further items were necessary to move away entirely from a textbook-driven curriculum. My principal and I discussed how to explain this curriculum change to the students and their parents. By articulating this transformation to the principal, I formed a clear sense of my reasons for choosing to teach for student understanding. I was then able to establish a rationale that was grounded in my emerging constructivist beliefs and supported by my study of the previous years' math coursework. This rationale empowered me to justify this decision to students, parents, and coteachers.

There was still more work to be done. Making this change to teaching for understanding meant that I had to make modifications in the standard system of evaluation required by my district. Our system relied on testing materials provided by the textbook company to determine individual student achievement. Our state department of education required standardized achievement tests during fourth and sixth grade. I specifically refer to my work as making modifications because these evaluation policies were not subject to change. I had to develop supplemental methods of evaluation that supported the spirit of teaching for understanding. To keep myself up-to-date with individual students' progress, I informally reviewed explorations that students wrote on *think paper*. As the title suggests, these explorations focused on mathematical thinking rather than computations. I noted responses, comments, and questions as constructive feedback for each student. I returned assignments to students and asked them to keep a folder, another tool for learning. In grading papers, I rated students for the processes they utilized—sometimes called *partial credit*—along with the appropriate response.

Inquiry Advice: An Experiential Continuum[1]

The narratives in this chapter were written to facilitate your understanding of a particular method of professional study. For two experienced teachers, the 4C virtues became the connective link between their career-long professional inquiry

[1] The continuum presented in this section is adapted from the works of M. Huberman (1993), *The Lives of Teachers*, New York: Teachers College Press; and F. F. Fuller and O. Bown, (1975), "Becoming a Teacher", in K. Ryan (Ed.), *Teacher Education (The Seventy-Fourth Yearbook of the National Society for the Study of Education, Part Two)* (pp. 25–52), Chicago: University of Chicago Press. The six points on the experiential continuum are somewhat arbitrary but represent critical points in teachers' career-long professional growth. The critical points have been identified through the application of research generalizations and may not be precisely applicable to individual teachers' careers.

and their current understanding of their evolving constructivist practices. In retrospect, these teachers came to the realization that the study of their teaching practices would have been enhanced by the use of a guiding framework, such as the 4C virtues.

You have a unique possibility to work with an inquiry structure that promotes and sustains your personal-professional development. Remember, the 4C virtues are scaffolding to serve as a guide for the study of teaching. You may now, or somewhere further along in the cultivation of your teaching practices, identify other important professional virtues. We encourage this exploration of meaningful teaching values.

Think of your career-long personal and professional development as part of an **experiential continuum**. The continuum divides your teaching career into six time periods according to significant experiences:

1. Educational experiences prior to professional course work
2. Early preservice field work in conjunction with professional course work
3. Concluding preservice field work as a student teacher or intern
4. Teaching: the first three years
5. Teaching: from the fourth to the sixth year
6. Teaching: from the seventh to the twenty-fifth year

Let's take a look at how you could use the 4C virtues to reflect on each period on this continuum.

Educational Experiences Prior to Professional Course Work

These experiences would include your own schooling as well as lessons you learned from parents and other adults. They may be experiences from participating in scouting, summer camp, Sunday school classes, music lessons, school plays, or team-centered activities. Can you remember a particular person in the role of teacher or leader who demonstrated any of the 4C virtues? What do you recall about the way that virtue was manifested in your experiences with this teacher? Were you aware of this quality while you were a student of this teacher, or has it become apparent to you after studying this book? Would this person serve as a model for the cultivation of one or more of the 4C virtues?

Early Preservice Field Work in Conjunction with Professional Course Work

These experiences might include tutoring or other classroom teaching activities. Which of the 4C virtues does your field-experience teacher exemplify? How is this apparent to you? What will you do with this information in light of your own professional development?

Consider this field work and your own interactions with students. Which of the 4C virtues do you exemplify? How is this virtue evident in your interactions with students? with teachers? within the school community? How do you intend to sustain further development of this particular virtue in your teaching? Would you try to establish a network of preservice teachers who aspire to cultivate the 4C virtues? How could you do this while you are also working on the pragmatic aspects of your teaching?

Concluding Preservice Field Work as a Student Teacher or Intern

According to research on student teaching (Britzman, 1991) and on adult development (Chickering, 1969), this is a time to be practical, to engage in intensive experiential learning. This may also be a time when you feel dissonance between your image of teaching and that of your cooperating teacher. How do you respond to perceptions of teaching that are different from your own? Do you consider different perceptions worthy of consideration in light of your understanding of teaching? Could this become an opportunity to broaden your understanding of diverse perspectives in the teaching profession? In what ways might you develop the willingness to accept the views of co-workers and colleagues as part of your personal-professional growth?

What 4C virtues do you want to cultivate during student teaching? Can you share your intentions with your cooperating teacher? Can this person help you cultivate these virtues?

Teaching: The First Three Years

It is common practice for a *mentor*, or experienced teacher, to work with first-year teachers (Reiman, Head, & Thies-Sprinthall, 1992, pp. 87–90). Consider that this assignment may be the ideal position in which your mentor encourages your empowerment as a teaching professional. You may find this mentoring arrangement to be less than ideal. However, it may be politically wise to cooperate while seeking out other, more sustaining relationships.

As you gain teaching experience, which of the 4C virtues have been the most difficult to cultivate? Cite some examples. Why are you experiencing difficulties? Can you do anything about the discrepancies between your teaching reality and the 4C ideals?

As you survey the landscape of professional opportunities, what avenues have you chosen to cultivate your "best self" as a teacher? What journals do you read regularly? What professional groups have you affiliated with to support your individual growth? Can you develop collaborative relationships that will enable you to openly and honestly explore your sense of teaching virtues?

Teaching: From the Fourth to the Sixth Year

Which of the 4C virtues is now well-defined in your reflective practice? Cite examples. Can you engage in discussion around your teaching virtues with others in your school building and in your district? How has your teaching matured? Cite examples. In light of the 4C virtues, do you feel the need to recharge your batteries, to renew your inspiration to be a virtuous teacher?

Teaching: From the Seventh to the Twenty-Fifth Year

What is your view of teaching as a profession at this point in your career? Have you been willing to provide leadership for professional empowerment? Will you celebrate a decade or a quarter-century of successful teaching? How do you envision this celebration? With whom will you celebrate? What personal-professional qualities and teaching practices have you refined that you originally thought would endure throughout your career? What are your plans for the continuous renewal of your constructivist practices? Have you made a personal commitment to a colleague by serving as a coach or mentor? Have you made a commitment to a professional network or organization beyond your school's learning community?

FURTHER READINGS

Ayers, W. (1993). *To teach: The journey of a teacher*. New York: Teachers College Press.

Barell, J. (1995). *Teaching for thoughtfulness: Classroom strategies to enhance intellectual development* (2nd ed.). White Plains, NY: Longman.

Butt, R. L. (1990). Autobiographical praxis and self-education: From alienation to authenticity. In J. Willinsky (Ed.), *The educational legacy of Romanticism*. Waterloo, Ontario, Canada: Wilfrid Lanier University Press.

Clandinin, D. J., & Connelly, F. M. (1995). *Teachers' professional knowledge landscapes*. New York: Teachers College Press.

Connelly, F. M., & Clandinin, D. J. (1988). *Teachers as curriculum planners: Narratives of experience*. New York: Teachers College Press.

Holly, M. L. (1989). *Writing to grow: Keeping a personal-professional journal*. Portsmouth, NH: Heinemann.

Jalongo, M. R. (1992). Teachers' stories: Our ways of knowing. *Educational Leadership*, *49*(7), 68–73.

Schubert, W. H. (1992). Our journeys into teaching: Remembering the past. In W. H. Schubert and W. C. Ayers (Eds.), *Teacher lore: Learning from our own experience*. White Plains, NY: Longman.

van Manen, M. (1991). *The tact of teaching: The meaning of pedagogical thoughtfulness*. Albany, NY: State University of New York Press.

Witherell, C., & Noddings, N. (Eds.). (1991). *Stories lives tell: Narrative and dialogue in education*. New York: Teachers College Press.

REFERENCES

Aoki, T. T. (1992). Layered voices of teaching: The uncannily correct and the elusively true. In W. F. Pinar & W. M. Reynolds (Eds.), *Understanding curriculum as phenomenological and deconstructed text* (pp. 17–27). New York: Teachers College Press.

Apple, M. W. (1993). *Official knowledge: Democratic education in a conservative age*. New York: Routledge.

Ayers, W. (1993). *To teach: The journey of a teacher*. New York: Teachers College Press.

Britzman, D. (1991). *Practice makes practice: A critical study of learning to teach*. Albany, NY: State University of New York Press.

Chickering, A. (1969). *Education and identity*. San Francisco: Jossey-Bass.

Eisner, E. W. (1994). *The educational imagination: On the design and evaluation of school programs* (3rd ed.). New York: Macmillan.

Freire, P. (1971). *Pedagogy of the oppressed* (M. Bergman Ramos, Trans.). New York: Herder & Herder. (Original work published 1970)

Garman, N. B. (1986). Reflection, the heart of clinical supervision: A modern rationale for professional practice. *Journal of Curriculum and Supervision, 2*, 1–24.

Greene, M. (1978). *Landscapes of learning*. New York: Teachers College Press.

Greene, M. (1988). *The dialectic of freedom*. New York: Teachers College Press.

Jagla, V. M. (1994). *Teachers' everyday use of imagination and intuition: In pursuit of the elusive image*. Albany, NY: State University of New York Press.

Noddings, N. (1984). *Caring: A feminine approach to ethics and moral education*. Berkeley, CA: University of California Press.

O'Loughlin, M. (1992). Engaging teaching in emancipatory knowledge construction. *Journal of Teacher Education, 43*, 336–346.

Reiman, A. J. , Head, F. A., & Theis-Sprinthall, L. (1992). Collaboration and mentoring in education. In T. M. Bey & C.T. Holmes (Eds.), *Mentoring contemporary principles and issues* (pp. 87–90). Reston, VA: Association of Teacher Educators.

Sierra Club (1962). *From Henry David Thoreau: "In Wildness Is the Preservation of the World."* New York: Ballantine Books.

Zeichner, K. M. (1993). Research on teacher thinking and different views of reflective practice in teaching and teacher education. Keynote address presented at the Sixth International Conference of the International Study Association on Teacher Thinking, Göteborg, Sweden.

8

Professional Collaboration

By engaging in different types of collaborative activities, teachers can help one another function as career-long students of their constructivist practices. The teachers at Bay Elementary School understood this important principle. We begin by examining their collaborative efforts.

At the end of the school year, the large numbers of students who failed at Bay Elementary School only confirmed what the teachers already knew: increasing numbers of Spanish-speaking children were not succeeding in school. After learning at the final meeting of the year about the number of children who would fail, the teachers decided they needed to take action. Even though their school had numerous classes that were taught in Spanish, the percentage of children who were failing in school was increasing rapidly.

The teachers at Bay wanted to look at their own teaching practices to examine what might be missing. They organized a collaborative team consisting of ten members, two from each of the following groups: students with university field experience, student teachers, novice teachers, teachers with four to six years of experience, and teachers with seven to twenty-five years' experience. The team decided to meet weekly during their lunch hour to discuss ways of dealing with the problem of student failure among the Spanish-speaking community.

The team began with brainstorming sessions to determine areas in which the Spanish-speaking students were weak. They generated a list of specific problems, such as low test scores, poor attention, and lack of motivation. They chose to focus on one problem at a time, each for a certain period of time. For example, the team decided to focus on the problem of poor attention during the first two weeks. Together they planned ways to increase the attention span of Spanish-speaking students who were failing. They planned specific activities, and they enacted these activities in their classes. They observed what took place following their enactment. Finally, they reflected on the entire process by writing in journals. Each team member kept a journal, and they shared their reflections at weekly meetings. As team members shifted their attention to other problems, they continued using the decision-making cycle to guide their collaboration.

During the entire collaborative process, each team member's distinctive ideas, opinions, and reflections were given a proper hearing. All ideas were respected, and diversity was celebrated. The team members were aware of their common goal of addressing student failure among Spanish-speaking students. Collectively they called themselves the *ADC Team*, referring to their shared values of autonomy, diversity, and commonality.

After several months of meetings, a student teacher made an observation. "We as teachers are growing by working together to solve a difficult problem. Wouldn't it make sense to give our Spanish-speaking students the same opportunity?" The other teachers began to buzz with excitement. The idea was so logical. All they needed was to work out the details.

During the next week, all the teachers on the team began to write in their journals about their reactions to creating a team of students from every grade level to work together. They were all in favor of such an idea, but no one was certain about its organization. They seemed to have reached an impasse.

At the next meeting when the teachers shared their journal entries, they all mentioned how "stuck" they felt. A novice teacher suggested that they examine what they needed to do to create a student team. After hearing the question, the teachers realized they needed more information about ways in which other schools might have solved problems like this one. They chose to look at literature on cooperative learning, talk with teachers in other schools, and gather as much information as they could on the subject. They set a goal of two months to collect the information.

These meetings became the place where the teachers learned what others had done in situations like theirs. They discussed what each team member had learned, and they wrote in their journals about the information they shared. They kept a running list of the aspects that they liked and thought would be applicable to their school.

At the end of two months, a plan emerged. They would form collaborative groups of Spanish-speaking students where more experienced, more successful students would work with those who were less experienced and less successful. The students would collaborate on general study skills and other educational topics.

Although the ADC Team was anxious to enact this plan, the members recognized that they needed to test it with a small group before offering it to all Spanish-speaking students in the school. They chose a group of students with particularly low grades to be part of the team. They wrote letters to the parents of these children, explaining the program and asking for their cooperation. Additionally, they chose a group of successful Spanish-speaking students to support their less experienced peers.

With the necessary approvals in place, the team began to meet in January. Their first task was to decide on a name for the team that would reflect the idea that all students could succeed at Bay Elementary. The team came up with the name *Éxito*, the Spanish word for success. Students met during their lunch periods to discuss any difficulties that the less experienced students were having. At the same time that the students were discussing their challenges, they also talked about their successes. The more experienced members of Éxito decided that their peers might benefit from rewards for their achievements, such as going out for lunch or getting tickets to special events in the city.

Parents of the students in Éxito began to notice an improvement in their children's work. They became more excited about their children's positive attitudes toward school. They wrote notes to their children's team thanking them for helping their children succeed in school.

At the end of the school year, the school held an assembly honoring all the participants in this program: the team of teachers, the student teams, and their parents. The remarks of Raúl, a second-grade student who had barely passed the previous year, summed up his response to being a part of the Éxito team:

Last year I didn't like school. I didn't want to come because I didn't know anything and I didn't have any friends. This year I have lots of friends. My friends can help me when I don't understand. I like school now. Maybe I can help someone too, some day.

As you read through this chapter, keep in mind what the Bay Elementary team's collaborative experience did for the team members and the school. Their study resulted in the establishment of cooperative learning activities for a team of students. Perhaps you have been part of collaborative study relationships as well. These relationships may also come to mind as you continue reading this chapter.

Introduction

Have you ever been on a team? If you have, you might be able to recall the feelings you had the first time you played in a big game. Maybe there was a more experienced player who helped you along the way, answered your questions, and encouraged you when you failed. In spite of all your talents, you may realize today that you succeeded because someone else helped you to do so.

This chapter will highlight a particular type of teamwork: teachers collaborating over the study of their reflective practices. This type of collaboration is partly based on respect for professional autonomy and diversity. The collaborative advice in this chapter is guided by a power-with (Kreisberg, 1992) orientation, which was discussed in chapter 6. This orientation means that people do not impose their interests on one another. Rather, they mutually "fulfill their desires by acting together" (pp. 85–86).

Think back to chapters 1 and 2. In those foundational chapters, you learned that the study of constructivist practices depends partly on the individual teacher's interpretation of educational constructivism. Furthermore, you learned that teachers cultivate unique styles of critical examination. In chapter 2 the four teacher-characters presented very distinct interpretations of educational constructivism, and they each discussed their unique critical style.

Collaborative study requires more than respect for professional autonomy and diversity. When taken to the extreme, too much autonomy and diversity can destroy the cohesive nature of collaborative groups (Luft, 1984). The result is that group members become isolated and alienated from one another. The group achieves balance when autonomy and diversity are mediated by a sense of common ground. Teachers cannot work well with one another if they don't possess the notion of a unifying ideal, or common ground. In this chapter the collaborative common ground is the teachers' willingness to become career-long students of their constructivist practices. In other words, collaboration will be discussed from the point of view that all parties are committed to supporting one another's reflective practices, that is, one another's pragmatic reconsideration and critical examination. This is the organizing theme of the book and, therefore, serves as the common ground referent for the collaborative advice in this chapter.

In this chapter we examine the definition of and the rationale for professional collaboration. You will also be introduced to a sampling of collaborative approaches. Finally, you will read advice on how to practice collaboration in your setting. We begin with a definition of collaboration.

Collaboration Defined

Collaboration must not be confused with **cooperation**, **congeniality**, or **power-over gamesmanship**. While cooperation may seem helpful for group work, it is only a "prerequisite to" (Henderson, 1992, p. 108) collaborative study. Henderson says that collaborative study, unlike cooperation, "is not an unconditionally supportive activity. Constructive criticism is accepted and encouraged" (p. 109). Cook and Cookingham (1980) note that while cooperation involves freedom of group members to talk to one another and ask for help, "there is little formal structure in the relationship" (p. 3). The skills employed for cooperation, such as mutual respect, help the collaborative process and serve as a foundation, but collaboration is much more than cooperation.

In the same vein, neither is congeniality the same as collaboration. Sergiovanni (1990) defines congeniality as "friendly human relationships and the development of strong, supportive social norms that are *independent* from the standards of the teaching profession and the purposes and work at school" (p. 119). Congeniality may engender positive feelings about a work environment, but it may also draw attention away from teaching. Teachers who collaborate discuss their teaching practices; they are not just pleasant with one another.

Collaboration can be inhibited when there is a power-over gamesmanship, which can be defined as competition "with one another for resources and influence" (Cummings & Worley, 1993, p. 153). Collaboration instead involves a common frame of reference where "members are motivated to work toward the group's common objectives" (Luft, 1984, p. 19). Group members place more value on operating within the confines of the group than on seeking personal gain (Luft, p. 7). This sense of mutuality permeates collaborative study.

If collaboration is neither cooperation nor congeniality nor power-over gamesmanship, then how can it be described? In this chapter, collaboration is defined as a facilitative relationship between people who are career-long students of their constructivist practices. When teachers collaborate, they support one another's professional autonomy and celebrate their diversity in the context of shared pragmatic reconsideration and critical examination. Collaborating professionals treat one another as fellow inquirers. When they work together, they facilitate one another's unique reflective practices.

This facilitation is reciprocal, but the benefits are not identical for each of the participants, as you will read shortly. For example, when teachers with varying experience collaborate, teachers with less experience may derive more immediate benefit than their more experienced counterparts. The sense of mutuality, however, is sustained when both parties voluntarily acknowledge and accept any dissimilarity in benefits.

Even when teachers with different degrees of experience collaborate with one another, more experienced professionals may find the relationship directly beneficial to their own reflective practices. Though teachers are different in many important ways, there is still a great deal of commonality to the teaching profession. As they help less experienced colleagues make sense of their teaching, more experienced teachers can also gain deeper insight into their own work. Stanulis (1994) and Stanulis and Jeffers (1995) studied mentor teacher–student teacher collaborations and noted the positive effects on both professionals' reflective practices.

Some teachers may willingly function as practitioners of the type of reflective teaching described in this book, but others may not. Under these circumstances, it is impossible to sustain the type of collaboration discussed in this chapter. The question of how to overcome this fundamental difference in professional disposition is explored in chapter 9.

The Value of Professional Collaboration

A review of the literature suggests that professional collaboration may be beneficial in four overlapping ways. Collaboration can facilitate professional development, provide a venue for new ideas, help build community, and serve as a means for professional generativity. Let us examine each benefit.

In support of the notion of facilitating professional development, Vygotsky (1978) states that individuals have the potential to learn more when working with others. He notes from his research with children that "learning awakens a variety of internal developmental processes that are able to operate only when the child is interacting with his [sic] environment and in collaboration with his [peers]" (p. 90). Applying the same psychological principle, Costa and Garmston (1994) argue that collaborative study enhances the intellectual capacities of teachers. It enables them to think about their teaching in ways they can't when they work alone. They feel more confident and better equipped to address complex educational issues.

Collaboration is also an important venue for new ideas. Working together exposes teachers to new information they might not have considered: a different way to define a student learning problem, a creative way to teach a topic, or a strategy for reaching out to disinterested parents (Clandinin, Davies, Hogan, & Kennard, 1993).

Collaboration can also provide new insights into teachers' personal-professional autobiographies—an idea that you read about in chapter 7. Clandinin (1993) explains this benefit in terms of her own collaboration with a group of student teachers, cooperating teachers, and university teachers. She notes that "as we worked with each other, our attention was drawn to . . . other ways of living and telling our own stories. This happened because we engaged with each other with intensity. . . " (p. 12). Collaborative practices can also assist community-building efforts (Berkey et al., 1990). Costa and Garmston (1994) note that collaborative study "develops positive interpersonal relationships which are the energy sources for adaptive school cultures and productive organizations" (p. 8). Working together, teachers feel more enthusiastic about their teaching. Their energy affects the entire school, making it a more positive and energized place in which to work. Hillkirk and Nolan (1990) document the improvement in a school district's "professional work culture" (p. 3) due in part to professional collaboration.

Finally, collaboration can provide opportunities for professional generativity. According to Erikson (1968), *generativity* is defined as "the concern for establishing and guiding the next generation" (p. 138). When experienced teachers work with less experienced colleagues, they may derive a great deal of satisfaction from knowing they are helping carry on the high standards of their profession. This sense of generativity may be passed on to the less experienced colleague.

Recalling a sense of appreciation for a mentor, one college professor writes: "there is no way to thank [that mentor] except to pass it on. So I try to see people's potential and try to always have the time to help" (Hardcastle, 1988, pp. 206–207).

Intellectual enhancement, acquiring new information, community building, and professional generativity are not the only benefits associated with professional collaboration. As you engage in your own professional collaborations, you may notice other important advantages.

Five Collaborative Approaches

Teachers can collaborate with one another in many unique ways. To help you consider how you might meaningfully engage in professional collaboration, five general and somewhat overlapping approaches will be identified: collaborative exchanging, collaborative modeling, collaborative coaching, collaborative supervision, and collaborative mentoring. The five approaches are organized on a continuum from the minimum to the maximum in levels of commitment, career influence, and intimacy. For example, at one end of the continuum, collaborative exchanging generally requires less commitment, has less impact on a professional's career, and is less intimate than collaborative mentoring, which is at the other end of the continuum.[1] The discussion of each collaborative approach begins with a definition. The approach is then illustrated by drawing an example from the literature on professional collaboration.

Collaborative Exchanging

Collaborative exchanging is found in relationships where new information is shared. This sharing may be a one-time event or part of a long-term study. The latter type of exchanging is especially relevant for this book since engaging in study projects is a characteristic of progressive decision-making.

As noted earlier, participants can be at the same level of experience, for example, student teachers exchanging ideas or experienced teachers working together, or at different levels of experience, for example, new teachers working with building principals or student teachers working with a university professor. Regardless of the level of experience, exchanging is based on the mutuality of participation. All parties feel free to share information.

Collaborative exchanging is part of the Teacher Development and Organizational Change Project. This project involves a collaborative group of teachers and building principals from the Holt (Michigan) public schools and university-based researchers from Michigan State University. For more than four years, these indi-

---

[1] For research that provides further insight into this continuum, see Hardcastle's Spiritual Connections, pp. 201–208, and F. A. Head, A. J. Reiman, and L. Thies-Sprinthall's The Reality of Mentoring: Complexity in its Process and Function, in T. B. Bey & C. T. Thomas (Eds.), *Mentoring: Contemporary Principles and Issues* (pp. 5–24), Reston, VA: Association of Teacher Educators.

viduals have worked together to promote "reflection as a way for teachers to direct their professional development" (Berkey et al., 1990, p. 204).

In this project, teachers reflect on their underlying beliefs about teaching and how these beliefs are manifested in their classrooms. They keep a journal of their reflections and periodically share journal entries with their colleagues. Zietlow, one of the teachers in the project, discusses the value of this type of collaboration:

> I gained so much confidence in myself, and I learned to respect myself as a professional and to trust my knowledge, that I have the courage to take risks, to try new things, and to be vulnerable. . . . I no longer need to strive to be someone else's ideal model of a teacher, but I can strive to be the best teacher I can be. (Berkey et al., 1990, p. 220)

Another teacher, Curtis, comments on the process:

> "Why did we collaborate?" To begin with, we had a sincere intrinsic desire to learn new knowledge, and collaboration provided us with an opportunity to learn more as a group of people than we could as individuals. . . . We experienced more . . . choice and autonomy. We began to tap into each other's energy and to develop mutually beneficial relationships. (Berkey et al., 1990, p. 216)

Collaborative Modeling

In **collaborative modeling**, one professional demonstrates a particular teaching practice to one or more colleagues. For example, an experienced teacher could model one of the constructivist practices introduced in chapters 3–6 to a group of new teachers.

The University of Florida's Elementary PROTEACH program utilizes collaborative modeling (Ross, Johnson, & Smith, 1992). In this teacher preparation program, faculty members use think-aloud procedures to demonstrate specific reflective practices to the preservice students, who have found this type of collaboration to be quite helpful.

Ross and her colleagues (1992) report:

> This type of modeling provides students with clear evidence that faculty not only urge them to be reflective but actually engage in the process. Additionally, sharing faculty reasoning provides students with a clear picture of the reflective process, a model of how one does it. (p. 31)

Collaborative Coaching

During **collaborative coaching** one professional, who is usually more experienced, provides constructive feedback to another as the latter is attempting to learn a new and personally relevant strategy or practice. Schön (1987) describes collaborative coaching:

> A coach has many ways of "telling." He [sic] can give specific instructions. . . . He can criticize a student's product or process, suggesting things the student needs to do. . . . He can tell the student how to set priorities. . . .

> Whatever the coach may choose to say, it is important that he say it, for the most part, in the context of the student's doing. He must talk to the student while she [sic] is in the midst of a task . . . or is about to begin a new task, or thinks back on a task she has just completed, or rehearses a task she may perform in the future. (p. 102)

Hillkirk and Nolan (1990) provide an example of collaborative coaching in their report on a semirural school district in the northeastern United States. In a year-long project twenty-five veteran teachers volunteered to be coached "to become more inquiring and thoughtful about what they do in the classroom and why" (p. 10). The coach served as "a second pair of eyes and ears in the classroom" (p. 5) in providing specific feedback to the teachers. To provide the teachers with specific information about new strategies and practices, ten content workshops were held on topics such as teacher expectations, cooperative learning, and learning styles. These workshops provided "basic knowledge and skills on a particular topic" (p. 6) and served as a focal point for the collaborative coaching.

As each teacher began to employ the new practices, the coaches provided feedback on specific strategies, such as waiting patiently for student responses to a question (wait-time), verbal interactions between student and teacher, and the use of higher- and lower-order questions (Hillkirk & Nolan, 1990, p. 9).

Because of their willingness to participate in collaborative coaching, the teachers noted many changes in their teaching practice. Evidence can be found in some of the following responses:

> The greatest change in my thinking about teaching is just that. I think about how and why and what I teach. I reflect on each lesson I teach and make mental and physical notes on it. I think about what I did well, what wasn't so good, and how I can improve on it. (Hillkirk & Nolan, 1990, p. 10)

> My thinking has shifted from concerns to content—to which is the best model to use to teach a given concept, to the particular group of children I have. (Hillkirk & Nolan, 1990, pp. 10–11)

Collaborative Supervision

During **collaborative supervision** one professional, who is usually more experienced, provides evaluative feedback to one or more colleagues. Schubert (1986) notes that this type of feedback relates to "teacher performance" (p. 397) and entails appraisal (Smyth & Garman, 1989) or value judgment of that performance. Current trends in the field are inviting teachers to become more active participants in their own evaluation. Discussion of these trends can be found in Garman (1993) and Newman (1994).

This collaborative approach is quite new and is therefore not well documented in the educational literature.

In the University of New Hampshire's teacher education program, collaborative supervision is understood as a "commitment to the belief that there are many ways to be a good supervisor" (Oja, Diller, Corcoran, & Andrew, 1992, p. 19). During the internship phase of this program, collaborative supervision is employed by both the cooperating teacher and the university supervisor. An integral part of the process is the feedback that the intern receives. The cooperating teacher and the university supervisor encourage deeper levels of reflection through the use of extensive questioning.

Another example of collaborative supervision is the practice of students evaluating their own teaching. This collaborative self-assessment has been practiced at Kent State University as a small-scale experiment (Newman, 1994). A student teacher is observed by a cooperating teacher and a university supervisor. The three individuals have a conference immediately following the observation. In these conferences, student teachers are asked to evaluate their own teaching based on responses to the following questions: How did you think the lesson went? What were some of the strengths of the lesson? What would you change in the future? Why? This line of questioning gives student teachers an opportunity to reflect on their teaching in the presence of the cooperating teacher and the university supervisor. The cooperating teacher and the university supervisor add their evaluative feedback to inform the students' appraisal.

Collaborative Mentoring

During **collaborative mentoring** a more experienced professional provides general counsel or advice to one or more less experienced colleagues. Levinson, Darrow, Klein, Levinson, and McKee (1978) note that a mentor welcomes "the initiate into a new occupational and social world . . . acquainting him [sic] to its values" (p. 98) and also provides counsel through "moral support in times of stress" (p. 98). Daloz (1986) validates this sense of guidance as he explains:

> Mentors are guides. They lead us along the journey of our lives. We trust them because they have been there before. They embody our hopes, cast light on the way ahead, interpret arcane signs, warn us of lurking dangers, and point out unexpected delights along the way. (p. 17)

The Comer Elementary School in rural Georgia has initiated a collaborative mentoring program. An experienced teacher, Lynne, served as mentor for Shawna, a student teacher. Randi, a university educator, documented their collaborative mentoring during a ten-week period. She did this by meeting with both of them every other week to discuss their interactions (Stanulis & Jeffers, 1995). As Shawna confronted challenges, especially in the area of classroom discipline, Lynne wanted to provide her with the opportunity to cultivate her own style. Responding to Lynne's desire to help Shawna develop her unique abilities as a teacher, Shawna notes during a conference:

> Oh, my gosh, she's [Lynne] been so supportive. . . . It was real good that when we have differences in how we feel about things, she lets me do what I need to do. She doesn't say, "Oh, that's wrong, she's messing up my class." She doesn't do anything like that. She's very tolerant of our differences. (Stanulis & Jeffers, 1995, p. 18)

Lynne writes of her need to both support and guide Shawna. She informs us that "I want her to learn on her own the fitting together of all the little pieces . . . yet I'm there to back her up if there are problems" (Stanulis & Jeffers, 1995, p. 20).

Examining the Opening Vignette

You have now been introduced to five general collaborative approaches. To further your understanding, you may want to examine this chapter's opening vignette in light of these approaches.

The following general questions can assist your inquiry: Which collaborative approaches did the teachers at Bay Elementary School use? How did they use these approaches? Who were the collaborative participants? How did the participants support each other's autonomy? How did they celebrate each member's diversity? What was their common ground?

Now that you know about these five approaches, can you envision other ways the Bay Elementary School teachers might collaborate with one another? Who might participate, and how might they productively collaborate? You may want to share your responses with a colleague.

The Collaborative Facilitation of Reflective Teaching

As mentioned in the introduction to this chapter, the five collaborative approaches are presented as ways to facilitate reflective teaching. Think back to the three forms of reflection mentioned in chapter 1: pragmatic reconsideration, critical reasoning, and critical engagement. In this section, you will have the opportunity to explore how the five collaborative approaches can facilitate these forms of reflection.

To help you visualize the ways in which the collaborative approaches facilitate reflective teaching, a blank matrix is presented in Figure 8.1. To demonstrate possible ways to fill in the matrix, you will receive guidance on how to complete the top row, which is an elaboration of collaborative exchanging. This guidance is summarized in Figure 8.2.[2] To spark your thinking, possible responses are presented in the form of questions, rather than statements. The questions that are offered don't cover all possible lines of thinking. You are encouraged to consider, discuss, and write down others as well.

To focus this inquiry advice, we will use a specific, well-known instructional strategy called *small group discussion*, which Kindsvatter, Wilen, and Ishler (1992) describe:

> Dividing the large classroom into small groups of students to achieve specific objectives permits students to assume more responsibility for their own learning, develop social and leadership skills, and become involved in an alternative instructional approach. . . . Although small groups are most appropriate for promoting problem

---

[2] You will have further opportunities to work with the matrix in the workbook that accompanies this text.

Forms of Reflection

	To facilitate pragmatic reconsideration	To facilitate critical reasoning	To facilitate critical engagement
Collaborative Exchanging			
Collaborative Modeling			
Collaborative Coaching			
Collaborative Supervising			
Collaborative Mentoring			

Collaborative Approaches

Figure 8.1
Matrix of Collaborative Practices and Reflective Teaching

solving, attitudinal change, and critical and creative thinking that coincides with the purposes of reflective discussions, they can also promote the understanding of subject matter. . . . To illustrate how reflection about a controversial issue might be stimulated, a government teacher could organize students into groups based on their points of view regarding [a current political issue]. . . . Each group might be charged with determining how they would gather evidence, collecting and organizing the evidence, and presenting it to the class in the form of a panel presentation. A variety of critical thinking skills would be developed as the students reflectively gathered and organized information and supported their points of view. (pp. 183–184)

Looking now at Figure 8.2, the first cell refers to using collaborative exchanging to facilitate pragmatic reconsideration. Collaborative exchanging involves the sharing of new information. To facilitate pragmatic reconsideration while using this collaborative approach, the following questions could be pursued:

- How can I use the small-group discussion strategy in my classroom?
- What new information can I share with my colleagues about this instructional strategy?

Forms of Reflection

	To facilitate pragmatic reconsideration	To facilitate critical reasoning	To facilitate critical engagement
Collaborative Exchanging	How can I plan to use Student Team Leaning in my classroom? What new information can I share with my colleagues about Student Team Learning?	How can I think about my reasons for using Student Team Learning in my classroom? How will I share these reasons with my colleagues?	Do I find the use of Student Team Learning to be inspiring? How could I share this inspiration with my colleagues?

Collaborative Approach (vertical label on left)

Figure 8.2
How Collaborative Exchanging Facilitates Reflective Teaching

You may think of other questions that apply to this cell and the other two cells in the matrix in Figure 8.1. As you think of them, it may be valuable for you to write them down so that you can use them later in the workbook.

Moving to the next cell to the right in the matrix, recall that critical reasoning examines the good reasons for particular teaching decisions. To facilitate critical reasoning, the teachers could ask themselves these two questions:

- What are my reasons for using the small-group discussion strategy?
- How will I share these reasons with my colleagues?

Looking at the last cell on the right in the matrix, keep in mind that critical engagement pertains to the awareness, feelings, and metaphors that inspire teaching. To facilitate critical engagement, the teachers could inquire:

- Do I find the use of the small-group discussion strategy to be inspiring?
- How could I share this sense of inspiration with my colleagues?

To further illustrate the ways in which the five collaborative approaches can facilitate reflective teaching, an additional vignette will be introduced. This vignette revisits the Bay Elementary School. As you read this vignette, look for evidence of pragmatic reconsideration, critical reasoning, and critical engagement in the teachers' collaborations. How is each form of reflection facilitated? What is the relationship between the collaborative approaches and these three forms of reflective teaching? Do you notice any type of pattern emerging? If so, how would you describe this pattern? Would you call it *professional interdependence*, or can you think of a better term?

Collaborative Teaching Vignette

Instead of faculty meetings with the entire staff, groups of teachers at Bay Elementary School meet once a week for a collaborative exchange of ideas on their constructivist practices. They focus on a particular instructional strategy for a period of time until the group feels satisfied with the new information and is ready to move on.

One of the teachers in the group is Jan Griggs, a teacher with five years of experience. Jan has just returned from a week-long workshop where she was introduced to a variety of cooperative learning techniques. She is excited about sharing her knowledge with her colleagues. At one team meeting, she talks about what she has learned. Over the course of the next few meetings, the teachers consider different ways they might incorporate cooperative learning strategies into their lessons. Their deliberations focus on the use of one particular cooperative learning strategy: Jigsaw.

The Jigsaw strategy is a way to structure individual learning responsibilities in a group learning context (Slavin, 1991). Students are organized into four- to six-member teams of varying abilities to study a particular topic. Each member of the team will be required to inquire into a portion of that topic. During the planning phase, the teacher divides that topic into sections that are manageable for student study. After team members complete their separate inquiries, they must serve as instructors for the other members of their group. At the end of this process, the teacher evaluates the group's understanding of the entire topic.

The teachers choose to document their ideas, questions, and concerns about the use of the Jigsaw strategy in their journals, and they decide to share their journal entries at group meetings. They also decide to observe Jan and other teachers in the Bay School District who are using Jigsaw.

To honor the last of these considerations, the teachers in the group make requests to visit classes within the district where Jigsaw is being applied. During their observations, they learn that one of their colleagues, Dawn Rowan, does an excellent job modeling the Jigsaw strategy. Two teachers in the group, Richard Hughes and Prentice Tuttle, plan to visit Dawn's class. They both have been teachers for two years. Dawn makes careful preparations for this visitation, and she reviews her planned demonstration with a colleague, who encourages her to provide clear reasons for her actions. As a firm believer in the use of the Jigsaw strategy, she hopes her demonstration will inspire her guests.

When Richard and Prentice come to observe her class, Dawn reminds herself to be consistent with her rationale. Following the demonstration, Dawn meets with the two observers to help them understand how the Jigsaw strategy can be applied in their classrooms. She answers their questions and concerns and encourages them to give it a try. She also invites them to observe her again to enhance their understanding and application of this instructional technique.

Dawn has seven years of teaching experience, but she just recently started modeling selected cooperative learning strategies such as Jigsaw. Her path to becoming a collaborative model began with developing an interest in cooperative learning. She went to workshops and observed colleagues. Finally, she worked with a collaborative coach named Sarah James.

With ten years of experience, Sarah is a veteran teacher like Dawn. To initiate their collaborative coaching relationship, Sarah asked Dawn to write down her professional development goals. One of Dawn's goals was to develop her ability to use the Jigsaw strategy in her social studies class.

To help Dawn make progress toward her goal, the two agreed on a plan. Dawn wanted Sarah to observe her class every two weeks so that she could receive feedback about her use of Jigsaw.

In addition to the observations, they scheduled time to confer before and after each observation. Prior to the observation, Dawn explained to Sarah what she planned to do. Following the observation, Sarah's coaching feedback was guided by the following questions: How did you help student team #2 work together? How did you work with the student who was wasting her time? Questions like these provided Dawn with an opportunity to think about the reasons for her actions and consider ways to change those actions if needed.

Sarah learned to coach by developing her expertise with student team learning and then refining her techniques by engaging in collaborative supervision with Carol Delaney. Like Dawn, Sarah had been fascinated by Jigsaw and was eager to employ it in her class. She observed an experienced teacher model this strategy in a class, just as Dawn, Richard, and Prentice did later. She was then coached on the use of this technique, as she later coached Dawn.

As she developed more confidence in using Jigsaw, Sarah felt the need to receive more evaluative feedback. To this end, Carol, another veteran teacher in the Bay School District who had 13 years of experience, met with Sarah to plan their course of action for collaborative supervision. They agreed on a schedule in which Carol would observe Sarah on a regular basis, talk with her before and after each observation, and encourage her to evaluate her own teaching.

As a proponent of constructivist learning, Carol expressed her evaluative feedback in the form of questions to encourage Sarah to reflect on her teaching. She made these inquiries: How do you think the lesson went? What were some of the strengths of the lesson? What would you change if you taught this lesson again? Why?

Sarah and Carol both expressed a specific concern regarding Jamie, a particularly resistant male student who refused to participate in his Jigsaw group.

The teachers worked together to plan ways to help Jamie participate with his team. To enhance Sarah's reflections, Carol posed these questions: How have you planned to encourage this student? How do you think the student will respond? Does your plan reflect any assumptions that you have about this student? What might those assumptions be?

As Sarah enacted her plan, Carol observed, noting questions and suggestions that she would share with Sarah. Following the lesson, Carol supported Sarah's self-evaluation of her work with these inquiries: Regarding this student, did you overlook anything in planning your lesson? What might you have overlooked? How will that information help you plan for the next lesson? What did you appreciate regarding the student's response to the lesson? What would you like to change?

Carol, now a veteran in the Bay School District, began teaching at Bay Elementary School with ten years of experience already under her belt. Because she was new to the district, Carol asked to work with a collaborative mentor. Tara Bradley, a veteran teacher with 15 years' experience, agreed to serve as Carol's mentor. They maintained their mentoring relationship for a two-year period.

At the onset of their collaboration, the two teachers decided to focus on an interest of Carol's: the Jigsaw strategy. They used the steps in the decision-making cycle to determine when Carol wanted to be observed, what she wanted Tara to notice in her observations, how Carol might practice pragmatic reflection, and how and when critical reflection and critical engagement would be appropriate for each of them.

One of Carol's reasons for wanting to use Jigsaw was the history of this particular class. These students had not been interested in school work throughout their years at Bay Elementary. Any students who expressed a desire to learn were quickly ridiculed by their peers.

As a veteran with ten years of experience, Carol was determined to change this attitude. She shared her hopes for improvement with Tara, along with her idea to use Jigsaw to help remedy the lack of student interest and involvement.

In spite of her years of experience, Carol felt anxious about initiating the collaborative relationship. She and Tara agreed to share a journal, making and reading each other's entries to provide Carol with a chance to express her feelings with a trusted colleague. In addition, Carol could receive support from Tara throughout the process.

The journal became an indispensable tool as Carol encountered numerous challenges. Carol was especially troubled by her impatience with many of her students' lack of motivation to learn. After all her hard work, Carol was extremely frustrated and depressed.

Tara knew from years of experience as a mentor that Carol needed an inspiration. She found a special poem that she shared with Carol. The tears that appeared in Carol's eyes as she read the poem confirmed Tara's decision to inspire her protégé.

The Experiential Continuum and Collaborative Applications

Now that you are familiar with the reasons for professional collaboration and some ways in which teachers can collaborate with one another, you may want to consider how you can work with these ideas in your own setting. The general advice offered in the following questions is adapted to the continuum of personal-professional growth, which was presented in chapter 7. As you read through these questions, you may want to record your responses in a journal. As with all the other inquiries in this book, these questions are only illustrative. They do not exhaust all the ways you can examine your personal-professional collaboration.

1. In your experiences prior to preservice field work, have you been involved in any of the five forms of collaborative study: collaborative exchanging, modeling, coaching, supervision, or mentoring? Describe the experience. With whom were you involved in collaborative study? Which of the 4C virtues—calling, caring, creative, centered—did these people demonstrate? What was the length of these relationships and/or the nature of the commitment? Was there mutuality in these relationships? Did you run into any problems? If so, how did you solve them? How were your collaborations helpful?

2. During your early preservice field work and later preservice field work (student teaching or internship), do you have a chance to participate in any professional collaboration? What forms of collaborative approaches have occurred? Do the people with whom you collaborate demonstrate any of the 4C virtues? Which ones are they, and how are they demonstrated? If you do not receive collaborative support during these stages, what form of support would you like to have? Are there people who would have supported the career-long study of your constructivist practices at your school or university? What form of collaboration might have taken place?

3. Are you receiving support for the career-long study of your constructivist practices in the first three years of teaching? If so, what form of collaboration takes place? How mutual is the relationship? If you are not receiving support, what form of collaboration would you like to have? How can you go about receiving support in your school? How important is this type of support during your first three years of teaching?

4. As you cultivate the career-long study of your constructivist practices between the fourth and sixth years of teaching or between the seventh and twenty-fifth years of teaching, do you engage in collaborative practices with other teachers? What forms of collaboration do you use? How do you support less experienced teachers' career-long development? How do you demonstrate the value of collaborative practices to those with less experience? How do you support their continuing development?

FURTHER READINGS

This section is designed to refine your understanding of collaborative practices and illustrate the variety of applications that are possible with each of the five collaborative approaches. You are encouraged to refer to this section, which features a list of readings about ways in which teachers, company employees, doctors, attorneys, social workers, and other professionals around the world engage in collaborative activities.

The suggested readings are categorized according to collaborative approach; but because these approaches overlap to a degree, each reading may describe more than one approach. You are now invited to select some of these readings to further your thinking on professional collaboration.

COLLABORATIVE EXCHANGING

Comeaux, M. (1991). But is it "teaching"? The use of collaborative learning in teacher education. In B. R. Tabachnick & K. M. Zeichner (Eds.), *Issues and practices in inquiry-oriented teacher education* (pp. 151–162). London: Falmer Press.

Greenwood, D. J. (1991). Collective reflective practice through participatory action research: A case study from the Fagor Cooperatives of Mondragón. In D. A. Schön (Ed.), *The reflective turn: Case studies in and on educational practice* (pp. 84–107). New York: Teachers College Press.

Heron, J. (1985). The role of reflection in a co-operative inquiry. In D. Boud, R. Keogh, & D. Walker (Eds.), *Reflection: Turning experience into learning* (pp. 128–138). London: Kogan Page.

Houston, W. R., & Clift, R. T. (1990). The potentials for research contributions for reflective practice. In R. T. Clift, W. R. Houston, & M. C. Pugach (Eds.), *Encouraging reflective practice in education: An analysis of issues and problems* (pp. 208–222). New York: Teachers College Press.

COLLABORATIVE MODELING

Ciriello, M. J., Valli, L., & Taylor, N. E. (1992). Problem solving is not enough: Reflective teacher education at the Catholic University of America. In L. Valli (Ed.), *Reflective teacher education: Cases and critiques* (pp. 99–115). Albany: State University of New York Press.

McCaleb, J., Borko, H., & Arends, R. (1992). Reflection, research, and repertoire in the Masters Certification Program at the University of Maryland. In L. Valli (Ed.), *Reflective teacher education: Cases and critiques* (pp. 40–64). Albany: State University of New York Press.

Ross, D. D., Johnson, M., & Smith, W. (1992). Developing a PROfessional TEACHer at the University of Florida. In L. Valli (Ed.), *Reflective teacher education: Cases and critiques* (pp. 24–39). Albany: State University of New York Press.

COLLABORATIVE COACHING

Colton, A. B., & Sparks-Langer, G. (1992). Restructuring student teaching experiences. In C. Glickman (Ed.), *Supervision in transition, 1992 Association for Supervision and Curriculum Development Yearbook* (pp. 155–168). Alexandria, VA: Association for Supervision and Curriculum Development.

Hillkirk, K., Tome, J., & Wandress, W. (1989). Integrating reflection into staff development programs. *Journal of Staff Development, 10*(2), Spring, 54–58.

Langer, G. M., & Colton, A. B. (1994). Reflective decision making: The cornerstone of school reform. *Journal of Staff Development, 15*(1), Winter, 2–7.

Schön, D. A. (1988). Coaching reflective teaching. In P. P. Grimmett & G. L. Erickson (Eds.), *Reflective teacher education* (pp. 19–29). New York: Teachers College Press.

COLLABORATIVE SUPERVISION

Newman, C. S. (1994). *Emancipatory constructivism in supervision: A view of the garden.* Unpublished paper. Kent State University.

Oja, S. N., Diller, A., Corcoran, E., & Andrew, M. D. (1992). Communities of inquiry, communities of support: The five year teacher education program at the University of New Hampshire. In L. Valli (Ed.), *Reflective teacher education: Cases and critiques* (pp. 3–23). Albany: State University of New York Press.

Pamplin, L. (1993). Dusty images. In D. J. Clandinin, A. Davics, P. Hogan, & B. Kennard (Eds.), *Learning to teach, teaching to learn: Stories of collaboration in teacher education* (pp. 137–145). New York: Teachers College Press.

Putnam, J., & Grant, S. G. (1992). Reflective practice in the Multiple Perspectives Program at Michigan State University. In L. Valli (Ed.), *Reflective teacher education: Cases and critiques* (pp. 82–98). Albany: State University of New York Press.

COLLABORATIVE MENTORING

Applegate, J., Shaklee, B., & Hutchinson, L. (1989). *Stimulating reflection about learning to teach.* Paper presented at the Annual Meeting of the American Educational Research Association, San Francisco, CA.

Dollase, R. H. (1992). *Voices of beginning teachers: Visions and realities.* New York: Teachers College Press.

Field, B., & Field, T. (Eds.). (1994). *Teachers as mentors: A practical guide.* London: Falmer.

Reiman, A. J., Head, F. A., & Thies-Sprinthall, L. (1992). Collaboration and mentoring. In T. M. Bey & C. T. Holmes (Eds.), *Mentoring: Contemporary principals and issues* (pp. 79–93). Reston, VA: Association of Teacher Educators.

REFERENCES

Berkey, R., Curtis, T., Minnick, F., Zietlow, K., Campbell, D., & Kirschner, B. W. (1990). Collaborating for reflective practice: Voices of teachers, administrators, and researchers. *Education and Urban Society, 22*, February, 204–232.

Clandinin, D. J. (1993). Teacher education as narrative inquiry. In D. J. Clandinin, A. Davies, P. Hogan, & B. Kennard (Eds.), *Learning to teach, teaching to learn: Stories of collaboration in teacher education* (pp. 1–15). New York: Teachers College Press.

Clandinin, D. J., Davies, A., Hogan, P., & Kennard, B. (Eds.). (1993). *Learning to teach, teaching to learn: Stories of collaboration in teacher education*. New York: Teachers College Press.

Cook, D. L., & Cookingham, F. C. (1980). Interagency action; Cooperation, coordination, collaboration. *Community Education Journal*, 7, January, 3–4.

Costa, A. L., & Garmston, R. J. (1994). *Cognitive coaching: A foundation for renaissance schools*. Norwood, MA: Christopher Gordon.

Cummings, T. G., & Worley, C. G. (1993). *Organization development and change* (5th ed.). St. Paul: West.

Daloz, L. A. (1986). *Effective teaching and mentoring: Realizing the transformational power of adult learning experiences*. San Francisco: Jossey-Bass.

Erikson, E. H. (1968). *Identity: Youth and crisis*. New York: W. W. Norton.

Garman, N. B. (1993). Teacher directed evaluation of teaching: An interpretive perspective. Invited presentation at the Annual Meeting of the American Educational Research Association, Atlanta, GA, April, 1993.

Hardcastle, B. (1988). Spiritual connections: Protégés' reflections on significant mentorships. *Theory Into Practice*, 27, 201–208.

Henderson, J. G. (1992). *Reflective teaching: Becoming an inquiring educator*. New York: Macmillan.

Hillkirk, K., & Nolan, J. F. (1990). The evolution of a reflective coaching program: School-university collaboration for professional development. ERIC document.

Kindsvatter, R., Wilen, W. & Ishler, M. (1992). *Dynamics of effective teaching* (2nd ed.). New York: Longman.

Kreisberg, S. (1992). *Transforming power: Domination, power, and education*. Albany: State University of New York Press.

Levinson, D. J., Darrow, C. N., Klein, E. B., Levinson, M. H., & McKee, B. (1978). *The seasons of a man's life*. New York: Alfred A. Knopf.

Luft, J. (1984). *Group process: An introduction to group dynamics* (3rd ed.). Mountain View, CA: Mayfield.

Newman, C. S. (1994). *Emancipatory constructivism in supervision: A view of the garden*. Unpublished paper. Kent State University.

Oja, S. N., Diller, A., Corcoran, E., & Andrew, M. D. (1992). Communities of inquiry, communities of support: The five year teacher education program at the University of New Hampshire. In L. Valli (Ed.), *Reflective teacher education: Cases and critiques* (pp. 3–23). Albany: State University of New York Press.

Ross, D. D., Johnson, M., & Smith, W. (1992). Developing a PROfessional TEACHer at the University of Florida. In L. Valli (Ed.), *Reflective teacher educator: Cases and critiques* (pp. 24–39). Albany: State University of New York Press.

Schön, D. A. (1987). *Educating the reflective practitioner: Toward a new design for teaching and learning in the professions*. San Francisco: Jossey-Bass.

Schubert, W. H. (1986). *Curriculum: Perspective, paradigm, and possibility*. New York: Macmillan.

Sergiovanni, T. J. (1990). *Value added leadership: How to get extraordinary performance in schools*. San Francisco: Jossey-Bass.

Slavin, R. E. (1991). Synthesis of research on cooperative learning. *Educational Leadership*, *48*(5), February, 71–77, 79–82.

Smyth, J., & Garman, N. (1989). Supervision-as-school reform: A critical perspective. *Journal of Educational Policy*, *4*, 343–361.

Stanulis, R. N. (1994). Fading to a whisper: One mentor's story of sharing her wisdom without telling answers. *Journal of Teacher Education*, *45*, 31–38.

Stanulis, R. N., & Jeffers, L. (1995). Action research as a way of learning about teaching in a mentor/student teacher relationship. *Action in Teacher Education*, *16*(4), Winter, 14–24.

Vygotsky, L. S. (1978). *Mind in society: The development of higher psychological process* (M. Cole, V. John-Steiner, S. Scribner, & E. Souberman, Eds. and Trans.). Cambridge, MA: Harvard University Press.

9

Transformative Teacher Leadership

"Appearances can be deceiving," Cameron reminded me as we pulled into the parking lot. I knew what she meant. I certainly was not impressed with the rambling old building. Who would have ever imagined that we would come back to Barber School in the first place? We were successful in our current schools. We were tenured teachers with well-established classrooms and congenial working relationships with our fellow teachers and the principal. One of us had a Master's degree, the other had numerous professional workshops and postgraduate course work to her credit. Why were we placing ourselves in such a vulnerable situation? Why were we interviewing with a faculty team for positions in a center of inquiry school?

One reason was that we decided providing a better quality of educational services to our students meant more than maintaining the status quo—a familiar and apparently outwardly successful work routine. Yes, our students did well on standardized tests, and the community was generally pleased with our teaching. We were dissatisfied, however, with the isolated and fragmented nature of classroom teaching. We found it cumbersome to support each other's teaching inquiry in a setting where teaching and learning were maintained as individual endeavors. It was our sense that professional growth depended on a school setting that encouraged time for dedicated study, planning, observation, and review.

The interviews were the first clue that this truly was an extraordinary school. Since Cameron and I were applying to teach in the primary team, we were interviewed together. The interviewers were the entire primary staff, including the teachers, librarian, principal, student interns, and the parent resource committee. Instead of the typical series of questions directed at a candidate by a principal with a team of teachers observing, the interview was more a conversation among all of us about center of inquiry schools. It was the most thoughtful dialogue about teaching and learning that I had ever been part of. We talked about ideas such as our individual interpretations of constructivist teaching and the role of public schools and teachers in a democratic society. We were asked to describe our personal sense of being called to the education profession and our views on caring and creative teaching. The primary team was clearly interested in our pragmatic and critical development. At the conclusion of the interview, we were asked to share our view of teacher leadership. In preparation for the interviews, Cameron and I had prepared the following brief statement which we read to the interview team:

Transformative teacher leaders believe in the generative power of collaborative study. They feel that this study should support progressive decision-making. We recognize that teachers will study their practice in different ways, and we will be sure to celebrate those differences as long as teachers are committed to pragmatic reconsideration and critical examination. We also recognize that over time, a center of inquiry school may need to undergo fundamental organizational changes.

Today I am pleased to say Cameron and I are in our third year as teacher leaders at Barber. Working in a teacher-initiated school-restructuring project has been a challenging, complex business. We agree that the greatest challenge has been cultivating the professional relationships that support collaborative study. We co-construct curriculum, team teach, plan, enact the plan, observe and review together, organize schedules, interview potential interns, and serve as mentors to current interns. Teaching in a school that is organized to provide time for individual and collective reflection on practice enhances and sustains our personal-professional development. We are guided by the insights and questions of our teammates and we appreciate the sense of professional accountability that is developing in our school.

At the heart of our center of inquiry school is the belief that there is a harmony created by a strong sense of responsibility for planning, supporting, and facilitating career-long personal-professional development. The teachers that originally proposed the charter for our school sought the commitment of the school district's administration to support professional growth for all faculty. This agreement designates six percent of our school operating budget for professional development activities. This money is managed by the faculty. It supports twenty percent of our time—the equivalent of one day per work week—for professional development, including curriculum planning, coaching and mentoring student interns, action research, and other activities. This time is made possible by including two interns in our school's six teaching teams.

With the support of veteran teachers, the interns take over a classroom, which enables the teacher to engage in professional development activities.

We strive to create and sustain our visions of a learning community through collaborative problem solving, dialogue, and the cultivation of community trust. We have grown beyond independence and self-reliance to the most empowering position of all: interdependence. This provides the safe environment needed to practice, to risk, and to grow.

Yes, as Cameron said, "Looks are deceiving."[1]

This book portrays for you a particular ideal of reflective teaching, which is described as progressive decision-making. It illustrates actions that will facilitate your becoming a career-long student of your constructivist teaching. The study of your educational practices is guided by three forms of reflecting: pragmatic reconsideration, critical reasoning, and critical engagement. If you feel called to becoming a progressive decision-maker, the ideal venue for your development will be a professional learning community. This chapter will offer suggestions and illustrations on how you might lend your support to the creation of such a community.

The school community described in the vignette, Barber School, exists only in the collective understandings of the authors of this book. It was envisioned as a response to two questions:

- What could a school, staffed with teachers who share the progressive decision-making ideal, become?
- Who helps create and sustain such a school?

Transformative Leadership

For a school to become a center of inquiry, which can be defined as a place where teachers are continuously learning through their individual and collaborative reflective practices, it must be staffed with teachers who believe they can influence, as well as be influenced by, the school's professional culture. This sense of community-based agency lies at the heart of transformative leadership. Burns (1978) argues that transformative leaders promote empowerment by establishing a social environment that fosters "principled levels of judgment" (p. 455). In contrast, traditional school leadership focuses on attainment of goals and objectives instead of "consciousness raising on a wide plane" (p. 43). Transformative leadership is "conceived not in terms of control, but rather in terms of guiding others to higher levels of judgment and self-governance" (Snauwert, 1993, p. 7).

---

[1] The collaborative work of the faculty of the Edward Devotion School in Brookline, Massachusetts, as described by K. Boles and V. Troen in their paper, *Teacher Leadership in a Professional Development School*, which was presented at the annual meeting of the American Educational Research Association, New Orleans, 1994, served as an inspiration for this vignette.

Many people can serve as transformative leaders in a progressive learning community. There might be a committee of parents and teachers who desire to create a more meaningful way to communicate students' progress than the common letter-grade report card. There might be a building principal and a dedicated group of teachers and interns working together, who are willing to critically examine their practices with respect to the National Council of Teachers of Mathematics (NCTM) Standards for teaching mathematics. There might be a group of teachers who want to focus on expanding their capabilities to use computers more effectively for teaching. Whoever assumes the responsibilities of transformative leadership in a school or school-community context is attempting to initiate and support activities that promote teachers' individual and collective progressive decision-making.

Transformative Teacher Leadership

Our focus in this chapter is transformative teacher leaders—professionals who help create collaborative cultures that support reflective practice. Teachers who are willing to undertake the challenges of transformative teacher leadership, like the imaginary Cameron and Barb in the opening vignette, will need to assume a broad range of overlapping **reform responsibilities**:

1. Changing staff development by encouraging a commitment to career-long study.
2. Encouraging individual and group curriculum and teaching deliberations.
3. Encouraging collaboration between teachers and other direct service providers.
4. Establishing a collaborative climate based on responsible diversity.
5. Altering power relationships and organizational structures.
6. Creating opportunities for **job enhancement** for teachers and other direct service providers.
7. Providing local policy leadership within the school and between the school and its neighboring community.

As you gain experience with the study methods discussed in chapters 3–6, you will be better prepared to engage in your own brand of transformative leadership. By becoming a reflective teacher, you are practicing a service ideal that can help unite teachers as true professionals.

Our country needs teachers who will accept the challenge of transformative leadership to support the development of teachers as true professionals working in schools that are centers of inquiry. If you work in an institutional environment that does not support your development as an empowered professional, consider these two questions:

1. How can I become an adept progressive decision-maker when confronted by administrators and administrative policy with a top-down management orientation?
2. How can I cultivate a study group that will help me develop as an empowered professional?

The first question is especially relevant if you are not a practicing teacher. If you are about to do field work in conjunction with your professional course work or concluding your field work as a student teacher or intern, you may find three problem-solving strategies useful. Goodman (1988) calls these strategies critical compliance, accommodative resistance, and transformative action.

Critical compliance is the least radical strategy. When you are critically compliant, you examine disruptions to progressive decision-making in your everyday relations, but you don't immediately try to alter your circumstances. Instead, you bide your time until you become more "politically" secure, for example, until you become tenured. Though you don't exhibit empowered behavior, you engage in necessary critical inquiry to keep your hopes alive and prevent yourself from being co-opted by a disempowering organization. When you have established the necessary political base, you can begin to act as a transformative teacher. Goodman (1988) describes one student teacher who followed the school district's phonics approach to reading but remained critical of this mandated curriculum. In effect, she patiently waited for the day when she could teach in accordance with her best professional judgment. She remarked:

> I don't know if grouping words by phonics is the best way to teach spelling. We [adults] don't learn to spell by having it on a list, writing it three times, and then having a test over it. Usually, if people read [and write] a lot, they will learn to spell. (p. 32)

Accommodative resistance is a step up from critical compliance in political engagement. In this strategy you publicly comply with school policy, but you look for small ways to function as an empowered professional. For example, you find ways to facilitate constructivist learning while still following your school district's mandated skill instruction, which is usually controlled through administration of standardized tests, such as proficiency exams. Goodman (1988) describes an accommodative resistance strategy that student teachers used to supplement the morning lessons they were mandated to teach:

> Several student teachers brought in instructional games they had developed. For example, Joan set up a learning center board game that helped children (first- and second-graders) recognize antonyms, homonyms, and synonyms. The children were told that they could play this game after they had finished their morning work. (p. 33)

The third strategy is *transformative action*, in which you begin to take major steps to transform the work you do as a teacher. You may act either as a single agent or in a coordinated effort with others. For example, you develop teaching units that directly challenge the mandated curriculum of the school district. Equally significant, you are willing to publicly defend your alternative classroom curriculum leadership. As another example, you might work with other teachers to develop meaningful collaborative coaching and supervision as an empowering substitute for the type of supervision currently mandated by the administration. A third example would be to devise collaborative professional development activities as alternatives to the school district's typical staff development offerings.

Consider how you might apply these three strategies to your own personal-professional development as a transformative teacher leader. Can you think of any other strategies that might be useful? Critical compliance, accommodative resistance, transformative action, and other potential empowerment strategies will be difficult to practice if you are not part of a school learning community that supports your progressive decision-making. A secondary education preservice student who inquired into her personal-professional development describes how she has already begun to create her own support group.

> One of my most important priorities is networking to provide myself with a supportive base. My peers will help to encourage me, brainstorm with me, and advise me. I, in return, will make myself available to help them. Together we can support each other as we grow more knowledgeable through pursuit of our personal educational ideas.
>
> Setting up my own support group began as easily as trading phone numbers with my fellow students. At first, it was natural to do this in case either of us missed class, but the action soon took on more significance. I found myself talking over my philosophies of education with my peers, and we also talked about how much we could use some peer support during student teaching. Soon I found myself with a group of students, who, like myself, wanted to band together.
>
> As I did the required field experience hours, I became acquainted with many teachers. I looked for support from many different types of teachers, and I have found some. I also keep my eyes and ears open.
>
> I've met teachers in restaurants, at wedding receptions, and at alumni functions. In fact, my wedding photographer was a moonlighting teacher. He was so eager to encourage me that when I bumped into him at a friend's wedding reception, he took a lot of time to share his teaching experiences with me.
>
> Teachers are like air. They are everywhere, and they always seem to be supportive and open. I find it amazing to listen to the inspiring stories some of these teachers have shared. My parting note is always, "Would you mind if I gave you a call sometime?" I haven't had anyone say "no" yet. (Henderson, 1992, pp. 166–167)

The rest of this chapter is devoted to a more careful examination of the seven reform responsibilities listed earlier in this section. This examination will clarify the activities of transformative teacher leadership. As you study these activities, keep in mind that the overall goal of a transformative teacher leader is to help articulate the creation of a school as a center of inquiry, which was defined earlier as a place where teachers are continuously learning through their individual and collaborative reflective practices.

Staff Development

Transformative teacher leaders understand staff development as teacher-generated pragmatic reflection and critical inquiry. The developmental focus is on teachers' questions in a particular school community. As Lieberman (1995) notes, "traditional staff development involves workshops and conferences conducted outside of school [often] with the help of a long-term consultant" (p. 591). This conventional view of staff development as inservice assumes that "other people's understanding of teaching and learning is more important and that the knowledge gained from the dailiness of work with students is of far less value" (p. 592). In traditional staff development topics are often selected by principals and curriculum specialists. Teachers are not supported as proactive learners with their own professional development purposes.

Transformative teachers have a dramatically different understanding of staff development. They are committed to collaborative study that is centered on teachers' work, and that generates new personal-professional knowledge. They have a strong commitment to "making organizational learning a way of life" (Senge, 1990, p. 24). They believe that teachers can serve as catalysts for one another's learning (Troen & Boles, 1994). They would agree with Goodlad (1994) that the mark of a professional is someone who is "continuously engaged in self-improvement" (p. 38).

Lieberman (1995) describes this new approach to continuing professional development. Her discussion includes the following three points. First, staff development must include the creation of a culture of inquiry, where professional learning is expected, sought after, and an ongoing part of teaching and school life. Second, teachers are involved in the decision-making about the substance, process, and organizational supports for individual and collective teacher inquiry and deliberation. Third, the staff development activities should facilitate long-term professional study aimed at changing teaching practices and the school culture (pp. 592–596).

Curriculum and Teaching Deliberations

The center of inquiry school in the opening vignette is grounded in Sirotnik's (1989) argument that a school should be a center of change, rather than a target for change. Transformative teacher leaders work as initiators of change, engaging in various meaningful deliberations to enhance constructivist learning. This type of decision-making must be thoughtful and patient and not a hasty response to policy mandates or administrative questions.

Schubert (1986) calls this deliberative reasoning "practical curriculum inquiry." He writes: "In deliberation, human beings are creators of knowledge who inform actions in situations they encounter" (p. 286). When teachers decide in this way, they increase their "capacity to act morally and effectively in pedagogical situations" (p. 289). Henderson and Hawthorne (1995) discuss curriculum and teaching deliberations from the perspective of a school-community partnership. They write: "Practical curriculum inquiry is also directed toward examination of the beliefs, thoughts, decision-making and judgments of teachers and others as they engage in curriculum design, development, enactment and evaluation practices" (p. 57).

A case study of the Fratney Elementary School in Milwaukee described how one staff used collaborative curriculum and teaching deliberations to solve an educational problem. The faculty at Fratney practiced the whole-language approach to reading and writing and, as a result, their students were not accustomed to the fill-in-the-correct-response type of testing the district uses. The teachers were not surprised "by the lower-than-average (but somewhat higher-than-expected) test scores for students on the district-wide reading tests" (Wood, 1992, p. 260). Wood (1992) further describes the faculty's deliberations:

> The staff has begun to attack this challenge on two fronts, first by just teaching kids what is not-so-lovingly called "reading-test-reading." Recognizing that kids will, for the short run, frequently be facing such tests, teachers are showing kids how the tests work, how to understand the questions asked, and the proper way to fill in the test forms. On the second front, the staff is researching and developing alternative ways to measure reading success that are consistent with their approach to teaching reading. While they hold little hope for that, the entire district will soon change its approach to testing. They feel confident they will find more accurate ways to report to parents what their kids are learning. (p. 260)

Collaboration with Direct Service Providers

Children have many needs that, while not clearly the responsibility of their school, certainly have influence over the quality of their educational experiences. Transformative teacher leaders accept the responsibility to work cooperatively with community agencies and organizations to coordinate the delivery of services that meet the developmental needs of children and their families. The Alberta Teachers' Association (1994) has addressed this concern:

> While the school may serve as the *site* for delivering such noneducational services as lunches, family counseling, and health care, teachers should not be the *agents* of delivery. A consolidation and coordination of services to children would better meet the needs of children and would better allow teachers to meet children's educational needs. (p. 10)

Another area within education in which teachers would most likely identify a need for a broad-based, interprofessional collaboration is what has been commonly called *special education*. Special education services are being restructured to reflect the movement toward a more fully inclusive society through legislation such as the Americans with Disabilities Act of 1990 (ADA), Individuals with Disabilities Act Amendments of 1991 (IDEA), and Goals 2000: The Educate America Act (1994). Strawderman and Lindsey (1995) describe the concept:

> The full inclusion model places children with disabilities in regular classrooms with support from specialists for all or a greater part of the school day. The roles and responsibilities of both the general and the special educator are dramatically altered in this model. An inclusive school environment demands more collaboration and cooperative planning among professional educators, administrators and parents and more specific modifications to existing curricular expectations and assessment practices. (p. 95)

A first-year teacher describes her success in facilitating these connections:

I taught a Down's Syndrome child who was very frustrated. I convened a meeting that included the district's experts, [the child's] parent, and a resource teacher, suggesting a change in educational strategy. All agreed to the pilot plan, and things have worked more smoothly ever since. It was a very rewarding experience. (Daugherty, 1994, p. 11)

Encouraging Responsible Diversity

Transformative teacher leaders respect and are willing to support the diverse professional development activities of their colleagues. They understand that teacher growth has unique personal dimensions. They tolerate and, when appropriate, even celebrate the differing beliefs of their colleagues. They would be comfortable working in a school that had several Johnny Jacksons, Amy Nelsons, Dennis Sages, and Silvia Riveras. They accept the complex ideological foundations of the education profession and do their best to establish a collaborative climate based on the commonality of continuing professional development in a context of personal-professional diversity. They respect teachers' idiosyncrasies as long as these differences don't undermine a collaborative ethic.

Henderson and Hawthorne (1995) provide an overview of how this type of professional climate can be initiated and sustained:

Just as dissonance is the impetus for self-reflection, it can also generate group reflection and changes in . . . [the] climate of a culture. Two ingredients are needed to foster the dissonance, reflection, and action cycle of a learning community: (a) descriptive data analyzed and interpreted by the group, and (b) a context of trust and honest dialogue. Without authentic and contextually based information and a willingness to confront the realities of the group's collective actions, school faculty and community groups will not have or sustain a learning community. A safety net of caring participants is a necessity when confronting the realities of . . . a school's own . . . policies and practices, resolving the conflicts that necessarily emerge in such intense and important work, and taking the risks needed to try on new beliefs and actions. A closely related virtue is that of the capacity for forgiveness (Huebner, 1966). To take on the challenges, the risks, and the uncertainty of a learning community requires the ability to forgive errors, blunders, stupidity, and arrogance—particularly when we are the guilty parties. (Henderson & Hawthorne, 1995, p. 96)

Initiating constructive dialogue with a diverse group of professionals who may not have much collaborative experience is an ambitious undertaking. Boles (1992) cautions leaders to plan carefully and address the problems of professional collaboration. The teachers in Boles' study noted three main problems: having difficulty scheduling meetings, having feelings of personal-professional intrusion, and struggling to reach compromises. Boles (1992) writes: "These findings demonstrate how complicated it will be to move from [the] parallel work of isolated classroom teachers to the interdependent work of collegial professionals" (p. 201).

The transformation of a school into a collaborative learning community will take time and patience. Drawing on the work of Schmuck and Runkel (1985), Henderson and Hawthorne (1995) identify three overlapping, long-term stages in this leadership work:

Stage I focuses on training members of the community to examine how they communicate, resolve conflicts, and express trust and regard toward each other. It also provides training directed toward the development of "groupness"; how to deliberate and develop consensus about what is important and what is not, and how to construct a common vision.

Stage II focuses on developing the analytic and critical aspects of community life. The group is trained to identify concerns, gather and analyze data about its own beliefs and functions, engage in problem solving and action planning, and critically assess the overt and covert meanings of their organizational life.

Stage III represents the full integration of human interaction skills, analytical and critical perspectives, and pragmatic problem-solving skills. Here the culture of the learning community develops a spiritual commitment and expresses it through a shared pedagogical covenant (Sergiovanni, 1992). The qualities of life within the community and the qualities of doing curriculum become one. (Henderson & Hawthorne, 1995, pp. 97–98)

Stage I work would include such activities as conducting workshops on group communication, receiving training in conflict resolution, and organizing retreats for community-building. Examples of Stage II activities include undertaking a collaborative action research project on a pertinent question, conducting a school climate survey, and initiating and sharing teacher journals. Stage III work would focus on the creation of broad-based curriculum designs, the establishment of common professional development expectations, and the formation of collaborative programs such as collaborative coaching and collaborative supervision.

The professional development advice in this book is geared to Stage III organizational activities. Translating the reflective teaching scaffolding of this text into a school organization setting may take years of Stage I and II work by transformative teacher leaders, as well as transformative administrators, parents, community leaders, and others. From the perspective of organization development, this book establishes high professional ideals that will not be easy to incorporate into a school culture. The book's reflective teaching guidance can be more readily followed by individual professionals than by groups of professionals at the same organizational site. You need to keep this point in mind as you contemplate becoming a transformative teacher leader.

Altering Power Relationships and Organizational Structures

Transformative leaders must also help administrators, teachers, and other relevant individuals reconsider power relations and organizational structures in their schools. Transformative leaders do not expect to "receive" power from their school administration. They find little value in roles such as those of designated teacher leader, mentor, or coach that are established by administrative selection, policy mandates, or collective bargaining agreements. Transformative leaders empower themselves through professional relationships. They establish their relationships from a power-with orientation. This is sometimes called *power-sharing*. Recall the distinctions between power-over and power-with leadership from chapters 6 and 8. Teachers with a power-over perspective expect to implement the decisions of other authorities. They prefer to teach in a setting with a "traditional authoritarian, command and control hierarchy where the top thinks and the locals act" (Senge, 1990, p. 288). Teacher leaders working with a power-with perspective integrate thought and action. They see themselves as unique reflective practitioners who are willing to work with other unique reflective practitioners. They respect ideological differences within a context of responsible autonomy. By demonstrating respect for the thoughts and feelings of their professional peers, they help nurture a sense of personal and collective empowerment.

Transformative leaders are "system thinkers" (Senge, 1990) who sponsor the efforts of all members of their professional community to work collaboratively to solve complex social and learning problems. They collaborate to plan, enact, observe, and reconsider constructivist transactions. They view colleagues as resources with whom they want to share teaching and learning experiences.

Consider the practice of collaborative coaching described in chapter 8. The power in this type of professional relationship stems from a mutual agreement. Both parties agree that one person will help a colleague with that person's own unique teaching. There is no attempt to impose an interpretation of "good" teaching on an unwilling professional. While the person being coached is, hopefully, learning a new facet of teaching, the coach may also be learning how to support and encourage a fellow colleague's growth. Because their relationship is based on a power-sharing ethic, their collaboration can be mutually beneficial.

New conceptions of teaching and leadership will not mesh with the traditional structure of schools where the top—the administration—thinks and the locals—the faculty—react. Transformative teacher leaders promote an alternative view of the focus of educational decision-making. Wood (1992) summarizes their beliefs:

> The power of decision-making about the things that really matter—curriculum, school organization, the budget, the evaluation and treatment of students—must be moved from the statehouse and the central office to the schoolhouse and classroom. (p. 244)

This is not to say that teachers make all decisions. The point is to relocate decision-making to the place where the decisions impact the day-to-day operations of the school.

In a learning community, teachers need time for pragmatic reflection and critical inquiry. When decision-making is centered within the school community, faculties are able to reorganize their work to best meet the learning needs of their students along with the professional needs of the faculty.

Troen and Boles (1994) describe how creating teaching teams at the Learning/Teaching Collaborative in Brookline, Massachusetts, required new organizational structures:

> . . . Time as a facilitating factor. A key feature of the collaborative is the allocation of a significant amount of professional time to be used by the teacher at his or her discretion.

By providing full-time graduate-student interns to work in classrooms, the collaborative has managed to fulfill the promise of creating more time for teachers. Not only are there two teachers in the classroom during most of the week, but the presence of the interns has provided the teachers with time during the week to pursue their own professional development . . . six hours a week away from classroom responsibilities. (p. 281)

Job Enhancement

Working in a collaborative culture offers the practitioners a variety of opportunities to expand the scope of their professional responsibilities. While serving as catalysts for the creation of a learning community, transformative teacher leaders may get involved in a variety of curriculum and professional development activities, for example, chairing a mathematics reform committee, coordinating a mentoring program, or creating a teacher study group. Referring to the Learning/Teaching Collaborative, Troen and Boles (1994) note:

All teachers have assumed new responsibilities to fill the time. They speak about how busy they are, but they do not complain about their inability to accomplish their work because of a lack of time. Nor do they describe feeling guilty about being away from their children or being unable to accomplish their primary role of classroom teacher, though they all have taken on additional professional roles. (p. 281)

By expanding their professional responsibilities, transformative teacher leaders may experience the joys of increased professional collegiality. Troen and Boles (1994) quote one of the teacher leaders at the Learning/Teaching Collaborative:

This is teacher-run and there's more involvement with other teachers—and the whole idea that I'm part of this team of teachers has really changed my teaching life. (p. 9)

Local Policy Leadership

Transformative teacher leaders willingly enter educational politics to help create local policies that support schools as centers of inquiry. They seek the establishment of "*new policies* that foster new structures and institutional arrangements for teachers' learning" (Darling-Hammond & McLaughlin, 1995, p. 598). Transformative teacher leaders actively seek opportunities to influence local policy makers to establish "a more democratic approach to decision-making, one that involves teachers in structured and meaningful ways" (The Alberta Teachers' Association, 1994, p. 8). They believe that teachers should be involved in the development of policies that are devised to "*help* teachers do their jobs by creating the necessary conditions in which teaching and learning can flourish" (The Alberta Teachers' Association, 1994, p. 8).

The school board and district administration will need encouragement and support from teachers to establish the appropriate environment for a school that functions as a center of inquiry. According to Darling-Hammond and McLaughlin (1995), this means an environment that will "undertake strategic assessment of existing polices to determine to what degree they are compatible with a vision of learning as constructed by teachers and students and a vision of professional development as a [career-long] inquiry-based, and collegial activity" (p. 598). Policy makers who support schools as centers of inquiry will conduct their deliberations with a facilitative spirit. In this spirit they will generate procedures and agreements and allocate resources to promote and sustain teachers' progressive decision-making.

A common impediment to teachers' decision-making is a policy that requires subjects to be taught for a specified number of minutes each day. Wood (1992) summarizes the isolation created by the factory-like scheduling typical of most secondary schools:

> For secondary school teachers the clock is perhaps the most personal enemy. Meeting on a frenzied schedule of as many as eight class periods of forty-five to fifty minutes a day with twenty to thirty students in each, it's not surprising that many teachers resort to lectures and workbooks. (p. 241–242)

When a policy is designed to allow flexibility in content, teachers can restructure the school day to accommodate their students' learning needs, as well as facilitate the collective study of teaching and learning. Faculties can then design schedules that include "time structured into their days to work on their work" (Wood, 1992, p. 242). Wood describes many schools with such flexible policies in great detail. Although the detail is beyond the scope of this book, it is significant that each school has been able to creatively restructure their schedules to meet situation-specific educational needs.

A Vision of a Transformed Society

You have been introduced to seven responsibilities of transformative teacher leadership. Fulfilling all of these responsibilities is beyond the abilities of most individual teachers. Therefore, this type of leadership must be viewed as a collaborative undertaking. A school does not become a center of inquiry due to the efforts of any one individual. The creation of this type of school is both a collegial and school-community challenge. Transformative teacher leaders are catalysts for personal and organizational change. They facilitate the process indirectly, rather than directly command others.

How many transformative teacher leaders are necessary to facilitate reform in a particular school setting? This is a context-specific question that depends partly on the helping hands of other educational stakeholders. Although this chapter focuses on teachers as leaders, others can serve in this role: parents, administrators, and various community leaders.

Why is transformative teacher leadership a fundamental consideration in this book? Why must some teachers assume the responsibilities of this type of professional leadership for at least a period in their career? The answer to these questions is straightforward: *Without the help of at least a handful of transformative teacher leaders, schools cannot become centers of inquiry.*

Creating centers of inquiry and devoting those centers to providing **constructivist educational services** are the two themes of educational reform that guided the organization of this book, as mentioned in the preface.

Can you imagine an entire society of people who have been educated at schools that function as centers of inquiry? How comfortable would they be with subject matter inquiry, personal inquiry, and social inquiry? What kind of work would they do? What books would they read? What television shows and movies would they watch? What cultural events would they attend? Who would be their heroes and heroines? What kind of society would they support? What would be their politics?

Continue to ponder these critical questions, which serve as the philosophical backdrop for this book. We now invite you to reflect on the following statement composed by John Dewey. In 1939, on the eve of World War II, Dewey contemplated the challenges that democratic societies now faced from Communist Russia and Fascist Germany:

> . . . the democratic road is the hard one to take. It is the road which places the greatest burden of responsibility upon the greatest number of human beings. Backsets and deviations occur and will continue to occur. But that which is its own weakness at particular times is its strength in the long course of human history. Just because the cause of democratic freedom is the cause of the fullest possible realization of human potentialities, the latter when they are suppressed and opposed will in time rebel and demand an opportunity for manifestation. We have advanced far enough to say that democracy is a way of life. We have yet to realize that it is a way of personal life and one which provides a moral standard for personal conduct. (Dewey, 1939/1989, pp. 100–101)

The Experiential Continuum and Transformative Teacher Leadership

You may be hopeful that you can someday secure a teaching position in a school that is becoming a learning community, but perhaps you are a realist and do not anticipate finding one in the near future. The challenge for you is to imagine yourself as a potential transformative teacher leader and carry that vision with you wherever you are teaching. The suggestions and questions offered in the following experiential continuum are intended to facilitate your growth as a transformative teacher leader.

Experiential Continuum

1.   Educational experiences prior to professional course work.   Think back over your classroom experiences as a student. Can you identify a particular class or school setting that exemplifies any of the characteristics of a school as a center of inquiry? What activities and behaviors made these characteristics evident to you as a student?

2.   Early preservice field work in conjunction with professional course work.   These field work experiences will give you the opportunity to observe and respond to some of the qualities and characteristics of a learning organization. Keep a reflective journal of your observations.

Ask to attend staff meetings as an observer. Note the effective communication techniques used by the staff members to promote open, honest dialogue around school issues. Try to develop your own description of the beliefs that might be grounding their deliberations.

3.   Concluding preservice field work as a student teacher or intern.   During your student teaching or internship, work toward developing a collegial relationship with your cooperating teacher, rather than a congenial relationship as discussed in chapter 8. Promote discussion of how collegial relationships are fostered and sustained in the particular school culture. If you are part of a teaching team, extend yourself and work to build your collaborative skills with the other members. Note what specific actions and behaviors connote collegiality to you as well as to your team mates. Ask your cooperating teacher to offer reflections about your strengths in establishing collegial relationships. What suggestions can your teacher offer about your interpersonal skills?

4.   Teaching: the first three years.   The induction year of teaching is usually so intense that you may not have the time to pursue collegial relationships. However, establish a relationship with at least one significant colleague—someone to work with during this important year. This will help support your continuing development of constructivist practices. Focus on your interpersonal skills for open, honest dialogue about teaching. During the second and third years of your teacher career, try to expand your network of colleagues. Consider establishing or joining a professional study group.

5.   Teaching: from the fourth to the sixth year.   By now you may have developed an expansive repertoire of constructivist practices. Through the three forms of inquiry for practice, you have elevated your understanding of individual and collective progressive decision-making. Are you prepared to extend yourself and welcome a student teacher or intern into your teacher setting? This will provide you with an opportunity to re-examine your own experiences and beliefs as you open yourself to another's inquiry into your teaching practices. Can you begin to undertake any of the seven transformative teacher leadership responsibilities? If so, which ones? If not, what obstacles are you facing?

6.   Teaching: from the seventh to the twenty-fifth year.   Are you the teacher envisioned by your novice self a few years ago? What colleagues have been key factors in your professional development? What is the focus of your inquiry now? Have you continued your formal education in graduate school? Have you intentionally changed your job or school assignment to work in a situation more in tune to your beliefs? Are you now able to function as a transformative teacher leader in one of the ways described in this chapter?

REFERENCES

The Alberta Teachers' Association. (1994). *Trying to teach: Necessary conditions*. Edmonton, Alberta, Canada: Author.

Americans with Disabilities Act of 1990, Pub. L. No. 101–336, §1, *et seq.*, 104 Stat. 327 (1990).

Boles, K. (1992). School restructuring by teachers. *The Journal of Applied Behavioral Science*, *28* (2), 173–203.

Burns, J. M. (1978). *Leadership*. New York: Harper & Row.

Darling-Hammond, L., & McLaughlin, M. (1995). Policies that support professional development in an era of reform. *Phi Delta Kappa*, *76*, 597–604.

Daugherty, R. F. (1994). The greatest challenge was the transition from being a student myself to being a teacher of others [Summary]. *Proceedings of the Symposium on Quality Education* (p. 11). Washington, DC: Corporate Communications.

Dewey, J. (1989). *Freedom and culture*. Buffalo, NY: Prometheus. (Original work published 1939)

Goals 2000: Educate America Act, Pub. L. No. 103–227, §1, *et seq.*, 108 Stat. 125 (1994).

Goodlad, J. (1994). *Educational renewal: better teachers better schools*. San Francisco: Jossey-Bass.

Goodman, J. (1988). The political tactics and teaching strategies of reflective, active pre-service teachers. *The Elementary School Journal*, *89*, 23–40.

Henderson, J. G. (1992). *Reflective teaching: Becoming an inquiring educator*. Englewood Cliffs, NJ: Merrill/Prentice Hall.

Henderson, J. G., & Hawthorne, R. D. (1995). *Transformative curriculum leadership*. Englewood Cliffs, NJ: Merrill/Prentice Hall.

Huebner, D. (1966). Curricular language and classroom meanings. In J. Macdonald & R. Leeper (Eds.), *Language and meaning* (pp. 8–26). Washington, DC: Association for Supervision and Curriculum Development.

Individuals with Disabilities Act Amendments of 1991, Pub. L. No. 102–119, §1, *et seq.*, 105 Stat. 587 (1991).

Lieberman, A. (1995). Practices that support teacher development. *Phi Delta Kappa*, *76*, 591–596.

Schmuck, R., & Runkel, P. (1985). *The handbook of organization development in schools* (3rd ed.). Prospect Heights, IL: Waveland Press.

Schubert, W. H. (1986). *Curriculum: Perspective, paradigm, and possibility*. New York: Macmillan.

Senge, P. (1990). *The fifth discipline: The art and practice of the learning organization*. New York: Bantam.

Sergiovanni, T. J. (1992). *Moral leadership: Getting to the heart of school reform*. San Francisco: Jossey-Bass.

Sirotnik, K. A. (1989). The school as the center of change. In T. J. Sergiovanni & J. H. Moore (Eds.), *Schooling for tomorrow: Directing reforms to issues that count* (pp. 89–113). Boston: Allyn & Bacon.

Snauwert, D. (1993). *Democracy, education, and governance: A developmental conception*. Albany: State University of New York Press.

Strawderman, C., & Lindsey, P. (1995). Keeping up with the times: Reform in teacher education. *Journal of Teacher Education, 46*, 95–100.

Troen, V., & Boles, K. (1994). Two teachers examine the power of teacher leadership. In D. Wallings (Ed.), *Teachers as leaders: Perspectives on the professional development of teachers*. Bloomington, IN: Phi Delta Kappa Educational Foundation.

Wood, G. H. (1992). *Schools that work: America's most innovative public education programs*. New York: Penguin Books.

A

The Teacher-Character
Ideological Map

The creation of the four teacher-characters for this book emerges from a synthesis of two systems of ideological analysis. One system was created by Bernier and Williams (1973a) for the purpose of studying the ideological foundations of educational practice in the United States. Bernier (1981) summarizes their system as follows:

> Williams and I, in our analysis of the ideological foundations of American education, identified six major belief systems which give direction to education in the United States. In each case, a teacher model was suggested to illustrate the way in which these ideologies are activated in schools. The belief systems identified and their teacher models are: Scientism—behavior modifier; Romanticism—artist; Puritanism—moral exemplar; Progressivism—facilitator;

Nationalism—patriot or ethnic exemplar; Educationism—professional. (p. 297)

The basis for the other system is an adaptation of Kliebard's (1986) study of American educational curriculum between 1893 and 1958. According to Kliebard, this 65-year time span represents a period "when curriculum reform emerged from somewhat tentative beginnings to become a national preoccupation" (p. xiii). Kliebard identifies four ideological traditions, and his analysis has been adapted to the study of teacher education by Zeichner and Liston (1991). Zeichner and Liston identify four fundamental traditions of good teaching: academic, social efficiency, developmentalist, and social reconstructionist. Because Zeichner and Liston directed their work specifically toward the study of teaching, we will present the four traditions in their system first. We will then explain the ideologies of the teacher-characters including a discussion of Bernier and Williams's more basic foundational analysis.

ZEICHNER AND LISTON'S SYSTEM

Academic Tradition

In Zeichner and Liston's (1991) ideological map, academics argue that good teachers are liberal arts scholars and subject-matter specialists who can facilitate students' disciplined-based inquiries. They help students become conversant with the great ideas of western civilization. Hutchins (1952) summarizes the liberal education goals of academic teachers as follows:

> The liberally educated man [sic] understands, by understanding the distinctions and interrelations of the basic fields of subject matter, the differences and connections between poetry and history, science and philosophy, theoretical and practical science; he understands that the same methods cannot be applied in all these fields; he knows the methods appropriate to each. The liberally educated man comprehends the ideas that are relevant to the basic problems and that operate in the basic fields of subject matter. He knows what is meant by soul, state, God, beauty, and by other terms that are basic to the discussion of fundamental issues. He has some notion of the insights that these ideas, singly or in combination, provide concerning human experience. (pp. 3–4)

Social Efficiency Tradition

Social efficiency advocates believe that good teachers should follow the guidelines established by scientific studies of educational practices. These studies follow a three-part logic:

- Based on a study of society's social and economic needs, decide on appropriate learning achievement objectives for students. These will be the desired quality outcomes or "products" for effective teaching.
- Following statistically valid and reliable descriptive, correlational, and experimental procedures, examine efficient instructional methods or "processes" for achieving these educational products.
- Use the results of this research to establish good competency-based teacher education programs.

After providing a comprehensive literature review of this process-product research, Brophy and Good (1986) write:

> The myth that teachers do not make a difference in student learning has been refuted, and programmatic research reflecting the description-correlation-experimentation loop . . . has begun to appear. As a result, the fund of available information on producing student achievement . . . has progressed from a collection of disappointing and inconsistent findings to a small but well-established knowledge base that includes several successful field experiments. (p. 370)

Developmentalist Tradition

To developmentalists, good teachers practice a child-centered instruction that is based on the study of students' active, developmentally based learning interests. Zeichner and Liston (1991) describe the two-year Developmental Teacher Education Program at the University of California-Berkeley, a graduate program designed in accordance with this ideological frame of reference:

> This program . . . is guided by the view that understanding of developmental principles is the best preparation for teaching. Students

are exposed in their courses to theories of cognitive, social, moral, and language development and then focus in various practicums on the application of developmental principles to the teaching of mathematics, science, and literacy. (p. 12)

Social Reconstructionist Tradition

To social reconstructionists, good teachers address the real problems of social justice in their educational practices. They want to engage in specific emancipatory learning projects because they believe that education is an important avenue for sociocultural reform. Freire (1970/1971) articulates this goal:

> Education as the practice of freedom—as opposed to education as the practice of domination—denies that man [sic] is abstract, isolated, independent, and unattached to the world; it also denies that the world exists as a reality apart from men. Authentic reflection considers neither abstract man nor the world without men, but men in their [problematic] relations with the world. (p. 69)
>
> . . . Problem-posing education, as a humanist and liberating praxis, posits as fundamental that men [sic] subjected to domination must fight for their emancipation. To that end, it enables teachers and students to become Subjects of the educational process by overcoming authoritarianism and an alienating intellectualism; it also enables men to overcome their false perception of reality. The world . . . becomes the object of that transforming action by men which results in their humanization. (p. 74)

IDEOLOGIES OF THE TEACHER-CHARACTERS

The four teacher-characters have been given names and symbols denoting their ideological frame of reference.

Johnny Jackson advocates Zeichner and Liston's (1991) academic belief system. His symbol is an open book, standing for the love of great ideas.

Amy Nelson represents Zeichner and Liston's (1991) social-efficiency perspective. This teaching ideology is based on the authors' application of scientism to educational practices. According to Bernier and Williams (1973a) *scientism* is the belief "that reality is or can be rationally controlled by man [sic] and that such an ordering implies predictability through the empirical testing of phenomenon by methods designed to secure objectivity and control" (p. 66). Amy Nelson's symbol is the personal computer, denoting efficient information processing, rational control, and economic achievement.

The third teacher-character is Dennis Sage, and his personal symbol is a teacher clasping the hand of a student, standing for his faith in the power of personal relationships. Dennis is a creative developmentalist, representing a synthesis of Zeichner and Liston's (1991) discussion of the developmentalist tradition and Bernier and Williams's (1973a) analysis of *romanticism*, which they describe as follows:

> Romanticism is the ideology of the rebel. It is reflected in the life style and value system of the prophet, the visionary, the bohemian, the cynical philosopher, the vagabond, and the disenchanted bourgeois. It necessitates a demand for critical disaffiliation, for romanticists reject all *imposed* restrictions and standards. Romanticists are rugged individualists, especially in the realm of ethics, and they are uncompromising and often vociferous in their demand for the right of self-expression. In rejecting all external commandments, they rely upon their imagination and intuition in their search for truth. (p. 128)

The fourth teacher-character is Silvia Rivera, and her symbol is the scales of justice. She represents Zeichner and Liston's (1991) social reconstructionism, a teaching ideology that is further amplified by Bernier and Williams's (1973a) foundational analysis of *puritanism*:

> Puritanism views man [sic] holistically and from a moralistic perspective. It is an ideology which combines the spiritual, aesthetic, and social aspects of man into a politico-economic framework. Viewing man as a moral agent regardless of his role in society and holding him accountable for all of his actions, it demands integration of the human personality. (p. 230)

Bernier and Williams's (1973a) system of analysis also includes nationalism, progressivism, and educationism. One dimension of *nationalism*, the affirmation of nation-state patriotism, is tacitly incorporated into the teacher-character's opinions. They all function as Americans, though they draw on the work of people from other countries. Silvia Rivera also operates from a particular ethnic identity. As Bernier and Williams (1973a) argue, this is another aspect of nationalism possessing deep historical roots:

> In a general fashion, Nationalism may be viewed as an ideological thrust within a cultural community, a nationality, to achieve a degree of social and/or political autonomy (e.g., various forms of Afro-Americanism such as Black Pride, Black Capitalism, or Black Separatism), or as an ideological matrix within a political community, a nation-state, designed to achieve cultural homogeneity (e.g., the "melting-pot" type of assimilation which was utilized to characterize the United States in the heyday of immigration). (p. 239)

As Silvia Rivera explains in chapter 2, she was born in Puerto Rico in 1961, and she takes pride in her Puerto Rican/Hispanic identity. She believes in the American ideal of equal opportunity for all. However, she thinks that this ideal must be reinterpreted for social groups that, historically, have experienced oppression. She argues that equality of oppor-

tunity means different things to different people. For example, she believes that the principle of educational equity requires teachers to be sensitive to Hispanic students' culturally unique learning styles. She thinks it is not fair to treat first-generation Puerto Rican students the same as fourth-generation Irish students. In succinct terms, she is a strong advocate of multiculturalism in education.

All four teacher-characters express progressivist and educationist sentiments. Collectively they are committed to their professional development. They all accept the three principles that guide the creation of this text:

- Teachers should develop their reflective teaching repertoire, which is understood as an ensemble of specific constructivist practices.
- Growth as a reflective teacher is facilitated by three interrelated thought processes: pragmatic reconsideration, critical reasoning, and critical engagement.
- Reflective teaching requires collaborative and leadership support.

All three of these principles have progressivist overtones. Bernier and Williams (1973b) provide this synoptic overview of *progressivism*:

> Adhering to the old adage that moderation is the mother of virtue, progressivists dismiss both the rigid formalism of Puritanism and the rebellious individualism of Romanticism. They believe that Puritanism borders on tyranny, Romanticism on anarchy. Questions of value and ethical decisions may be open to individual response, but choices must be made within the social context with careful consideration given to the consequences of one's decision. Because man [sic] is by nature a social animal, the progressivists assert, the consequences of an individual's actions often effect other individuals. For this reason many decisions should be group decisions. (pp. 201–202)

The four teacher-characters are also advocates of *educationism*, or the belief in the professionalization of teaching. They all believe "that schooling influences positively the development of an individual's potential" (Bernier & Williams, 1973a, p. 340) and that teachers need to continuously cultivate their own personal-professional growth to be the best possible facilitators of their students' growth. As advocates of teacher inquiry, they all concur with Barth's (1990) point, which is cited in chapter 1: "Those who value . . . education, those who hope to improve our schools, should be worried about the stunted growth of teachers. Teacher growth is closely related to pupil growth" (p. 49).

REFERENCES

Barth, R. S. (1990). *Improving schools from within: Teachers, parents, and principals can make the difference*. San Francisco: Jossey-Bass.

Bernier, N. R. (1981). Beyond instructional context identification—Some thoughts for extending the analysis of deliberate education. In J. L. Green & C. Wallat (Eds.), *Ethnography and language in educational settings* (pp. 291–302). Norwood, NJ: Ablex.

Bernier, N. R., & Williams, J. E. (1973a). *Beyond beliefs: Ideological foundations of American education*. Englewood Cliffs, NJ: Prentice-Hall.

Bernier, N. R., & Williams, J. E. (1973b). *Education for liberation: Readings from an ideological perspective*. Englewood Cliffs, NJ: Prentice-Hall.

Brophy, J. E., & Good, T. L. (1986). Teacher behavior and student achievement. In M. C. Wittrock (Ed.), *Handbook of research on teaching* (3rd ed., pp. 328–375). New York: Macmillan.

Freire, P. (1971). *Pedagogy of the oppressed* (M. Bergman Ramos, Trans.). New York: Herder & Herder. (Original work published 1970)

Hutchins, R. M. (1952). *Great Books of the Western World: Vol. 1. The great conversation: The substance of a liberal education* (pp. 1–131). Chicago: Encyclopaedia Britannica.

Kliebard, H. M. (1986). *The struggle for the American curriculum: 1893–1958*. New York: Routledge.

Zeichner, K. M., & Liston, D. P. (1991). Traditions of reform in U.S. teacher education. *Journal of Teacher Education, 41*, 3–20.

B

Simulated Cases

There are five simulated cases in this appendix that you can use to practice solving complex learning problems in a constructivist way. Each case describes a complex, unbounded problem in a particular type of institution. The institutions are a primary school, a middle school, a junior high school, and two different senior high schools. The cases are based on the four-part format created by Harvard University's Business School: Flashpoint, Background, Situation, and Flashpoint Reprise (Christensen, Hansen, & Moore, 1987). The Flashpoint section opens the case, catches your attention, and foreshadows the problem. The Background section provides the necessary contextual information, while the Situation section describes the problem. The Flashpoint Reprise returns you to the starting point of the case so that you can begin your work. The format is quite dramatic. As McCarthy (1989) points out, a "good case is good drama" (p. 16), and good drama helps stimulate your thinking.

Each case is based on information carefully compiled through lengthy interviews with an experienced teacher, who was the actual protagonist of the story. The cases, therefore, simulate true-life incidents. You should reflect on the learning problem in each case as if you were the protagonist. As you recall from chapter 3, classroom learning situations are quite complex and often multi-layered. Since the simulated cases can't possibly replicate the rich contextual information in real learning situations, your case analysis must be somewhat imaginative and speculative in nature. Furthermore, in simulated case work, you cannot engage in the complete decision-making cycle. You have no chance to act, to observe and reflect on the consequences of your actions and, if necessary, to engage in further inquiry. Nevertheless, simulated case reflection can be a useful way to practice solving complex learning problems in a constructivist way.

To save you from referring back to chapter 3, here are the steps that were suggested for solving unbounded, complex learning problems.

1. Frame the problem for constructivist learning. Decide what aspects of the problem you want to focus on, based on your inquiry teaching and in light of your student's personal purposes and past experiences. This becomes the foreground for your problem-solving efforts.
2. Brainstorm possible constructivist solutions. These are solutions that encourage students to engage actively in meaning-making. This is often done best in collaboration with others. It is also helpful to review pertinent literature for new ideas.
3. Try out one or more solutions. Observe what is or isn't working.
4. Review the situation. Determine whether further inquiry or action is appropriate, usually by asking yourself whether the situation now promotes constructivist learning.

Remember also that you have a wide range of choices and possible actions available within a constructivist philosophy. There are no obvious right answers, and there are probably many "somewhat-right" answers that can slightly improve the situation while working in the best interest of the students' understanding of subject matter, themselves, and/or their democratic society.

CASE STUDY #1: HOLDING AMANDA BACK

Flashpoint

"I've got a tummyache." Amanda, a first-grader, looked up at her teacher with large, pleading eyes. "I don't want to eat."

Time for the stomachache routine again, Charlotte Porter thought to herself. But to Amanda she said, "Are you sure you don't want to try to eat? Not even a little bit?"

Amanda shook her unruly red curls decisively. The other children had already filed out to the lunchroom. "I want to stay here."

"Now you know you can't stay in here alone," Charlotte told her, as she had done at least every second day since school began three weeks ago. "Come on, I'll walk you down to the lunchroom."

Amanda trailed slowly behind her, looking as miserable as a six-year-old could look. Well, at least she doesn't actually get sick, Charlotte thought. Look on the bright side, it could be worse.

As she watched Amanda slowly walk over to a table and sit down by herself, Charlotte recalled her meeting the previous day with Amanda's mother, Molly Davis, and Sam Anderson, the principal of Austin Magnet School.

Ms. Davis is a divorced woman in her early forties, a librarian by education and trade. Apart from her owl-like spectacles, her appearance is somewhat flamboyant, with shoulder-length red hair that matches Amanda's. Both of the times Charlotte had seen her, Ms. Davis was dressed all in black, with chunky silver jewelry: large dangling earrings and a wristful of bracelets that jangled with every movement of her arm. She was obviously intelligent and well read, and she reminded Charlotte in her appearance and manner of a 1950s-style Bohemian. At their meeting yesterday, Ms. Davis did most of the talking, her glance alternating between Charlotte and Sam as she spoke.

"Amanda has been reading since she was three years old," she said. "I'm sure her behavior problems occur because she's bored in first grade. She needs to be challenged. You yourself said she's reading at about a third-grade level!"

"She may be reading at the third-grade level, but emotionally and socially she's still very much a first-grader," Charlotte replied.

"You shouldn't judge her on whether or not you like her personality. You're supposed to be judging her on her schoolwork. She is very well behaved at home. She just needs the proper stimulation. That's one of the reasons I wanted her to come here to the magnet school. It's unfair to hold her back when she is so clearly advanced."

Charlotte tuned out the rest of Ms. Davis's monologue. She wondered how a child's own mother could miss seeing what the real problem was. She was brought back by the sound of Sam Anderson's voice.

"Let me assure you, Ms. Davis, Ms. Porter and I will discuss the situation and see what can be done." He ushered Amanda's mother out the door. When she left, he turned to Charlotte.

"Okay! Let's think this over and get back together tomorrow."

"What do you mean?"

"I mean Ms. Davis. If we keep 'holding Amanda back,' as she claims, she may take her out of Austin. That would be a shame."

"Yes, it would be," Charlotte agreed. "It would also be a shame to skip an emotionally immature six-year-old up to a group of eight-year-olds, where she'll feel even more isolated than she does now."

"You don't have to give me an answer right now. Do me a favor, just think it over, all right? Then let me know tomorrow, at 3:00 p.m."

Background

The School

Austin Magnet School is located just outside the central business district of a large midwestern city. It is housed in a fairly modern, three-story glass and concrete building. Students at Austin are admitted on the basis of their standardized test scores, which must be in the upper one-fifth for their age group. After that, other criteria are considered, including financial resources and ethnic background. Austin admits no student whose parents make over $30,000 per year. The children are also carefully selected to maintain a diverse ethnic and racial balance. It is one of only three such magnet schools in the city, and competition for admission is intense. Because of this, most parents of students at Austin are very concerned with their children's academic progress. There is frequent communication between parents and teachers, and many parents take an active part in school activities.

The facilities at Austin are well maintained. Class size is limited, and resources are usually adequate to support the above-average status quo. A teaching position there is considered a plum assignment in the public schools. Faculty members are energetic, dedicated, and proficient in their areas of expertise. Sam Anderson, the principal, is a youthful-looking forty-five-year-old White man whose low-key but effective methods of dealing with faculty, parents, and students have earned him respect. Austin enjoys an excellent academic reputation. Students tend to be highly motivated achievers who graduate and then move on to magnet or private high schools where they usually do very well.

Because Austin is a magnet rather than a community school, students come from various areas of the city. They are united by their high potential, their limited family incomes, and their parents' desire for a high-quality educational experience for their children. All the children either are driven to school or take the school bus for transportation.

The Protagonist
Charlotte Porter, a young African-American woman, is fulfilling a career ambition by teaching at Austin. Charlotte attended the city's parochial schools, received a scholarship for the state university, and earned her degree in elementary education. A very successful student, Charlotte achieved high grades in her classes and discovered that she had a real knack for communicating with children. Students responded well to her, and she received excellent evaluations from her student-teaching supervisors and professors. These, combined with her energetic, positive personality, helped her to attain the position at Austin. She was in her first year of teaching there when the problem with Amanda Davis began.

Situation

Amanda Davis is a six-year-old girl who quickly distinguished herself on the first day of school by refusing to participate in the warm-up activities Charlotte had prepared for her class. Amanda didn't seem to be afraid, as younger students sometimes were at first. She just sulked, displaying a rather remarkable ability to resist the persuasion of her teacher and classmates. While the other students dutifully pulled up their chairs in a circle, eager to play a get-acquainted game, Amanda sat off to one side, refusing to join the group.

When another little girl approached her and asked her to join them. Amanda told her to go away.

Charlotte allowed her some extra time to become accustomed to the classroom, but now, almost a month later, Amanda was still having difficulties. She reluctantly followed directions, but when the students were left to explore, or carry out independent activities, Amanda didn't seem to know what to do. She had not made friends among the other first-graders and frequently expressed her inability to relate in hostile ways. If she joined a couple of children playing with blocks, she was as likely to knock down what they had built as to build something herself. At lunchtime she habitually complained of a stomachache and insisted on sitting by herself.

The only time Amanda seemed to interact in a positive way was during the reading hour. Charlotte had quickly noticed Amanda's advanced reading skills. While the other children were struggling to master the basics, Amanda breezed through her book in one sitting, afterwards pronouncing it "baby stuff." Charlotte encouraged her to select other books from the room's bookshelves on her own, which Amanda did, but Charlotte sensed that this might only deepen the rift that already existed between her and the other children.

Then Charlotte asked Amanda if she would like to help one of her classmates during the reading session. She put her together with Sara, a little girl of East Indian parents who was having difficulty with the text.

Amanda became a different person when helping Sara. The aloofness that characterized most of her peer interactions disappeared. She seemed to take a great deal of pleasure in the role of tutor, encouraging Sara, smiling and clapping when Sara completed a difficult passage, and patiently coaching her when she had problems.

Apart from her enthusiasm during reading time, however, Amanda continued to display the same difficulties in making friends and partaking in group projects. After the second week of school, Charlotte had called Amanda's mother to express her concern about the child's adjustment problems. Ms. Davis had seemed interested and supportive, requesting the meeting with Charlotte and the principal.

At yesterday's meeting Charlotte had been surprised when Ms. Davis stated that Amanda should skip a grade to match her reading level and that she was being treated unfairly. From that meeting Charlotte formed an impression of the kind of pressure Amanda might be under at home, and felt even more strongly that the child needed time for socializing with her own age group. Amanda was just beginning to warm up through tutoring Sara; she would lose that opportunity completely among children whose reading level matched her own.

Flashpoint Reprise

Charlotte stood outside her classroom door as the students returned from lunch. As usual, Amanda was last, walking alone. As Charlotte watched the little girl enter the room and slowly make her way to the space she had claimed for herself near the back, Sam Anderson rushed by, probably late for an appointment.

"Don't forget, today at 3:00! I'll be looking for you!" he called as he hurried down the hall.

Charlotte headed for the chalkboard. Damian, a first-grader, came running up to her. "Amanda took my crayons," he said. Charlotte looked up to see Amanda, with a small fistful of crayons, methodically breaking them in half and letting them drop to the floor, one by one.

Maybe it wouldn't be such a bad idea to put Amanda in the third grade, Charlotte mused. At least then I wouldn't have to put up with this!

CASE STUDY #2:
TOO CUTE FOR HIS OWN GOOD?

Flashpoint

Angela Harper placed the telephone receiver back in its cradle and sat for a moment, sorting out the conversation she just had with the mother of one of her students. "If you could even call that a conversation," she thought. No wonder Jeffrey was having problems in school, if this was any indication of the kind of support he was getting at home.

After almost four weeks of going through a frustrating cycle of failure with Jeffrey, Angela had decided to call his mother and discuss the problem. She knew that Mrs. Watson was raising Jeffrey and his two younger sisters by herself and that she worked during the day. Angela waited until 7:00 p.m. to call. The exchange took place as follows:

"Hello."

"Hello, may I speak to Mrs. Watson, please?"

"Who's this?"

"My name is Angela Harper. I'm one of Jeffrey's sixth-grade teachers. Mrs. Watson?"

"Yeah, so what?"

"Well, Jeffrey's been having some problems in school, and—"

"What the hell are you calling me for?"

"I thought it might be helpful if we could discuss—"

"Listen. Teaching the kids is *your* job. If you can't do your job without bothering me, that's your problem. I don't ask you for help with my job, do I? So don't call here again."

Angela was left holding the phone with the sound of Mrs. Watson banging down the receiver reverberating in her ear.

Background

The School

Regis Middle School is a public institution located on the near south side of Chicago. Until recently the area was populated by mostly lower- and working-class African-American families living in single homes or two- and three-room flats. There are no housing projects in the district. Because several large medical centers and colleges are flourishing in the area, a recent flurry of construction has displaced many of the former residents. Along with the new construction came an influx of middle-class professionals who are mainly White, Asian, or Hispanic. The student population at Regis is about seventy percent African-American, with the other thirty percent composed of an equal mix of the other ethnic groups. Although the school is housed in a newer building, it was cheaply constructed and lacks updated furniture and equipment.

There has not been much gang activity at Regis, but the overall achievement scores are somewhat below average. Many students have truancy problems, and few go on to graduate from high school.

The principal of Regis is Mr. Harrison, a dignified-looking, middle-aged African-American man. His overwhelming concern regarding the faculty at Regis is that they not make waves. Those who make no waves are rewarded with benign neglect from the administration. They seldom see Mr. Harrison except when their evaluations are due, and those are always glowingly positive. Those whom Mr. Harrison perceives as being too demanding or too zealous incur his silent displeasure, which manifests itself in increased surprise classroom visits, excessive criticism, and lackluster evaluations.

Because Regis is a middle school, there is a lot of interaction among the teachers. However, this is almost always confined to a lim-ited academic agenda. The "problem" of Mr. Harrison has never, as far as Angela knows, come up.

The Protagonist

Angela Harper is a 28-year-old African-American woman who has been teaching sixth-grade social studies in the public schools for the past four years. She loves working with children and had always wanted to be a teacher. Her own education began in a neighborhood public school. She attended a private high school and the state university. She went directly into education as her major, where she did very well both in her coursework and as a student teacher. She acquired her current position at Regis soon after graduation.

Angela has earned a reputation among the students for being firm but fair, and she is quite popular among the children. Angela believes that social studies lends itself to many exciting teaching possibilities. She enjoys teaching and constantly strives to make her classes better. However, she does this in an isolated way so as not to rock the boat. As a result, she has thus far enjoyed a fairly positive relationship with Mr. Harrison. On her own she has successfully coped with students who presented discipline problems or were poor academic achievers. However, she has never encountered a student like Jeffrey Watson before.

Situation

Jeffrey Watson is a twelve-year-old sixth-grader. He repeated fourth grade after he missed six weeks of class due to a prolonged illness.

Although he is a year older than most of his classmates, physically he is smaller: short in height, with a slight build. Jeffrey sometimes wears the same clothes to school all week, although he does not appear to be unwashed or dirty. Angela has never observed Jeffrey socializing with his classmates. He always seems to be alone, except when he meets his sisters, ages ten and nine, after school to walk them home. Angela often sees him sitting in the library or reading in the lunchroom. He appears to be a quiet, serious young man. He always sits right up front in class and is very attentive. He gives the impression of being eager to be called on and to participate in learning activities.

Based on her observations, Angela had first concluded that Jeffrey was highly motivated and was going to do well. She was therefore very surprised when, on his first test, Jeffrey left more than half the questions unanswered. Where he did attempt to respond, the answers were vague and disconnected. His handwriting was large and loopy, with lots of smudges and scribbles. Many words were misspelled. He did not even guess at some multiple-choice questions.

Immediately after taking that first test, Jeffrey had come to Angela after class. He smiled brightly at her, yet seemed a little shy.

"I'm sorry I didn't do good on my test today, Ms. Harper," he said. "Don't be mad at me. I know I didn't do too good, but I'm going to try harder, and next time I'll do better, you'll see."

"Of course I wouldn't be mad, Jeffrey," Angela replied. "But what happened to you this time? Why do you think you didn't do well?"

Jeffrey just smiled and shrugged his shoulders. "I don't know."

"Did you study?"

"Oh, yes ma'am, I did study! I guess I just forgot or something. But I'll study harder, I'll do better next time and get an 'A'."

Except that Jeffrey never did better. There were two more tests and four more homework assignments, and none of his even approached a passable quality of work. His homework had the appearance of having been hastily scribbled, and his papers were always messy and wrinkled. The tests continued to be extremely poor, with Jeffrey often barely making an attempt to respond to many of the questions.

And each time, Jeffrey came up to her, smiled, apologized, and promised to do better. Each time Angela spoke to him at length until she felt that he understood the problem. Jeffrey made a point of telling her how much he liked her class, how she was his favorite teacher, and how he didn't want to disappoint her. He seemed so sincere that each time Angela wanted to believe him. But now she had allowed the situation to go on for too long.

A little investigating into Jeffrey's record revealed that he was also doing poorly in his other classes. Yet his psychological testing last year had shown that he possessed an intelligence that was actually slightly above average. When she approached Jeffrey's other teachers about the problem, they did not seem to be overly concerned with his poor performance. They all spoke of him fondly, remarking to Angela about how "cute" he was, and how he was always trying so hard. That was when Angela decided to call Mrs. Watson, to see if she could learn a little more about Jeffrey's background and how she might address his problem.

Flashpoint Reprise

As she hung up the phone after talking to Jeffrey's mother, Angela looked at the papers she had spread out on her coffee table, intending to refer to them when she spoke to Mrs. Watson. She gathered them into a pile, shaking her head at the untidy-looking assignments.

Well, Mrs. Watson isn't going to be much help here, Angela mused. What should I do now?

CASE STUDY #3:
ON A DIFFERENT LEVEL

Flashpoint

Christopher Jordan watched as the forlorn figure of his student, Katie, receded slowly down the hall. He could see her silhouette against the bright light of the corridor's west window. He turned back to his empty classroom and slammed his fist down on the desk in frustration. It just wasn't fair that he had to be the one to tell Katie that she wasn't smart enough to enroll in the class she so desperately wanted to take. Not that we'd ever come right out and make such a blunt—or honest—statement, he thought, stuffing the day's papers into his briefcase. No, we use euphemisms and code words, like *Level 1* and *Level 2*—as if these kids couldn't see through that.

He sighed and started down the hall, replaying in his mind how Katie had come to see him, optimistic that somehow he would be able to help her. Instead, he had to watch her hopeful smile fade while he recited the official line about which classes Level 3 students could and could not take. She had just looked down at the floor as he added, "I wish I could help you, but there isn't anything else I can do." But wasn't there? he asked himself. Had he really done everything he could do?

Background

The Community

Fawndale is an upper-middle-class suburb of a midsized West Coast city. It is a community of tastefully elegant, single-family homes and manicured lawns. The citizens are mostly career professionals: white-collar corporation officers, physicians, and lawyers. Most families have two parents, and the mothers are as likely as the fathers to be highly educated. Nannies are not uncommon, but many moth-

ers have elected to stay home with the children and become full-time homemakers and community volunteers. The parents of Fawndale take pride in the excellent quality of Parker, their local junior high school, and most of them are active supporters of the institution. Because of this, many students go to Parker who might otherwise attend private schools.

The School

Parker Junior High is a public school located in Fawndale. The building is relatively new, about thirty years old, and is very well maintained. Equipment and supplies are plentiful and up-to-date. The student body at Parker reflects the ethnic makeup of the community: about ninety percent are White and ten percent are Asian or Hispanic.

Parker Junior High prides itself on its excellent academic reputation. The principal, Jane Reed, is an energetic, stately White woman in her late forties. Her enthusiasm about Parker's high national ratings on standardized tests is shared by the faculty. Parker's students are also well aware of their reputation, and the school attracts many excellent young scholars from the area.

Of course, not all students are academic achievers. Parker, along with the other schools in the Fawndale district, utilizes a tracking system that assigns students into three groups based on their standardized test scores. The groups are labelled College Prep Level 1, College Prep Level 2, and Pre-College Prep Level 3. Level 1 includes the above-average students and numerous outstanding achievers who supply Parker with a steady stream of awards and scholarships. Level 2 is for students who may excel in some areas, but on the whole are average to slightly above-average achievers. Level 3 includes those students who have borderline-average or below-average scores on standardized tests, and who for the most part do not intend or are not expected to go to college. The students themselves refer to the three groups as the *Brains*, the *Joes*, and the *Slugs*, respectively.

Jane Reed wholeheartedly endorses this tracking system. Since becoming principal nine years ago, she has seized every opportunity to expound on its many advantages to both parents and faculty. The above-average students are free to excel without being held back by less gifted classmates. These brilliant students are the pride of Parker, and many resources are poured into Level 1 programs. Level 2 students frequently become motivated to try harder to achieve Level 1 status, but they are neither artificially accelerated nor held back by mixing with the other two groups. Much of the Level 1 equipment and some of its programs are shared with Level 2 students, many of whom go on to attend local colleges and state universities.

Level 3 students are a different story. They seldom share in the resources or courses earmarked for the college-prep groups, ostensibly so they won't be overwhelmed academically. Class offerings for Level 3 include few options, and courses are more likely to have titles like *Intermediate Composition* than *Reflections of Society in American Fiction*.

Principal Reed adamantly supports this "realistic" system, and her enthusiasm is contagious. She enjoys the strong support of parents and faculty as she basks in the glory of Parker's many academic honors.

The Protagonist
Christopher Jordan is a twenty-nine-year-old White male science teacher. He came to Parker one year ago, thinking it would be a good compromise between the small town where he had taught for four years and a major urban area. He was very pleased to get the position at Parker. He liked the more sophisticated suburban atmosphere, and at first he was delighted with the modern facilities available for his biology classes.

It wasn't long, however, before the tracking system began to bother him. Although it could be exhilarating to conduct higher-level activities with his Level 1 group, he detected a lack of enthusiasm, even a sense of defeat, in the Level 3 students. Surely, knowing they were tagged *Slugs* couldn't do much for their self-esteem, he thought. So he tried to compensate by making their classes more interesting and enjoyable. His efforts often met with apathy: assigned chapters went unread, homework papers unwritten, challenging discussion questions answered with stony silence. It seemed only natural that he eventually redirected his best efforts to Level 1 students, who were always bright-eyed, attentive, and eager to learn more.

Despite nagging misgivings about the value, if not the efficiency, of the tracking system, Christopher allowed himself to be persuaded by the forceful views of Principal Reed and the indisputable successes of the Level 1 students.

At least he thought he had convinced himself, until Katie Winslow came to him with her problem.

Situation

Katie Winslow is a fourteen-year-old freshman at Parker. She has a plain, pleasant appearance and a placid, mild-mannered disposition. Katie's standardized test scores consistently place her solidly in the Level 3 category. Her grades in English, reading, math, and social studies have been fair at best. She has a low-average IQ (95), but no particular learning disability. Her neurological workup was completely normal. Katie is rather shy and quiet, and she often daydreams in class. When confronted with a question, she usually tries to respond, and never seems surprised or upset when her answer is incorrect.

Katie is the middle child of three. Her older sister, now eighteen, was an average student who got married immediately after graduation. Her younger sister, currently a sixth-grader, displays above-average scholarship and forceful leadership qualities that sharply contrast with Katie's. The two sisters live with their parents in a comfortable (though modest by Fawndale standards) single-family home. Katie's father is an insurance executive. Her mother works part-time in a florist shop. The Winslow family, though solidly middle-class, is at the lower end of the Fawndale social scale.

Katie's parents display interest in their daughter's schoolwork and attend parent-teacher conferences together. However, all the teachers have remarked that they do not seem overly concerned about Katie's borderline performance, and they tend to make passive, defensive comments such as, "As long as Katie is happy and well-adjusted and not having discipline problems, that's the important thing."

There is one area, however, in which Katie has shown marked enthusiasm and certain ability. Katie's interest became apparent in the first biology class she took with Christopher Jordan. Parker's biology rooms are stocked with a variety of flora and fauna: plants, tree seedlings, parakeets, canaries, hamsters, gerbils, turtles, frogs, and lizards, and an aquarium full of fish. Katie had instantly gravitated toward the animals. When Christopher requested volunteers who could stay after school a few days a week to help look after the menagerie, her hand was the first to shoot up. She stayed for an hour every day to tend to the animals and took great pleasure in caring for them. The animals benefited as well, and their living quarters were virtually spotless.

One day Christopher remarked on her affection for the animals. Katie smiled and said, "We can't have any pets at home. I wish we could have one."

That was at the beginning of the year. Now it was late April, and students were beginning to think about the next term.

About a week prior to the current incident, Katie had approached Christopher after class. Despite her avid interest in the pets, her biology grades were as marginal as those in every other subject. Christopher assumed she was going to ask about taking care of the animals next year. Instead she pulled out a list of courses offered for Level 1 students.

"Can I ask you something?" she said, smiling wistfully and waiting for an answer.

"Yes, of course, Katie. What is it?"

"Isn't this about animals?" She pointed to the class entitled *Introduction to Zoology*.

"Yes." He took the paper from her hands. "But these are Level 1 courses, Katie, these aren't—" He fumbled for a word. "These are the wrong classes. Do you want a list of the Level 3s?"

She shook her head. "I have one. But this class isn't there." She produced the list of Level 3 offerings and handed it to Christopher, but he didn't need to look. He knew she was right.

"Do you think I could take it?" she asked. "I'd really like to learn more about the animals."

"Did you ask Mr. Wyler? He's going to teach that class."

"No, I'm afraid to ask him. He doesn't know me. Could you ask him for me? You know how much I like animals."

"Yes, I know Katie. You've done such a good job taking care of our zoo here." She smiled broadly in response to his praise. "Well, OK, let me see what I can find out. I'll let you know next week."

But what he found out frustrated him. Bill Wyler, his biology colleague, is a man in his late fifties who has taught at Parker for twenty-five of its thirty years. He wears a gray suit every day. Christopher and the other faculty members had wondered among themselves, was it the same suit, or did he have a closet full of them? He always remains somewhat aloof, though he is not really unfriendly. He is a big fan of Principal Reed and the tracking system, as Christopher found out when he brought up the subject of Katie. Wyler frowned, pushed his glasses up onto his head, and put his hands up to his pursed lips in a praying gesture as Christopher explained the situation to him at lunch. Wyler listened silently until Christopher ended with, "Well, what do you think?"

"Hmm," said Wyler, settling his glasses back onto his nose. "Do you think she's capable of doing the work? Perhaps she is in the wrong track?"

"No, she's really not that good of a student, but I do think her love of animals might motivate her to do better than she usually does."

"Yes, but remember, even if she does, you're still talking about Level 3. I'm sure she'd be in over her head. It wouldn't be fair to her."

"I know she'd do her best. It's the only thing she's really interested in. If you were willing to take her, I'm sure Jane would let her do it."

"Well, you see, that's the other problem. Why don't you ask her? Because even if I did agree, I don't think it can be done."

"But you will agree?"

"See what Jane says first."

Christopher ran up against a brick wall with Principal Reed. He explained the situation to her in her office while she attended to some paperwork. When he finished, she stopped, looked up, and replied crisply, "I understand your good intentions, but I'm afraid it's out of the question."

Christopher's guard was down, and he blurted out, "But why? What harm could it do?"

"Well, Christopher, it probably doesn't seem likely that one girl in one class could do much harm. But I'm sure you're aware that if we made an exception for one student, we'd have to make exceptions for everyone. And then there wouldn't be much of a system left, would there? I'm sure you're aware that our system has been very successful. I'm afraid your student will just have to be content with some other class."

"But Wyler even agreed to give her a chance."

Reed's left eyebrow arched skeptically. Christopher could tell that she knew he was, in effect, lying.

"Did he really? I'd be very surprised. But even if he did," she leaned forward for emphasis, "it's not up to the individual teacher to make such decisions. We need to have everyone's cooperation." She leaned back again. "Trust me. Your student will be happier among others of her own ability. Now, was there anything else you wished to discuss?"

No, he hadn't wished to discuss anything else. Later that evening he received a phone call from Katie's mother.

"Katie says that you're going to let her take zoology," Mrs. Winslow said. "Is that true? Can you really get her in that class? I know it's not one of her regular courses, but she would really love to take it."

"I don't know, Mrs. Winslow, I just said I would try." He didn't have the heart to tell her he had already failed.

Flashpoint Reprise

After Katie left the biology room—for the first time ever she hadn't checked on the animals on her way out—Christopher headed for his car. In the parking lot he met Ellen Chung, a social studies teacher with whom he frequently ate lunch.

"What's the matter?" she asked. "You look like your dog just died."

Christopher spilled out the whole story. When he finished, Ellen said, "Well, too bad her parents aren't big wheels."

"What do you mean?"

"You know. If they could throw their weight around a little bit—"

Christopher was dumbfounded. "Are you serious?"

"No, I'm just being cynical. Forget it."

But as Christopher drove home, he couldn't forget it. He couldn't forget the look on Katie's face. And, come to think of it, he couldn't name one student in his Level 3 group whose parents were physicians, lawyers, or bank presidents.

CASE STUDY #4:
IS YOUR CLASS MORE IMPORTANT THAN A MAN'S FUTURE?

Flashpoint

Tim Foster stood at the front of his classroom and surveyed his group of twenty-five high school seniors. A few of them were on task, writing an in-class essay; the others were talking with each other, listening to radio headphones, or just daydreaming.

"Keesha, quiet down, now, and finish your essay," he called to one of a group of students who had gotten a little too boisterous. They laughed, and Keesha made little effort to hide her annoyance at being singled out for comment.

Tim pretended not to notice. As he looked at their faces, he silently reviewed what he knew about their lives. Keesha had been held back a year as a sophomore, the year that her father had been shot and killed in the street, an apparently innocent bystander in a gang dispute. Frederick, the gang-banger, had carried a beeper to class to keep track of business until they were banned this year. Jeremy had been caught with a gun in his jacket yesterday; when it was confiscated, he protested that he

needed it for protection. Marcella had missed a few days of school last fall when she was arrested for soliciting, apparently as part of a gang enterprise. Michael had an obvious drug problem and came to school high more often than not. Monica had one baby at home and, apparently, another on the way. Up front sat Clement, one of the few serious students, whose brother had been knifed right outside school last month when he refused to give his baseball jacket to another kid; he was still in the hospital. Tanya, whose building had burned down two weeks ago, was living in a hotel for transients with her mother and five siblings. Maurice never knew his father, and his mother was in jail, leaving him to be raised by an older sister. Stories of promising young lives being ground beneath the wheels of poverty and hardship were depressingly frequent, not just in Tim's class, but throughout the school.

And then there was Darryl. Six-foot, five-inch Darryl Smith, who even now was sitting with his head tilted backwards, eyes closed, apparently fast asleep. Darryl, who Tim suspected was a casual drug user. Darryl, who lived with his grandmother because his new stepfather didn't like him. Darryl, who had almost single-handedly brought the basketball team into the state semifinals, providing the only taste of school pride Wright High students had ever known. Darryl, who was flunking his senior English class and seemingly unconcerned about his precarious academic situation.

Tim walked down the aisle to the dozing young man, whose desk could not begin to accommodate his long, lanky frame. "Darryl," he said loudly. Darryl's eyelids barely fluttered. Tim was careful to avoid physical contact. All the students were watching him.

"Darryl, are you sick?" he continued. Laughter erupted in the class. "He ain't sick, he's just tired." "Hey Darryl, wake up, man."

Darryl looked at Tim through bleary eyes.

"You'd better get started on that essay," Tim advised.

"Yeah, yeah." Darryl sat up a little straighter. He appeared to have neither paper nor pen. "That goes for all of you, too," Tim added, walking to the back of the room. He stood by the back door, thinking. His body grew tense as he recalled his confrontation earlier in the day with Harold Carter, the phys. ed. teacher and basketball coach. How could Carter, even in his wildest dreams, expect Tim to give Darryl a passing grade?

Background

The Community

Wright High School is located in Knoxburg, an impoverished inner-city neighborhood of a large New England city. The streets of Knoxburg resemble a war zone. The buildings are old and crumbling. Some stand vacant, windows and doors long since broken. Some buildings have been razed, leaving trash-strewn empty lots. Few trees or green lawns relieve the bleak landscape. Several newer housing projects in the area are cheaply built, poorly designed and maintained, and universally regarded as "vertical slums." Numerous shops along Knoxburg's main street are boarded up and abandoned. The residents of the community are almost exclusively African-Americans. Unemployment and crime rates are high, with significant gang and drug problems. Incomes of the Knoxburg residents are low. Many are on welfare or unemployment compensation, and those who are working tend to have low-paying jobs. It is an economically and socially depressed area. With the exception of a small, dedicated core group of parents, little interaction takes place between the neighborhood residents and Wright.

The School

Wright High School is a dilapidated, three-story brick building that dates back about eighty years. The walls are covered with graffiti, and the first-floor windows have been permanently boarded up. Because of over-crowding, several trailers parked in the former school yard serve as adjunct classrooms for the overflow of students, who number about 1,200.

Wright is a school in crisis. Standardized test scores are in the lowest percentile ranges. Discipline is almost nonexistent, even with teachers spending most of their time on class-room management tasks. Student drug use is widespread, and gang activity is rampant, despite a growing list of rules that forbid the wearing of gang colors, multicolor shoelaces, baseball caps, off-center belt buckles, gang symbols, or beepers.

Both student and faculty absenteeism are high at Wright. An average class of thirty to thirty-five students has five to ten missing at any given time. The average teacher misses about one day per month. The student dropout rate is over fifty percent. The administration of Wright is also in a crisis. Four principals have come and gone in the past six years. The most recent, Mrs. Claire Burns, has been in the position for eight months.

Mrs. Burns is a serious, professional-looking African-American woman in her mid-thirties. Most faculty members believe she is totally overwhelmed in her current situation. At first she issued memos and called meetings to address the problems at Wright. Faculty, students, and parents—having been through this before—were lackluster in their response. Mrs. Burns now spends a good deal of time in her office, issuing periodic missives to inform teachers of her plans for the school.

The faculty at Wright is about one-third African-American and two-thirds White. Although many of the African-American teachers have been there for a number of years, the White teachers tend to be young and on their first job. There is not much social interaction between the White and African-American teachers, although the groups are not hostile. The annual teacher turnover is about forty percent.

The one positive aspect of Wright is its athletic program, in particular, the basketball team. The Hawks have brought home winning records for the past four years and went to the state semifinals this year. Enthusiastic students crowded into the tiny gymnasium after school to watch team practice sessions. The send-off rally for the first round of the state tournament was the most exuberant display of school spirit any of the teachers at Wright could remember seeing. Student volunteers made decorations and hung clever banners around the school. At the rally, some of the kids recited original poems or raps to the team, much to the delight of the crowd. Even the faculty was impressed. Harold Carter, the head coach, had coordinated these activities. Mr. Carter is a large, physically imposing figure with a stern expression and a no-nonsense attitude. He is by far the most popular teacher at Wright. He seems to have boundless enthusiasm and encouragement for the kids on his teams. The students respond well to Mr. Carter, partly because they are happy to have found an area in which they can feel good about their achievements. Also, because Mr. Carter is an African-American teacher who has been at Wright for about twelve years, many students find it easier to relate to him on a personal level.

The Protagonist
Tim Foster, age twenty-five, is a White, first-year teacher at Wright. He originally obtained a Bachelor's degree in English, then stayed in college to get a teaching degree. Tim grew up across town in a mostly White, ethnic, work-ing-class area. Because he student-taught at what he had considered to be an inner-city school, Tim thought he was prepared to deal with the problems he expected would exist at Wright. But after less than a year, Tim was already beginning to reconsider his vocation. Nothing could have prepared him for the apathy—and occasional hostility—of the Wright students, the chaos of their lives, the oppressive ugliness of the surroundings, or the ever-present feelings of mistrust and despair he saw reflected in the other faculty members, who seldom walked outside the building alone.

Tim was an idealist who had come to Wright feeling confident that with lots of patience, caring, and understanding, he would be able to do a good job. But his resolve had been worn down by the relentless struggle to merely get his students' attention. He often felt overwhelmed and at a loss for ways to make his English classes more accessible and interesting. No matter what he tried, it seemed, his efforts were in vain.

His morale had reached a low point in December. Just before the Christmas break, he purchased coupons good for a free hamburger at the local fast-food restaurant and gave one to each student. Although they seemed to appreciate the gesture, they were no better behaved, and a fight actually broke out in class when someone claimed another student had stolen his coupon. When Tim inserted himself between the two battling students, he was pushed and accidentally hit in the face, causing his lip to bleed slightly. An onlooking student yelled, "Come on, let's get him," and the rest of the class laughed.

After that incident, Tim became disheartened. He got through the days by concentrating on the few good students he had in each class, the handful of kids who motivated him to keep trying. Clement, for example, had a natural talent for writing and had even won honorable mention in a civic essay contest

Tim had urged him to enter. Keeping up in school was nevertheless a struggle for Clement. Tim realized one day with a certain shock that Clement came to Wright each morning looking for some stability and order in his life.

Talking informally to other faculty members, Tim had discovered that many had demoralizing experiences of their own. The prevailing attitude was one of grim pessimism.

Harold Carter seemed to be just about the only teacher who had not been deterred by the conditions at Wright. Carter seldom mingled with the other faculty, usually eating lunch on the run in the gym. Tim decided to approach Carter to see if he might be able to offer some advice. But before he had a chance to do so, Carter approached him first.

Situation

The fifth of six grading reports for the year had gone out the week before. Tim was heading for the faculty lunchroom when he saw Harold Carter striding purposefully toward him. Tim smiled in greeting; Carter did not.

"You Tim Foster?" he asked in a deep bass voice. When Tim nodded, Carter stuck out his hand. "Harold Carter, phys. ed."

"Yes, I know you," Tim replied, shaking his hand.

"Let me get right to the point, Foster," Carter said with a heavy sigh. "It's about your student, Smith. The senior."

"Darryl Smith?"

Carter nodded. "He's flunking your English class."

"Yes, I know."

Carter looked impatient. "Well then, Foster, let me tell you something maybe you *don't* know. Smith has a chance, a slim one, to make something out of himself. He's the big man

on our team, and several colleges are interested in him."

"College? Darryl—go to college?" The concept seemed incongruous to Tim. "I mean he—he can barely put two words together, when he even bothers to try, but—"

Carter cut him off. "You don't get it, do you, Foster? Look, I am talking about a man's *life* here. If he can get into college, who knows how far he could go? He's a good athlete, and this may be his only chance to pull himself out of the kind of life he has now, you see what I'm saying?"

Tim hesitated. "I'm not sure that I do."

Carter sighed again, a deep, exasperated sigh. "Okay then, let me spell it out for you. Smith won't be eligible to graduate and get into college with an 'F' in your English class. Now do you see what I'm saying?"

Tim just looked at him in silence.

"Ask yourself this, Foster. How important is this one class compared to being able to give a young man like Smith with a natural ability the chance to make something of his life? You can see that he doesn't get the kind of breaks in life that you got. Just what do you suppose will happen to him if he leaves here without even graduating? Is your class more important than a man's future? Think about it, Foster. I'm sure there's *something* you can do."

Flashpoint Reprise

"Okay, time's up," Tim called out to his class. "Please hand in your essays on the way out. Remember, for next week, finish reading the story we began on Monday." His last words were nearly drowned out as the students, talking and laughing, headed out the door.

As he passed by, Darryl handed Tim a piece of paper with his name and a few lines written on it in pencil.

"Darryl, can I talk to you for a minute?"

Darryl frowned. "I got to go," he replied.

"Just one minute?"

"What for?" The young man was clearly displeased.

Tim looked down at the essay. The first line was a sentence fragment that had little relationship to the assignment.

"On this essay—I think you can do better."

"Man, I ain't got a minute for that," Darryl said, and kept walking.

Tim almost called out after him. If I told him I had talked to Carter, that would get his attention, he thought. But then what would I say?

As the next class began to file in, Tim felt a growing sense of anger and hopelessness. Carter's words echoed in his mind: "Is your class more important than a man's future?" Sure, he would like to give Darryl a break, but how far did Carter expect him to go?

CASE STUDY #5: *SO, YOU'LL BE EXPERIMENTING ON US?*

Flashpoint

Mary Bloom stood by the window in the empty second-floor classroom and watched the kids from Edison High School spill out onto the street. The clock on the wall told her it was 3:25; apparently Lisa was not going to come to see her after school as Mary had requested. Running footsteps echoed in the hallway as the last few students left. Mary sat down at her desk, realizing that all this time she had been clenching the paper she had confiscated from Lisa during class. Thinking of how Lisa had once again demonstrated her lack of respect for her, Mary unconsciously crumpled the paper in her fist. Why had this particular student taken such a dislike to her?

Background

Edison High School is located in a working-class neighborhood of an industrial city. At the time it was built in 1912, the brick and stone structure had won architectural awards. Now it is in a sorry state of disrepair. The walls are scarred with graffiti. The small, once-grassy campus has given way to dirt and weeds. The first-floor windows are reinforced with wire and bars.

The slow decline of Edison High mirrors the history of the neighborhood. Once a solid, middle-class enclave of White European-American ethnic groups, the economic level of the area declined as the earlier residents moved to the suburbs. The neighborhood was now a mixture of Hispanic, African-American, and White working poor. The student population at Edison reflects this mix fairly well, with about fifty percent Hispanic, thirty percent African-American and twenty percent White students.

The Protagonist

Mary Bloom is a thirty-year-old White English teacher, a recent graduate in her first teaching job. After getting an undergraduate degree in English, Mary worked for several years for one of the city's newspapers before returning to school to pursue a second career in teaching. An excellent student, Mary felt that she had finally found her calling. She possessed a special affinity for adolescents and was looking forward to teaching high school. Mary's teacher-mentor at Edison, where she had done her student teaching, praised her highly. She had developed a good rapport with her classes and was confident about starting her teaching career.

On the job Mary encountered a few minor problems at first, but in general her classes were running fairly smoothly. Until the situation with Lisa came along.

Situation

Mary taught three freshman composition classes, but the class she really looked forward to was the American Literature class with the juniors. The class consisted of twenty-three students, fourteen girls and nine boys, with a racial mix consistent with the rest of the school. Lisa Hernandez, a petite, attractive sixteen-year-old, had made an impression on Mary the first day. In telling the students a little bit about herself, Mary mentioned how pleased she was to be teaching her first literature class. "So, that means you'll be experimenting on us," Lisa said aloud, to which Mary replied, "In a good class we should all be able to learn from each other."

Since then, nothing Mary did seemed to satisfy Lisa. She sometimes noticed Lisa smirking during class, but never being overtly disruptive. When she spoke to another teacher, Mary discovered that Lisa was a fairly bright student who was doing "A" and "B" work in her other classes. In Mary's class, however, she was turning out only average work. Challenged by Lisa's negative attitude, Mary made a point of looking at her, calling on her frequently, and trying to get her more involved. Lisa's responses in class were consistently weak and confused, usually accompanied with comments such as, "I don't think that was explained very well," or "I don't see why we need to know that." Mary overlooked Lisa's mumbling to herself or another student presumably about her unhappiness with the class. Because it was not obtrusive, Mary felt it best to ignore the verbal sniping. Lisa continued to turn in "C" papers that were more lackluster and careless than incorrect. The rest of the class ran the gamut, from a straight "A" student to those who were doing below-average work.

Mary had decided to write Lisa off as a chronic complainer and get on with the rest of the class until that morning, when one of her other juniors had stopped by to speak to her. Nancy was the shy, quiet, sixteen-year-old African-American girl who was getting straight "A's" in class. She seemed nervous as she approached Mary.

"Hello, Nancy. What can I do for you?" Mary said.

"Hi, Ms. Bloom." Nancy fiddled with her book. "Ms. Bloom, you know Lisa?"

"Yes, of course. Why?"

"Well, don't say that I told you, okay? She's got this paper that she's passing around the class."

"You mean an assignment she's letting other people see?"

"No, Ms. Bloom. Like a petition or something. It's about you." Mary was too surprised to respond immediately. Before she could question Nancy further, the student turned to go. "Please don't say I'm the one who told you, Ms. Bloom. I just thought you ought to know. I don't agree with it myself. I don't think it's right."

"Well, thank you for sharing this with me, Nancy," Mary managed to say as Nancy disappeared out the door.

In class that afternoon, Mary kept a close eye on Lisa while the class worked on a writing assignment. After several minutes, she noticed that one of the boys slipped Lisa a folded piece of paper. Immediately, Mary was standing next to her.

"Let me see that paper, Lisa."

"What paper?"

"That paper that Carl just handed you."

"He didn't hand me anything."

"Look, I just saw him do it. That paper is right here." Mary pulled on a sheet of paper that Lisa had tucked into her closed textbook.

"Hey, you have no right to do that," Lisa yelled. By now the whole class was buzzing.

"Okay, quiet now, everyone. Continue with your assignment." She looked down at Lisa. "Lisa, see me right after school today."

Lisa looked down at the desk and did not respond. Mary walked back to her desk, unfolded the piece of paper, and read:

> We the undersigned think that Ms. Mary Bloom is not qualified to teach American Literature to juniors. She has no prior experience, and many students are not doing well in her class because she does not know how to explain the subject and how to teach. We would like to request that the administration please do something about this situation as it is unfair to the students.

Even more surprisingly, the petition had been signed by six of the students. Mary recognized four names of people she had seen Lisa hanging out with in the halls. Then the bell rang and class was over.

Flashpoint Reprise

Back in the empty classroom, Mary gathered her things together. "I wonder how many more of the students might have signed, if given the chance?" she thought. I wonder if any were asked and refused? She tried to fit the pieces together, but she wasn't sure where to begin.

REFERENCES

Christensen, R., Hansen, R., & Moore, J. (1987). *Teaching and the case method.* Boston: Harvard Business School Press.

McCarthy, M. (1989). *Teaching cases at the Harvard Business School: A model for teacher training and faculty development.* Paper presented at the meeting of the American Educational Research Association, San Francisco.

Glossary

4C scaffolding A guide to professional inquiry that is based on the 4C virtues: calling, caring, creativity, and centeredness.

4C virtues The four virtues integral to constructivist teaching, so called because they all begin with the letter *C*: calling, caring, creativity, and centeredness. To view teaching as a calling highlights the personal and social significance of the educational profession. Caring teachers regularly confirm, have dialogue with, and cooperate with their students. Creative teachers seek ways to imaginatively and aesthetically engage their students. Centered teachers operate on the basis of deliberate moral choice; they know themselves through years of pragmatic and critical reflection.

academic meaning-making A constructivist orientation that focuses on helping students actively understand academic disciplines, particularly the traditional disciplines that incorporate the great ideas of Western civilization. This is the preferred orientation for teacher-character Johnny Jackson.

academic problem solving A strategy in which teachers create bridges between the formal knowledge of a subject and the personal purposes and past experiences of their students. This is the preferred problem-solving approach of teacher-character Johnny Jackson.

action research A thoughtful approach to social problem solving that includes seven key dimensions: analyze a problematic situation, gather additional useful information, define the problem, hypothesize a solution, act to solve the problem, observe the results, and make a judgment as to how best to proceed.

administrative problem solving A strategy that refers to solving problems that are administrative rather than educational in nature. The distinction is important because administrative and educational problems are often confounded. For example, solving a busing problem, which is administrative, does not necessarily help teachers solve the educational problem of improving students' literacy.

authentic evaluation The activity of reviewing how a learning activity facilitates active meaning-making for students. This is an ongoing type of evaluation that is the culminating phase of a teacher's day-to-day use of the decision-making cycle (planning, acting, observing, and reflecting). This evaluative activity usually involves realistic, performance-based activities. Portfolio assessment is often used as a basis for authentic evaluation.

autobiographical reflection The critical examination of personal experiences so as to create a meaningful narrative of one's life. This type of reflection can provide personal coherence and can supplant any superficial, inappropriate, stereotypical, or fragmentary scripts that are interfering with authentic existence.

calling A view of teaching that recognizes, and even celebrates, the personal and social value of the educational profession. Possessing a sense of calling is a virtue for constructivist teaching.

caring A professional ethic whereby teachers regularly confirm, engage in dialogue with, and cooperate with their students. Cultivating this ethic is a virtue for constructivist teaching.

centered Operating on the basis of deliberate moral choice. Centered teachers know themselves through years of pragmatic and critical reflection. Developing one's centeredness is a virtue for constructivist teaching.

centers of inquiry A place where employees think for themselves instead of rotely following the directions and procedures of supervisors, administrators, and others. They exercise their pragmatic intelligence, function as action researchers, grow through experiential learning, and engage in various types of meaningful professional collaboration. When a school is a center of inquiry, it operates as a learning community. This book has been designed to help teachers initiate and work in a school that is a center of inquiry.

cognitive dissonance A feeling of discomfort engendered by experiences that are perceived to be in conflict with fundamental constructs.

collaboration A facilitative type of human interchange. For the purposes of this book, collaboration is defined as a professional relationship in which teachers actively support and encourage one another's reflective practices. Collaborative efforts can focus on pragmatic reconsideration, critical reasoning, and/or critical engagement. The text explains and illustrates five general collaborative approaches: exchanging, modeling, coaching, supervision, and mentoring.

collaborative coaching A type of professional collaboration in which one or more individuals provide descriptive, procedural feedback to a colleague or group of colleagues who are engaged in enacting a technique or a general practice.

collaborative exchanging A type of professional collaboration focusing on sharing new information on a topic, a technique, or a general practice. The sharing may be a one-time event or part of a long-term study by an individual or a team. The latter type of exchanging is especially relevant to this book, since engaging in study projects is one of the highlighted characteristics of progressive decision-making.

collaborative mentoring An intimate form of professional collaboration in which one individual provides guiding advice and counsel to a colleague. The mentor has generally engaged in more professional learning than the individual receiving guidance.

collaborative modeling A type of professional collaboration in which one or more individuals demonstrate a technique or a general practice to a colleague or group of colleagues.

collaborative supervision A type of professional collaboration in which one or more individuals provide evaluative feedback to a colleague or group of colleagues concerning the enactment of a technique or a general practice.

congeniality A friendly type of human interchange that may engender positive feelings about a work environment. People who are congenial may make no attempt to be either cooperative or collaborative.

conscious agents An understanding of students that encourages constructivist teaching. Students are viewed as having their own purposes or intentions as well as a background of prior knowledge and dispositions.

constructivist educational services Deliberate educational activities designed to facilitate students' active understanding. These activities focus on teaching for meaning-making rather than for memorization or rote-skill practice. This book has been designed to facilitate thoughtful constructivist practices in education.

constructivist learning A complex interaction between students' personal purposes, their prior knowledge and dispositions, and the requirements for specific subject matter inquiry.

context sensitivity The thoughtful responsiveness of teachers to the unique circumstances of their work. This is one of the four characteristics of progressive decision-making.

cooperation A type of human interchange in which the parties have dialogue with, help, and/or support one another. Cooperation differs from collaboration in the following ways. Though cooperative professionals can be supportive of one another, they do not work at establishing mutual interests and common ground; nor do they engage in a more penetrating analysis and evaluation of one another's practices. There is a lack of mutual support for personal-professional

reflection, that is, for pragmatic reconsideration, critical reasoning, and critical engagement.

covenant A solemn and binding agreement between two or more parties. This type of agreement provides for reciprocal rights, duties, and obligations and serves as a guideline for action. It may take years of organization development work before teachers and other interested parties are able to create a covenant for their school.

creative Imaginatively and aesthetically engaging students in learning activities. Cultivating creativity is a virtue for constructivist teaching.

criterion-referenced test An evaluation instrument in which students demonstrate the competencies they have had the opportunity to practice. The use of this instrument is advocated by teacher-character Amy Nelson.

critical engagement A type of critical examination of one's personal-professional knowledge. It is the reflective process of becoming attuned to the tacit awareness, feelings, and metaphors that inspire one's teaching. It is an aesthetically immediate, qualitatively aware form of reflection. This is one of the three forms of reflection featured in this book. The other two forms are called pragmatic reconsideration and critical reasoning.

critical reasoning A type of critical examination of one's personal-professional knowledge. It is the reflective process of considering good reasons for particular teaching decisions. It is the examination of why something should be done a particular way. This is one of the three forms of reflection featured in this book. The other two forms are called pragmatic reconsideration and critical engagement.

critical style The preferred approach for teachers to use in the critical examination of their practical decisions. Because of our rational and intuitive natures, a balanced critical examination involves analytical reasoning and aesthetic attunement. Using the decision-making cycle encouraged in this book, teachers can focus critical examination on their planning, actions, observations, and/or pragmatic reflections.

curriculum design The general framework or blueprint for an educational program. Without a curriculum design, educational services would lack coherence.

decision-making cycle An approach to teaching that integrates four thoughtful phases: (1) fluid planning, (2) teaching enactment, (3) participant observation, and (4) pragmatic reconsideration. The final phase is one of the three forms of reflection featured in this book.

empirically sound argument An argument that can be supported by evidence gathered through careful research, either formal or informal. This type of argument serves as a key referent for the problem-solving approach of teacher-character Amy Nelson.

existential will The ability to decide what is right for one's life without being intimidated by others' expectations. This type of personal assertiveness serves as an important constructivist referent for teacher-character Dennis Sage.

experiential continuum A time line delineating six significant periods of personal-professional experience: educational encounters prior to preservice field work, early field work, student teaching or interning, first three years of teaching, fourth to sixth years of teaching, and seventh to twenty-fifth years of teaching. Research indicates that teachers may shift their perspectives as their career progresses from one period to the next. This continuum is used to orga-

nize the inquiry advice in chapters 7 through 9.

experiential learning A way of learning from experience by balancing acting and observing with participation and thoughtful detachment. The text's decision-making cycle, described in chapter 1 and used to create the four constructivist practice protocols in chapters 3 through 6, provides a blueprint for experiential learning.

formative evaluation Critical feedback from a teacher on students' learning performances for the purpose of facilitating personal growth and improving educational programs. This feedback can be offered to students, their parents, and other interested parties. Teacher-character Dennis Sage argues for this type of curriculum evaluation.

great ideas The vital concepts that have withstood the test of time in Western cultures. New ideas from non-Western cultures may be added to this list. The great ideas serve as a constructivist referent for teacher-character Johnny Jackson.

historical agents People who believe they can discover and cultivate the personal and social emancipatory possibilities in their lives. This sense of agency serves as an important constructivist referent for teacher-character Silvia Rivera.

ideology A perception of reality that becomes internalized and guides behavior, whether consciously or tacitly.

intuitive problem solving A strategy of solving problems through intuitions based on carefully cultivated relationships. Teacher-character Dennis Sage argues for this type of problem solving. He believes that teaching requires a tactfulness that must be based on sensitive teacher-student bonding.

job enhancement Expanding the scope of a particular type of work. Job enhancement is a relevant consideration in this book for several reasons. First, the chapters in Section 2 (chapters 3–6) encourage a sophisticated and empowered educational professionalism that integrates curriculum and teaching responsibilities. This type of integration may substantially expand the scope of a teacher's work. Second, chapter 8 encourages professional collaboration; teachers who have worked in isolation will find that collaborative activities can enhance their work beyond their daily routines. Finally, as explained in chapter 9, teachers who accept the challenges of transformative leadership will broaden their professional activities to include a wide range of reform responsibilities. One of these is to help other colleagues respond positively to the increased scope of their work.

learning community An association of people dedicated to the diverse, continuing educational growth of all participants. This association can be characterized as a virtuous and sacred social commitment. Chapter 6 presents a five-phase protocol for building a classroom learning community. Changing the context of professional development from discrete staff development activities to learning community collaborations is one of the eight reform responsibilities of transformative teacher leadership.

liberal professional inquiry This type of teaching study promotes empowered educational professionals who are able to function responsibly in a participatory democracy and who can help their students function likewise. This is the study method used in this book.

metacognitive guidance Mental reminders that help guide thoughtful activity. This thinking support can also be called scaffolding. All the study advice in this book is organized as metacognitive guidance.

micro-management A top-down administrative style in which teachers' behavior is carefully controlled.

naive eclecticism The superficial adopting of selected elements of a person's ideology without a critical examination of practices and underlying beliefs.

organizing center A theme, problem, project, or some other integrating strategy for organizing content that serves four purposes: various parts of the content are connected together in some coherent manner, the content is inviting and accessible to students, the content supports multiple learning styles, and the content encourages individual construction of meaning. Teacher-character Dennis Sage advocates the use of organizing centers.

participatory democracy An understanding of democracy that highlights the creation of a common good in the context of acknowledging the diversity of people and, when appropriate, celebrating that diversity. The four teacher-characters in this text are ideologically diverse; however, they all share the view that good teachers are progressive decision-makers. Guided by this common orientation, they willingly collaborate with their peers in curriculum and professional development.

personal-professional knowledge A term that highlights the personal and professional aspects of teachers' knowledge. This hyphenated term, which first appears in the preface, is used throughout the book. It is an acknowledgment that personal circumstances and beliefs strongly impact teachers' decisions, actions, and subsequent reflections.

postmodern multiculturalism An approach to multiculturalism that celebrates human differences without overtly or tacitly promoting dominant American middle-class values. This multicultural approach can be contrasted with traditional multiculturalism, which focuses on understanding human differences from the point of view of certain dominant values. The postmodern multicultural approach takes the point of view that others are intrinsically equal simply because they are human. This approach focuses on the critical struggle to undo negative stereotyping from the perspective that there is no ideal way of being a human.

power-over Power understood as command, control, and/or competition for scarce goods, in which one individual has power over another. This understanding of power inhibits the creation of classroom and school learning communities as well as the practice of professional collaboration.

power-over gamesmanship A type of human interchange characterized by competition over resources and/or influence.

power-with Power understood as the facilitation of co-agency, in which individuals share power in a collaborative relationship. This understanding of power is an important building block for the creation of classroom and school learning communities and for the enactment of various collaborative approaches.

practice A complex activity guided by the decision-making cycle of planning, acting, observing, and reflecting. Four constructivist practices are each explained and illustrated in chapters 3 through 6.

pragmatic intelligence An understanding of human intelligence associated with the philosophical tradition of pragmatism. This understanding highlights people's ability to learn through individual and collaborative problem solving.

pragmatic reconsideration The practice of reflecting on one's personal-professional teaching knowledge as the final phase in the four-stage decision-making cycle of planning, enacting, observing, and reflecting. This type of reflection, which may involve cognitive dissonance and resolution, can lead to new knowledge. Pragmatic reconsideration is one of the three forms of reflection featured in this book. The other two forms are called critical reasoning and critical engagement.

praxis A reflective practice informed by social analysis and utopian, visionary thinking. Teacher-character Silvia Rivera is an advocate of educational praxis.

progressive decision-makers Teachers whose decision-making is informed by (1) context sensitivity, (2) a planning-enacting-observing-reflecting cycle, (3) a critical examination of personal-professional knowledge that blends critical reasoning with critical engagement, and (4) continuing study projects. This understanding of thoughtful teaching serves as this text's referent for reflective practice.

reform responsibilities Challenging activities that are associated with the facilitation of human and organizational change. Eight reform responsibilities of transformative teacher leadership are explained and illustrated in chapter 9.

social liberation A general category for attempting to resolve problems of human injustice. This visionary type of activity serves as an important constructivist referent for teacher-character Silvia Rivera.

socially aware problem solving A strategy of understanding the social context of a learning problem and using that knowledge to guide the efforts to solve the problem. This is the preferred problem-solving approach of teacher-character Silvia Rivera.

summative evaluation The activity of making a final judgment about a student's educational progress. Teacher-character Dennis Sage argues against this type of curriculum evaluation.

symbolic-analytic work An important category of work in an information-based society that involves engaging in analytical thinking, problem solving, collaboration, and team work. This work category serves as a constructivist referent for teacher-character Amy Nelson.

teacher enactment An integral part of an empowered teacher's practice that builds on fluid planning and is informed by participant observation and pragmatic reconsideration. This type of activity differs from teacher implementation.

teacher implementation A teacher activity controlled through top-down administration. This type of activity can be contrasted with teacher enactment.

teacher-characters Imaginary characters who represent a dominant ideological position in the teaching profession. This book intro-duces four teacher-characters: Johnny Jackson, Amy Nelson, Dennis Sage, and Silvia Rivera. They provide commentary on a variety of topics in chapters 2 through 7, and they have been created to facilitate critical reasoning and critical engagement, two of the three forms of reflection highlighted in this book. Collectively, the four teacher-characters provide an ideological overview of beliefs about good teaching. Appendix A provides a background discussion of this ideological overview.

technical problem solving A strategy of following a precise procedure to solve an educational problem. This type of problem solving serves as a contrast to the constructivist protocol in chapter 3.

technicism A term for thinking only about the means and not the ends of what you do.

thinking skills Explanations, predictions, problem-solving strategies, and other higher order applications of subject matter content. These types of skills serve as the constructivist referent for teacher-character Amy Nelson.

transformative teacher leadership A form of collaborative leadership focusing on the facilitation of progressive decision-making and the creation of organizational structures that support teaching as a reflective practice. Eight reform responsibilities of transformative teacher leadership are identified in chapter 9.

Index